812113

DATE			

Barnes & Noble

General Editor: Anne Smith

BLACK FICTION:
New Studies in the
Afro-American Novel
Since 1945

BLACK FICTION:
New Studies in the Afro-American Novel Since 1945

edited by

A. Robert Lee

BOOKS
10 East 53d St., New York 10022
(a division of Harper & Row Publishers, Inc.)

Barnes & Noble Books
Harper & Row, Publishers, Inc.
10 East 53rd Street
New York

ISBN 0-389-20012-3

First published in the U.S.A. 1980

Printed and bound in Great Britain
MCMLXXX

Contents

5

Introduction

by A. ROBERT LEE

The eleven essays which make up this collection, by critics from both sides of the Atlantic (four are American, seven British), offer a fresh estimate of the Afro-American novel since Richard Wright. Not every writer, or tendency, is covered in what has been an extraordinary body of fiction, though no writer of importance has been neglected. Further, these readings offer a fair degree of cross-reference and the recognition of common themes. Each of the essays has its own critical voice, and I haven't sought to homogenize differences of tone or approach. What they very clearly give emphasis to is the diversity and depth of the post-war black American novel, an efflorescence which continues despite the diminishing taste, especially in America, for things 'ethnic'.

When *Native Son* made its appearance in 1940, it signified the close of a previous era which had lasted through the exuberant, hopeful years of the Harlem Renaissance and the subsequent shock of the Depression. It gave evidence of a new stir of literary energies, a perspective on black social culture which admitted of little compromise or evasion. It wasn't that Wright judged his predecessors less than essential to Afro-American cultural tradition, especially forbears like Paul Dunbar, W. E. B. DuBois, James Weldon Johnson, Claude McKay, Jean Toomer and Arna Bontemps (indeed in 'The Literature Of The Negro In The United States', the third essay in *White Man, Listen!* (1957), he paid them explicit acknowledgement), but that in Bigger Thomas he sought voice for a world whose boundaries were the Northern city ghetto, the domain of the street and the tenement, and whose idioms had still to be transcribed. The contrast with, say, the impressionistic canvases of Jean Toomer's *Cane* (1923), or Countee Cullen's lyrics, or even Claude McKay's lively fiction and autobiography, is evident even at a first glance. Wright's novel, especially when read with his classic autobiography, *Black Boy* (1945) and its continuation in *American Hunger*, issued posthumously in 1977, took the tradition of black American letters decisively out of its first classic phase and into the recognizably 'modern'. For that reason, Wright acts as the point of departure for this volume.

In the opening essay, Ian Walker argues for a Wright less bound by the legacy of naturalism than is generally assumed, and for a view of his imagination whose truths lie closer to inward realms of the psyche and the human heart than to the 'realism' of the city colour-line and his depictions of the South and the north-wards Great Migration. Brian Lee, in turn, argues for the sophistication of Langston Hughes's ingenuous-seeming fiction, and locates Hughes's best strengths in the Jesse Simple stories. Theodore Gross examines the social vision behind the fiction of Ann Petry, a leading voice of Wright's 'school', bringing to bear assumptions she herself has said gave shape to her work. In their accounts of Ralph Ellison and James Baldwin, both Laurence B. Holland and William Wasserstrom pay homage to the two crucial shaping forces of black literary modernism after Wright, whose fiction was to the fifties and to a subsequent decade what *Native Son* had been to its time. Ellison and Baldwin published their epochal novels, *Invisible Man* (1952) and *Go Tell It On The Mountain* (1953) in the context of work by other 'Wrightians'—Chester Himes, William Gardner Smith, Willard Motley and Ann Petry notably—but overwhelmingly they wrote as literary sons who had assumed their own creative paternity. They provide the bridge into the contemporary.

Of these contemporaries, LeRoi Jones and Ishmael Reed are considered in separate essays partly because they have been responsible for a body of writing, and in Jones's case, a politics, clearly responsive to the cultural energies of the sixties and beyond. I should explain that Eric Mottram's essay on Jones has a special history. It was initially written for another collection and dealt with Jones's prose writings up to 1971. Mr. Mottram kindly agreed to extend his consideration to Jones's more recent activities and to locate the fiction and political writing within the changing body of ideas which took Jones into his re-birth as Imamu Amiri Baraka. The essay, I believe, is indispensible to an understanding of Jones's complexities and I have let it stand in the length which follows from its two phases of composition. Frank McConnell

8

approaches Ishmael Reed's fiction also as a wholly contemporary phenomenon, a 'Hoo-Doo' imagined world whose inside geography he maps with a gusto to match Reed's own.

The four concluding essays were deliberately conceived as attempts to confront a large range of material from within a single perspective. C. W. E. Bigsby identifies and analyses the pre-occupation with a world turned upside down, a racial order wrested free of arbitrary white control, in novels by John A. Williams, John Oliver Killens, William Melvin Kelley and Alice Walker. Faith Pullin offers a feminist perspective on the fiction of contemporary black American women, noting the place of Zora Neale Hurston, Nella Larsen and Gwendolyn Brooks before evaluating novels and short-stories by Alice Walker, Toni Cade Bambara, Toni Morrison and Gayl Jones. Graham Clarke, in seeking to establish the case for an achievement which goes beyond 'realism', and into 'the real thing', looks to the novels of Julian Mayfield, Ronald Fair, Cyrus Colter, Robert Deane Pharr and Hal Bennett. My own essay takes up a complementary body of fiction, novels consciously given to innovation, and concentrates upon five novelists—William Demby, John Wideman, Charles Wright, Carlene Hatcher Polite and Leon Forrest—paying acknowledgement to Chester Himes's contribution to contemporary styles of experiment.

This is not, as I have said, a collection which offers literary history. Rather, it represents an effort to take new critical soundings in a striking body of recent fiction, the post-war novels of black America. The concentration upon novels rather than short stories, upon some writers more than others, I recognize to be in some degree arbitrary. But the selections were made in the hope of gaining a clearer overall focus for the volume. The essays, I believe, speak perfectly well for themselves. They are offered as a tribute to creative endeavour whose critical passage has rarely been easy, or appropriately recognized.

A.R.L.

1

Black Nightmare:
The Fiction of Richard Wright

by IAN WALKER

> To discuss, . . . in the light of pure reason the Negro problem in
> the United States is to falsify its essential mystery and unreality;
> it is a gothic horror of our daily lives.
> >   Leslie Fiedler: *Love and Death in the American Novel* (1960)

> And when I contemplated the area of No Man's Land into which
> the Negro mind in America had been shunted I wondered if there
> had ever existed in all human history a more corroding and
> devastating attack upon the personalities of men than the idea of
> racial discrimination.   Richard Wright: *American Hunger* (1977)

From the start, Richard Wright has commonly been identified with
the naturalist tradition in American writing, particularly with the
literature of social protest and political commitment that emerged
in the wake of the Depression; and since he has been evaluated
largely within the confines of that tradition, the social and political dimensions of his fiction have been emphasised, while his
explorations into the fearful, and often bizarre inner layers of
black experience, have been neglected. Thus, Alfred Kazin concluded prematurely that 'Wright was only the child of his generation, and his resources no different in kind from the left-wing
conception of life and literature to which, like many Negro writers,
he surrendered his thinking because of the general indifference or
hostility to Negroes and Negro writing'.[1] James Baldwin, who early
in his career was inspired and encouraged by Wright, later denounced *Native Son* for its artistic and psychological distortions,
likening it to Harriet Beecher Stowe's *Uncle Tom's Cabin*: 'Bigger
is Uncle Tom's descendant, flesh of his flesh, so exactly a portrait
that, when the books are placed together, it seems that the contemporary Negro novelist and the dead New England woman are

11

locked together in a deadly, timeless battle; the one uttering merciless exhortations, the other shouting curses'.[2] Ralph Ellison, too, has disowned Wright's literary example on the grounds that he was guilty of subscribing to 'that much abused idea that novels are "weapons"—the counterpart of the dreary notion, common among most minority groups, that novels are instruments of good public relations'.[3]

But Wright, an outsider by temperament and experience, was too proud and too independent to surrender himself unreservedly to any ideology or group; and while political opinion clearly invades his fiction, it never completely takes control or defines its deepest meanings. Wright's relationship with the Communist Party, which he joined formally early in 1934 via the Chicago John Reed Club, was often strained, and ended a decade later in disillusion, withdrawal, and mutual recriminations. The Party offered him for the first time in his life friendship, respect, opportunity, and a vision of a better world based upon ideals of human equality; but it also demanded intellectual obedience from its followers, and he was unwilling to accept the leadership's attempts to interfere with and direct his art along Party lines—he admitted, 'I wanted to be a Communist, but my kind of Communist'.[4] Moreover, Wright was aware of the shortcomings of Marxist literary didacticism; in his essay entitled 'Blueprint for Negro Writing' (1937) he declared:

> And yet, for the writer, Marxism is but the starting point. No theory of life can take the place of life. After Marxism has laid bare the skeleton of society, there remains the task of the writer to plant flesh upon those bones out of the plenitude of his will to live. . . . And if the sensory vehicle of imaginative writing is made to carry too great a load of didactic material, the artistic sense is lost. And if imaginative writing is required to perform the social office of other professions, then the autonomy of craft is submerged and writing fused detrimentally with other interests.
>
> The relationship between reality and artistic image is not always direct and simple. The imaginative conception of a historical period will not be a carbon copy of reality. Image and emotion possess a logic of their own. A too literal translation of experience into images is a defeat for imaginative expression. And a vulgarized simplicity constitutes the greatest danger in tracing the reciprocal interplay between the writer and his environment.[5]

12

For Wright, being born black and poor in the 'alien land' of Mississippi meant, of course, 'race hate, rejection, ignorance, segregation, discrimination, slavery, murder, fiery crosses and fear'; but he also recognized racism as a disease of the mind which distorts and torments human emotions in grotesque and terrible ways, and he wrote of this in *American Hunger*:

> What could I dream of that had the barest possibility of coming true? I could think of nothing. And, slowly, it was upon exactly that nothingness that my mind began to dwell, that constant sense of wanting without having, of being hated without reason. A dim notion of what life meant to a Negro in America was coming to consciousness in me, not in terms of external events, lynchings, Jim Crowism, and the endless brutalities, but in terms of crossed-up feeling, of psyche pain. I sensed that Negro life was a sprawling land of unconscious suffering, and there were but few Negroes who knew the meaning of their lives, who could tell their story.[6]

The nature of black experience in America as Wright perceived it was a psychic nightmare as well as a social and historical tragedy. But nightmares are hardly the material of social protest, so while one line of Wright's literary descent leads to Dreiser and naturalism, another, less well acknowledged, goes back to Poe, Hawthorne, and Dostoevsky, writers who explored private realms of guilt, terror, 'nothingness', and 'crossed-up feeling', using techniques of irony and metaphor. It is significant that in his discussion of 'How Bigger Was Born', Wright suggested that had Poe and Hawthorne been writing in the modern world, they would have had available to them an immediate and tragic theme: 'we have in the oppression of the Negro a shadow athwart our national life dense and heavy enough to satisfy even the gloomy broodings of a Hawthorne. And if Poe were alive, he would not have to invent horror; horror would invent him'.

Wright was born in 1908 near Natchez, Mississippi; his father was an illiterate sharecropper, his mother a rural schoolteacher. His early life was marked by poverty, repression, anomie (his father abandoned the family in 1914, and Richard was moved around a succession of relatives), and a justified fear of white people. He had little formal schooling, and after menial jobs in Jackson and Memphis, he moved to Chicago in 1927 determined to escape the expectations of the South. There he worked as a post office clerk, hospital orderly, and burial society agent; but it was not until he became involved in the John Reed Club, the cultural arm of the Communist Party set up to foster proletarian art and literature, that he began to think of himself as a writer. By 1937 when he moved to New York to become the Harlem correspondent of the *Daily Worker*, he was a prolific author of poems, essays, and stories in the left-wing press; and in 1938 he persuaded Harpers to publish four of these stories—or 'novellas' as he preferred to call them—under the title of *Uncle Tom's Children*.

The title of Wright's first book refers the reader back to the notorious racial stereotype in Mrs. Stowe's novel; a figure characterized by his servile humility and passive acceptance of degradation and suffering. In contrast, the stories in *Uncle Tom's Children* assert black pride and courage, and are dedicated to the death of Uncle Tom. But the Uncle Tom stereotype had private as well as cultural significance for Wright, as an important episode in his autobiography, *Black Boy* (1945), reveals. Wright's actual Uncle Tom, an authoritarian retired school teacher, takes it upon himself to thrash the 'sassyness' out of his nephew and teach him humility and obedience: 'And now a strange uncle who felt that I was impolite was going to teach me to act as I had seen the backward black boys act on the plantations, was going to teach me to grin, hang my head, and mumble apologetically when I was spoken to.' Richard, however, has the courage not to accept his uncle's authority or example, and when he confronts him with violence Uncle Tom breaks down:

> 'You think you're a man,' he said, dropping his arm and letting the switch drag in the dust of the yard. His lips moved as he groped for words. 'But you'll learn, and you'll learn the hard way. I wish I could be an example to you . . .'
>
> I knew I had conquered him, had rid myself of him mentally and emotionally; but I wanted to be sure.
>
> 'You are not an example to me; you never could be,' I spat at him. 'You're a *warning*. Your life isn't so hot that you can tell me what to do.' He repaired chairs for a living now, since he had retired from teaching. 'Do you think I want to grow up and weave the bottoms of chairs for people to sit in?"

14

He twitched violently, trying to control himself.
'You'll be sorry you said that', he mumbled.

(Chapter 6)

The first story in *Uncle Tom's Children* is one of Wright's finest compositions. 'Big Boy Leaves Home' is a dramatic tale of gross racial violence, as well as a searching study of the psychopathology of lynching, and a moving parable about growing up black in the South. The opening scene describes four black boys walking and running happily through summer woods: they joke and sing, invent smutty rhymes, and wrestle together on the grass. Then, after ignoring the 'No Trespassing' notice, they swim in a white man's pool, and play in naked innocence. Suddenly, the peace of the idyllic landscape scene is broken: a young white woman appears, and although the terrified boys try to hide and cover themselves, the woman stares 'eyes wide' and her screams mark the end of their innocence and freedom. From here the story deals with their initiation into the racist world of adult life; a twisted world of suffering, fear, violence, and humiliation. The woman's scream immediately brings an armed man to her defence, and he shoots two of the defenceless boys before being killed with his own gun by Big Boy. As Big Boy and his surviving friend, Bobo, flee from the lynch mob, they find that their environment has symbolically changed: nature which had been warm and gentle is now cruel and hostile—vines trip them as they run, and the 'sun stretching out over the fields was pitiless'. The lynching of Bobo is a grotesque orgy, a carnival of cruelty motivated by sadism:

'LES GIT SOURVENEERS!'
He saw the mob close in around the fire. Their faces were hard and sharp in the light of the flames. More men and women were coming over the hill. The long dark spot was smudged out.
'Everybody git back!'
'Look! Hes gotta finger!'
'C'MON! GIT THE GALS BACK FROM THE FIRE!'
'He's got one of his ears, see?'
'Whuts the matter!'
'A woman fell out! Fainted, Ah reckon . . .'
The stench of tar permeated the hillside. The sky was black and the wind was blowing hard.
'HURRY UP 'N BURN THE NIGGER 'FO' IT RAINS!'

15

Big Boy watches the lynching while lying in a hole in the ground clasping the body of a dead dog, and he sees enacted before him an archetypal ritual of racism in which the black man is cast in the role of sacrificial victim.

Other stories in the collection dramatize black fortitude and heroism, but seem psychologically less complex. In 'Down By the River Side' a Black named Mann, trapped in a flooded Southern town, kills a hostile white man in defense of his family. After Mann's wife dies in childbirth, he heroically if improbably returns into the flood to rescue the family of the man he shot. Inevitably, he is denounced by the white family he saves, and is shot down like an animal as he attempts to escape. In 'Long Black Song' the defiance is more positive and the narrative more credible. A lonely young black woman, dreaming of the lover she did not marry, is talked into bed by a smooth-sounding white salesman. When her husband discovers what has happened he kills his wife's seducer, and then faces the lynchers with dignity and tough fatalism. In each of these stories the black protagonist faces his white oppressors alone; resistance is a matter of personal will and nerve, and the outcome has no immediate social relevance. In 'Fire and Cloud', however, individual courage brings about political change. The setting is a Southern town during the Depression; black folk are starving while the authorities cynically refuse to distribute Federal aid. Dan Taylor, a preacher and spokesman for the black community, is torn between his moral duty to help his people, and fear of offending his white masters: 'Lawd, Ah don know whut t do! Ef Ah fight fer things the white folks say Ahma bad nigger stirrin up trouble. N ef Ah do nothin, we starve . . .' Taylor is initially an Uncle Tom figure: he begs charity from the whites and prays ardently for Divine intervention. But he has around him more positive examples in the two white Communist organisers who are planning a march through the town, and in his own son who is prepared to fight and if necessary die for justice. During a meeting with the mayor and his henchmen, Taylor for the most part acts out his Uncle Tom role; but he refuses to ask the people not to march in support of their rights, and for his disobedience he is savagely beaten and humiliated:

> Warm blood seeped into his trousers, ran down his thighs. He felt he could not stand it any longer; he held his breath, his lungs

16

swelling. Then he sagged, his back a leaping agony of fire; leaping as of itself, as though it were his but he could not control it any longer. The weight of his body rested on his arms; his head dropped to one side.

'Ahhlll ppprray,' he sobbed.

'Pray, then! Goddam you, pray!'

He tried to get his breath, tried to form words, hearing trees sighing somewhere. The thong flicked again, *whick*!

'Ain't you going to pray!'

'Yyyyyyessuh ...'

He struggled to draw enough air into his lungs to make his words sound.

'Ooour Fffather ...'

The whip cut hard, *whick*! pouring fire and fire again.

But instead of teaching him obedience, Taylor's ordeal teaches him the futility of his Uncle Tom role; he joins the people, and walks triumphantly at the head of the united black and white workers:

A baptism of clean joy swept over Taylor. He kept his eyes on the sea of black and white faces. The song swelled louder and vibrated through him. This is the way! he thought. Gawd ain no lie! He ain no lie! His eyes grew wet with tears, blurring his vision: the sky trembled; the buildings wavered as if about to topple; and the earth shook ... he mumble out loud, exultingly:

'Freedom belongs t the strong!'

In comparison with Taylor's sufferings and dilemmas, this ending seems contrived and crudely rhetorical. Here, and in the didactic and unconvincing 'Bright and Morning Star' included in the second edition of *Uncle Tom's Children* (1940), Wright briefly suspended his concentration on the bleak realities of Southern life to indulge in a sentimental political dream.

Wright's first novel, *Lawd Today*, was probably completed in 1937, but for reasons that are not clear but may be political, it was not published until 1963. The novel relates in unrelenting detail one day in the life of Jake Jackson, a postal worker living in Chicago's Black Ghetto; and the particular day is, ironically, 12 February—Lincoln Day. In part one, 'Commonplace', Jake wakens ill-tempered from a frustrating dream: he is running up an endless flight of stairs but can never make any progress. He bathes, dresses, eats, quarrels with his wife, goes out into the streets; he visits the 'Black Gold Policy Wheel', calls in at 'Doc Higgins' Tonsorial Palace', plays cards with his aimless friends, and generally seeks amusement. 'Squirrel Cage' deals with Jake's life at the post office: he is harassed by his supervisors and is in danger of being dismissed because of his wife's complaints; but he finds escape from the tedium of his job in gossip and peurile fantasies. The last section, 'Rats' Alley', describes his night-time misadventures in a black club/brothel and his drunken homecoming to another bout of violence with his wife.

Jake is clearly not an heroic or even a likeable character: he is lazy, selfish, feckless, and stupid; moreover, he is almost entirely uninterested in the nature of the racial and economic prison in which he exists. His life is filled with trivia, distractions and frustrations, on which Wright does not attempt to impose an artificial pattern or extract a specific significance. But what the novel does offer are marvellously sharp vignettes of Black life; here, for example, is the scene of Jake and his pick-up in the club:

> Jake hugged Blanche and screamed. When the song ended she danced. Her flaccid buttocks and bosom shivered like fluid. Her eyes were closed, her face lifted ceilingward, her lips tightly compressed. She seemed absorbed in an intense feeling burning in her stomach and she clawed her fingers hungrily in the air.
> 'Pick them cherries, gal! Pick 'em!'
> Abruptly the dance changed; her legs leaped into the air; her body ran riot with a goal of its own. The muscles of her stomach rose and fell insatiably. The music whirled faster and she whirled faster. She seemed to have lost all conscious control, seemed possessed by the impelling excitement of her nervous system. The climax came as she clasped her knees together in a steel-like clamp and wrapped her arms tightly about her heaving bosom.
> A thin black woman grabbed her boy friend and bit his ear till the blood came.
> 'Lawd, today!'
>
> (Part 3, Chapter 2)

Although *Uncle Tom's Children* attracted a good deal of attention (it won a prize offered by *Story* magazine and was widely and favourably reviewed), Wright was troubled that it expressed black suffering rather than black rage and frustration; in 'How Bigger Was Born' he declared: 'I found that I had written a book even bankers' daughters could read and weep over and feel good about. I swore to myself that if I ever wrote another book, no one would weep over it; that it would be so hard and deep that they would have to face it without the consolation of tears. It was this that made me get to work in dead earnest.[7] *Native Son*, published in 1940, was the outcome of this resolve.

Native Son has usually been considered a typical example of proletarian social protest literature: the plot, as indicated by the section headings 'Fear', 'Flight', 'Fate', is highly deterministic, and the central character, a poor brutalized urban black youth, was based in part on actual people Wright had known or heard about in Chicago. But if *Native Son* was intended as social protest fiction, the result is disappointing. The novel covers only a narrow range of experience, and, as James Baldwin pointed out in his essay 'Many Thousands Gone', we know little more about the political and economic dynamics of American society at the end of the book than we did at the beginning. Moreover, the white environment is only sketchily documented, and, as Baldwin has protested, we get little sense of the black community. The entire focus of the novel is on the mind and emotions of Bigger Thomas, and the remaining characters, both black and white, are important only in so far as they contribute to our understanding of the myth Bigger Thomas embodies. Bigger's tragedy takes place on the streets of Chicago, but it concerns the inner world of mind and spirit; it reveals with terrible clarity the destruction of a personality acting out the implications of inhuman racist beliefs.

The opening scene of the novel in which Bigger hunts a black rat in the narrow confines of a tenement room, is a microcosm and forewarning of his eventual fate:

> 'Hit 'im, Bigger!' Buddy shouted.
> 'Kill 'im!' the woman screamed.
> The rat's belly pulsed with fear. Bigger advanced a step and the rat emitted a long thin song of defiance, its black beady eyes glittering, its tiny forefeet pawing the air restlessly. Bigger swung the skillet; it skidded over the floor, missing the rat, and clattering to a stop against a wall.

19

'Goddamn!'

The rat leaped. Bigger sprang to one side. The rat stopped under a chair and let out a furious screak. Bigger moved slowly backward toward the door.

'Gimme that skillet, Buddy,' he asked quietly, not taking his eyes from the rat.

Buddy extended his hand. Bigger caught the skillet and lifted it high in the air. The rat scuttled across the floor and stopped again at the box and searched quickly for the hole; then it reared once more and bared long yellow fangs, piping shrilly, belly quivering.

Bigger aimed and let the skillet fly with a heavy grunt. There was a shattering of wood as the box caved in. The woman screamed and hid her face in her hands. Bigger tiptoed forward and peered.

'I got 'im,' he muttered, his clenched teeth bared in a smile. 'By God, I got 'im.'

He kicked the splintered box out of the way and the flat black body of the rat lay exposed, its two long yellow tusks showing distinctly. Bigger took a shoe and pounded the rat's head, crushing it, cursing hysterically:

'You sonofabitch!'

(Book one)

Bigger arouses exactly the same emotions among white people during his trial as the rat had provoked in his own family: revulsion, fear, hysteria, and violence.

The 'Fear' section of *Native Son* is dominated by imagery of exclusion and envy. The white world has no more reality to Bigger than the fantasy films he watches; indeed, the whole spectrum of white life lies beyond his vision, and the only way he and his friends can approach it is through play acting: thus we see tough black street boys 'playing white' and pretending to be important white people such as 'J. P. Morgan' or the 'President'. But this white world not only fascinates Bigger, it also terrifies him; and when he is faced with the prospect of robbing a white shopkeeper, he rejects the plan at the last moment, and takes out his frustration in attacks upon his Black friends.

Bigger's relationships with his white employers are remote and uneasy; and when the daughter of the house, Mary Dalton, and her Communist boyfriend attempt to patronize and understand him,

20

he responds with feelings of discomfort, shame, and fear. At the end of his first evening at the Dalton home, Bigger finds that he has by accident wandered into an archetypal scene from black nightmare: he and the helpless white girl are alone in a sexually compromising situation,[8] and when Mary's blind mother enters the bedroom he cannot behave in a rational manner. Instead, he responds to what Franz Fanon calls 'the world's anticipation'—he becomes the leading actor in a grotesque racial melodrama, and kills and mutilates his white female victim, as is expected of him in his role as the Black Brute. The gruesome Poe-esque dismemberment and burning of Mary in the cellar (there is a white cat in attendance), is not merely a means of disposing of the body; it is also an act of sadism carried out with a mixture of revulsion, desire and excitement. Locked in a world of racial myths and perversions, Bigger's sexual desire for the hated and feared white woman is expressed with the knife:

> Wistfully, he gazed at the edge of the blade resting on the white skin; the gleaming metal reflected the tremulous fury of the coals. Yes; he *had* to. Gently, he sawed the blade into the flesh and struck a bone. He gritted his teeth and cut harder. As yet there was no blood anywhere but on the knife. But the bone made it difficult. Sweat crawled down his back. Then blood crept outward in widening circles of pink on the newspapers, spreading quickly now. He whacked at the bone with a knife. The head hung limply on the newspapers, the curly black hair dragging about in blood.

Later, Bigger and his lawyer, Max, argue that the killing was 'an act of creation', the only possible outcome of an existence twisted by fear and frustration. After the murder, Bigger felt for the first time in his life a sense of his own dignity and power: 'And, yet, out of it all, over and above all that had happened, impalpable but real, there remained to him a queer sense of power. *He* had done this'. Eldridge Cleaver confessed to similar emotions after violating a white woman: 'I considered myself to be mentally free—I was an "outlaw". I had stepped outside of the white man's law, which I repudiated with scorn and self-satisfaction. I became a law unto myself—my own legislature, my own supreme court, my own executive.'[9] But the killing of Mary Dalton is, as the powerful dream sequence in 'Flight' makes clear, a bitter act of

21

self-hatred. In his dream Bigger is running in blind terror through the streets carrying a wet, slippery, paper-wrapped package:

> . . . and the paper fell away and he saw—it was his *own* head—his own head lying with black face and half-closed eyes and lips parted with white teeth showing and hair wet with blood and the red glare grew brighter like light shining down from a red moon and red stars on a hot summer night and he was sweating and breathless from running and the bell clanged so loud that he could hear the iron tongue clapping against the metal sides each time it swung to and fro and he was running over a street paved with black coal and his shoes kicked tiny lumps rattling against tin cans and he knew that very soon he had to find some place to hide but there was no place and in front of him white people were coming to ask about the head from which the newspapers had fallen and which was now slippery with blood in his naked hands and he gave up and stood in the middle of the street in the red darkness and cursed the booming bell and the white people and felt that he did not give a damn what happened to him and when the people closed in he hurled the bloody head squarely into their faces . . .
>
> (Book two)

'Fate' has generally been considered the weakest part of *Native Son*, and Wright has been accused of allowing the novel to deteriorate into a socio-political lecture; for instance, Margaret Just Butcher complained that 'The book is marred only by the author's overreliance on the Communist ideology . . . ideological commitment . . . cheated him of a classic in American literature'.[10] In this last movement, Bigger does at times seem more important as a social type than as an individual, but this is because Wright deliberately makes him the focus of the racist rantings of the prosecution and the windy rhetoric of his defence lawyer, Max. Because Max is so articulate and rational, and so sympathetic to Bigger's predicament, the reader is inclined to overlook the inherent ironies and contradictions he embodies. Wright by this time had enough experience of the Communist Party to realise that its involvement with the 'Negro problem' was not entirely altruistic; and in the novel Max admits to Buckley, the prosecution lawyer, that his defence of Bigger was politically motivated: 'If you had not dragged the name of the Communist Party into this murder, I'd not be here. . . .' Moreover, some of Max's pleas during the trial seem primarily defences of the Party rather than Bigger; his attack on the Dalton family seems unnecessarily cruel, while his long socio- logical explanation of Bigger's conduct does not seem suitable for the occasion. Bigger's immediate problems are racial and psycho- logical rather than political and economic, and Max's idealism is of no more practical use to him than his mother's religion had been. Bigger is black and lost; he kills alone and suffers alone, and notions of comradeship mean little to him. Bigger cannot be ex- plained rationally; he is the black Brute of white mythology, an extension of the primitive savage of Thomas Dixon's lurid novels, and Buckley, the viciously racist prosecutor, invokes the full horror of the hate-filled myth: 'Every decent white man in America ought to swoon with joy for the opportunity to crush with his heel the woolly head of this black lizard, to keep him from scuttling on his belly farther over the earth and spitting forth his venom of death!' Wright promised that *Native Son* would not offer the consolation of tears, and he kept to his word.

There were thirteen years between *Native Son* and the publica- tion of Wright's next novel—*The Outsider* (1953)—by which time, restless and disillusioned with the racial intolerance he found in America, he had moved into permanent 'exile' in France. All his life Wright had no choice but to be aware of anxiety, dread, self- hatred—the basic tenets of existentialism—but in France he found these concepts being deeply and formally explored by writers he admired, notably Camus and Sartre, and in *The Outsider* he too tried to write a philosophical novel incorporating existential themes. But despite Wright's ambitions, *The Outsider* is a disap- pointing novel, and its indifferent reception in America was prob- ably merited. It is too long; the characters are poorly motivated and inadequately developed; and the melodramatic plot is inter- rupted by lengthy passages of tedious philosophical discussion. The first part of *The Outsider* appears to be a reworking of the material that went into *Lawd Today*, but without the life, humour, and feeling for language and place which the earlier novel pos- sesses. Cross Damon is an intellectual version of Jake Jackson; he works at a routine job in the Chicago post office and has problems with money and women; but unlike Jake he can rationalize his sense of alienation: 'The three men looked silently at Cross. He

23

knew that they liked him, but he felt that they were outside of his life, that there was nothing that they could do that would make any difference. Now more than ever he knew that he was alone and that his problem was one of the relationship of himself to himself.' Damon escapes from his unhappy existence through an accident on the underground railway in which he is thought to have been killed; and after observing his own funeral and murdering his gross black friend who discovers his secret life (both dramas of black self-hatred), he escapes to New York where he takes on the identity of Lionel Lane, a recently dead man. In the second part of the novel where Cross Damon is drawn into the web of the Communist Party (as Wright thought that he had been), the narrative is disturbed by long and frequent polemics on existential themes (' "Maybe man is nothing in particular," Cross said gropingly. "Maybe that's the terror of it." '), delivered in jargon-laden speeches either by Cross himself or by his white outsider counterpart, Ely Houston, a deformed New York district attorney. Embittered by the Party's cynical betrayal and exploitation of Black people, Cross embarks on a gruesome orgy of retribution. First he watches Gil Blount (the cold, unscrupulous Party official in whose home he lives) and his fascist landlord beat themselves to bloody pulps with a poker, then he steps in and kills both of them with a table leg; afterwards, 'The universe seemed to be rushing at him with all its totality. He was anchored once again in life, in the flow of things; the world glowed with an intensity so sharp it made his body ache.' Next he kills the local Communist organizer, Jack Hilton (perhaps the Brother Jack of Ellison's *Invisible Man*), ostensibly to destroy the evidence of his earlier murders—a bloody handkerchief! By this time he has declared his love for Eva, the innocent long-suffering widow of Gil; his love is returned, but Eva, not surprisingly commits suicide when Cross tells her his history. Inevitably, he too is killed—gunned down by the Party as he leaves a movie house—and he dies with Houston at his side and a homily on his lips: ' "The search can't be done alone. . . . Never alone. . . . Alone a man is nothing. . . . Man is a promise that he must never break. . . ." '

It is clear from this outline that *The Outsider* is not at all a realistic novel, but rather a work of grotesque fantasy embodying versions of Wright's private bitternesses—Margaret Walker Alexander has observed that 'Cross Damon has a lot of Richard Wright in him that Bigger Thomas was not big enough to understand'.[11] But *The Outsider* is a poorly controlled and often badly written book, and it signifies an emerging crisis in Wright's career: he had come near the end of the great literary vein in his life.

A more compelling treatment of the outsider theme is to be found in Wright's long story 'The Man Who Lived Underground' (originally published in 1942, revised and enlarged in 1944, and collected in the posthumous miscellany, *Eight Men*, 1961). Images of black invisibility recur throughout Wright's fiction and autobiographical pieces; in *American Hunger*, for example, he recalls his experiences in a Chicago hospital: 'The hospital kept us four Negroes as though we were close kin to the animals we tended, huddled together down in the underworld corridors of the hospital, separated by a vast psychological distance from the significant processes of the rest of the hospital—just as America had kept us locked in the dark underworld of American life for three hundred years—and we had made our own code of ethics, values, loyalty.'

In Wright's story, a black man having been forced by the police to confess to a crime he did not commit, takes refuge in the sewers of the city. There, in the darkness, amidst the rats and the 'abysmally obscene' debris of life, he begins painfully and slowly to discover a new man and build a new existence. From his underworld cave the black explorer makes excursions into the now unfamiliar regions of the outer world and discovers absurdity everywhere; he watches a cinema audience:

> These people were laughing at their lives, he thought with amazement. They were shouting and yelling at the animated shadows of themselves. His compassion fired his imagination and he stepped out of the box, walked out upon thin air, walked on down to the audience; and, hovering in the air just above them, he stretched out his hand to touch them . . . His tension snapped and he found himself back in the box, looking down into the sea of faces. No; it could not be done; he could not awaken them. He sighed. Yes, these people were children, sleeping in their living, awake in their dying.

Man's life, he learns, is not only absurd and cruel, it is also permeated with guilt (a variety of absurdity), and it is guilt which

25

forces him to return to the outside world to confess to his 'crimes'. But the police think he is mad and dangerous, and they kill him: ' "You've got to shoot his kind. They'd wreck things." ' Wright did not need existentialism to teach him that life might be nothing more than an absurd joke, and the Black man could hold the key to its meaning; in *White Man, Listen!* he said: 'The Negro is America's metaphor'.

Wright's next novel, *Savage Holiday* (1954), further reveals his artistic debility. It concerns Erskine Fowler, a white, middle-aged recently redundant insurance executive, who finds himself in a black comedy situation: he is locked out of his apartment with no clothes on, and his hairy nakedness so frightens a neighbour's small boy that he falls to his death from a balcony. Motivated by guilt and sexual curiosity, Fowler pursues the dead boy's promiscuous mother, but when she continues to associate with other men, he kills her with a butcher's knife—we later learn that he was re-living childhood traumas. *Savage Holiday* is a comprehensive failure: it is badly written and constructed, the characters and their problems are unconvincing, and Harpers may have been wise to turn it down.

At the end of *Black Boy* Wright said, 'I fled the South so that the numbness of my defensive living might thaw out and let me feel the pain—years later and far away—of what living in the South had meant'. And in his last novel, *The Long Dream* (1958), he returned again to the familiar environment of the South in an attempt to resurrect the pain and bitterness of Black life there. The story focuses on two black lives—those of Tyree and his son Fishbelly Tucker. Tyree is a prosperous undertaker with a sideline in brothels; but his prosperity has been bought at a terrible expense to his dignity as a human being, for in order to survive in the white dominated world he had had to learn to play the cringing Uncle Tom with consummate skill. When he ceases to play the role he is damned as a 'bad nigger', and when he stands up to the white police collaborator in the brothel business, he is killed like a dog. Tyree's life—his shame and his eventual stoic dignity—is one of many examples and warnings offered to Fishbelly. Early in the novel, for instance, Fishbelly and his friends visit a fairground, and watch with fearful fascination the happenings at the 'HIT THE NIGGER HEAD' stall:

26

They pushed their way delicately into a packed, shouting mass
of white men and saw, about fifty feet behind a wooden barrier,
a black man's head protruding from a hole in a thick canvas.
Trembling gas flares made the whites of the man's eyes gleam
and gave his flashing white teeth a grisly grin. A barker shouted:

'Come on, folks, and hit the nigger! He's chained and can't
run! His skull's iron and his head's solid rock! Here's a chance
to hit a nigger like you really want to hit 'im! Buy a bargain:
three big-league baseballs, all genuine, for fifty cents! Who wants
to hit the nigger!'

Fishbelly gaped at the 'nigger' head nightmarishly spotlighted
by gas flares. A tight-lipped white man handed up fifty cents,
saying:

'I'm going to kill that nigger.'

(Part one, chapter 7)

Fishbelly, sickened by the degrading spectacle, recognises that the
'obscene black face was his own face'; later after witnessing and
experiencing the total nightmare of racism in the South, he understands that the poor 'nigger head' is the potential identity trap of
all black people in America. The alternatives are to resist like his
father and be destroyed, or flight; Fishbelly chooses flight, and at
the end of the novel he is on his way to France, able to look a
white woman in the face for the first time in his life.

It is not easy to account for Wright's literary decline after he
left America. Perhaps cut away from the roots of his hate and
anger, he could not summon back the anguish and emotional intensity that makes his greatest work so memorable—this, at least,
is how his friends Arna Bontemps and Saunders Redding have
explained his failures.[12] Compared with his finest work, *The Long
Dream* lacks freshness and tension: Fishbelly's story had already
been better told in *Uncle Tom's Children* and *Black Boy*. It is as
if Wright had nothing new to say, but was going back over the
old terrors and nightmares in a desperate attempt to make them
live again. A further novel about Fishbelly's exile in France was
written, but it remains unpublished. To a later generation of black
radicals, Richard Wright has seemed one of the most important
American authors; Eldridge Cleaver probably spoke for many
when he declared: 'Of all black American novelists, and indeed
of all American novelists of any hue, Richard Wright reigns

supreme for his profound political, economic and social reference. But this response now seems too parochial, too far from the central grotesqueness of his fictional world; James Baldwin comes closer to understanding Wright's lasting worth when he directs us to look inward: 'It now begins to seem, for example, that Wright's unrelentingly bleak landscape was not merely that of the Deep South, or of Chicago, but of the world, of the human heart.'

NOTES

1 Alfred Kazin, *On Native Grounds*, (New York, 1956), p.301.
2 James Baldwin, 'Everybody's Protest Novel', in *Notes of a Native Son*, (New York, 1957), p. 17.
3 Ralph Ellison, 'The World and the Jug', in *Shadow and Act* (New York, 1966), p. 121.
4 'I Tried to Be a Communist' (1944), reprinted in *American Hunger*, (New York, 1977), p. 107.
5 This essay was originally printed in *New Challenge*; a fuller version is published in *Amistad 2* (New York, 1971), pp. 1–20.
6 *American Hunger*, p. 7.
7 'How Bigger Was Born' is conveniently reprinted as the preface to the Penguin Books edition of *Native Son* (Harmondsworth, 1977).
8 See on this subject Calvin C. Hernton, *Sex and Racism*, (London, 1969), especially chapter 3, 'The Negro Male'.
9 Eldridge Cleaver, *Soul on Ice*, (New York, 1968), p. 25.
10 Margaret Just Butcher, *The Negro in American Culture*, (New York, 1957), p. 142.
11 Margaret Walker Alexander, 'Richard Wright', *New Letters*, (Winter, 1971), p. 200.
12 'A Symposium on an Exiled Son' in *Anger and Beyond*, ed. Herbert Hill, (New York, 1966).

2

'Who's Passing for Who?' in the Fiction of Langston Hughes

by BRIAN LEE

Richard Gilman's famous—or infamous—review of *Soul on Ice* in *The New Republic* (reprinted in his essay collection *The Confusion of Realms*, 1970) set down, in a general way, the only possible answers to the question I have posed myself in this essay. I am not attempting to pursue here the particular motivations or neuroses of Hughes's characters and create a map of his fictional world. Nor am I proposing to concern myself primarily with such things as his style and technique. As critical exercises these would seem to me to have little or no value beyond establishing the fact that, judged by conventional literary standards, Hughes is not a very accomplished writer. Having admitted the irrelevance of these standards, though, is it still possible to say anything illuminating about Hughes's work that is not merely obtuse or patronising?

Writing about a later generation of artists Gilman came to the conclusion that it was not, and he ended his review by saying that 'the kind of *black writing* I have been talking about, the act of creation of the self in the face of that self's historic denial by our society, seems to me to be at this point beyond my right to intrude on'. He meant by this, autobiographical writing, and that of Fanon, Malcolm X, and Eldridge Cleaver, rather than that of Booker T. Washington. Autobiographical works do make different demands on us, necessarily; but to insist on that discrimination is to miss a more important difference, between what Gilman calls 'the work of authors who *happen* to be black' and those for whom 'one's condition is not a pretext, not the raw material of art, but the very subject of the work'. Such a distinction, subtle and complex as it often is, applies equally to fiction, poetry, and

29

drama, and perhaps the most important critical task for any critic—white or black—is to discover and apply techniques for describing and judging works of the former kind and works of the latter.

In the case of Langston Hughes this is more difficult than with a novelist like James Baldwin, say, whose search for authenticity depends upon a degree of self awareness and sophisticated introspection of the kind that Hughes is continually trying to reject. Baldwin's black protagonists often fail in their attempts to break out of the restrictive mould of American life; more rarely they succeed. But in either case, the living space they create, in imagination or fact, is well defined and well lighted, even if it is narrow. The self that is created is one created out of refusals and rejections, it is true, but the very strength of its resistance gives it clear form and substance. The same is true of characters in the work of Richard Wright, Ralph Ellison and LeRoi Jones, writers whose work all exhibits a firmness of dialectical structure usually lacking in Hughes's fiction. In a speech to the *National Assembly of Authors and Dramatists* in 1957, Hughes set out to itemize some of the ways in which black writers are discriminated against, and to enforce his point told an anecdote that characterises the negative aspect of his attitude towards his own fictional beings:

> Another story of mine which did not concern race problems at all came back to me from one of our best known editors of anthologies of fiction with a letter praising the story but saying that he, the editor, could not tell if the characters were white or colored. Would I make them definitely Negro? Just a plain story about human beings from me was not up his alley, it seems. So before the word *man* I simply inserted *black*, and before the girl's name, the words *brown skin*—and the story was accepted.

The fact that he believes himself capable of writing 'a plain story about human beings' sufficiently distinguishes him from his successors. So too, in a more positive way, do the multiple ironies directed at racism in his short story 'Who's Passing for Who?'.

It is set during the time of the Harlem Renaissance and involves a group of what Wallace Thurman called the 'niggerati'. Three young artists have met to drink and talk at Small's and are accosted there by a black social worker, Caleb Johnson, and his three white acquaintances. Caleb is the kind of man who, 'if it were the

30

white race that was ground down instead of Negroes . . . would be one of the first to offer Nordics the sympathy of his utterly inane society, under the impression that somehow he would be doing them a great deal of good'. This evening he has got hold of some nondescript people from Iowa and is intent on showing them the sights of Harlem. In return for free drinks the young black writers entertain them:

> The drinks came and everything was going well, all of us were drinking, and we three showing off in a high-brow manner, when suddenly at the table just behind us a man got up and knocked down a woman. He was a brownskin man. The woman was a blonde. As she rose he knocked her down again. The red-haired man from Iowa got up and knocked the colored man down.
>
> He said, "Keep your hands off that white woman."
>
> The man got up and said, "She's not a white woman, she's my wife."
>
> One of the waiters added, "She's not white, sir, she's colored."
>
> Whereupon the man from Iowa looked puzzled, dropped his fists, and said, "I'm sorry."

After that, the party moves on but the man from Iowa leaves after being criticized for his behaviour. Eventually the remaining white couple confide to the Blacks that they, too, are really coloured and have been passing for white for fifteen years. At this revelation the young writers drop their 'professionally self-conscious "Negro" manners' and settle down to a relaxed and joyous evening with their new friends, eating, drinking and laughing about the earlier incident. When it is time for the 'light-colored' people to leave they finally reveal the truth to the Blacks, that they are in fact white—passing for coloured, passing for white. The point is that in the dumbfounded bewilderment of the three self-conscious black artists, there is the seed of awareness that they are the ones who have been trapped by the rigidity of racial stereotypes, not the whites. Even so, what is most surprising about this story, and what makes it typical of Hughes's work, is the benign way in which he ends it: 'Whatever race they were, they had too much fun at our expense—even if they did pay for the drinks.'

There are some early stories, mostly published in *The Ways of White Folks* (1933), in which the irony is more direct, and in

31

which anger is not subverted by laughter. 'Slave on the Block,' another story of the twenties, lays bare the pretentious patronage of white intellectuals, and their prurient interest in the lives of their black servants. The Carraways are typical of the kind of middle-class whites who 'went in for Negroes':

> In their collection they owned some Covarrubias originals. Of course Covarrubias wasn't a Negro, but how he caught the darky spirit! They owned all the Robeson records and all the Bessie Smith. And they had a manuscript of Countee Cullen's. They saw all the plays with or about Negroes, read all the books, and adored the Hall Johnson Singers. They had met Dr. Dubois, and longed to meet Carl Van Vechten. Of course they knew Harlem like their own backyard, that is, all the speakeasies and night clubs and dance halls, from the Cotton Club and the ritzy joints where Negroes couldn't go themselves, down to places like the Hot Dime, where white folks couldn't get in—unless they knew the man. (And tipped heavily).

They add to their collection a young Negro, Luther, ostensibly hired to look after the garden and tend the furnace, but who is employed in fact as an ornament to their liberal conscience, and as a nude model for Mrs. Carraway's romantic paintings.

Luther eventually starts sleeping with the maid, Mattie, and proceeds to live his own subterranean life with her, ignoring as far as possible the demands of his employers. The ironies of the story are developed in the juxtaposition of the Carraways' growing sense of moral outrage as Luther and Mattie reject the roles forced upon them, and their continued protestations of delight in the natural simplicity of the Negro servants. In one of his letters to James A. Emanuel, Hughes claimed that 'Through at least one (maybe *only* one) white character in each story, I try to indicate that "they are human too" '. In 'Slave on the Block' this can only be Michael Carraway's mother who makes no pretence of appreciating Luther's 'jungle' qualities, and who takes the first opportunity to have him fired for impudence.

With a few changes in idiom and emphasis, 'Slave on the Block' could easily pass as a story from a much later period; the intellectuals of the fifties and sixties who tried to imitate Negro culture were just as confused in their life-style as the Carraways. Hughes's satire is exact and corrosive, but the story's weakness lies in his failure to do more than merely indicate the real life of Luther and Mattie in contrast to the self-caricaturing fantasies of the Carraways.

The twenties and thirties were years in which Hughes travelled the world, and despite his involvement in the Harlem Awakening, he could hardly be said to have any real roots in New York until the last years of his life, when he settled down to produce the long series of Simple sketches. In fact, most of the stories in *The Ways of White Folks* were written either in Moscow or California, and of these, the one that explores his 'soul-world' most profoundly, reaches back to the life he knew as a boy in a variety of small, mid-western towns. 'Cora Unashamed' is the story of a black woman who, unashamed herself by the inescapable facts of life and death, lays bare the shame and disgrace of her employers' squalid lives. Cora's own child, the product of a brief love affair with a passing white worker, dies of whooping-cough and is buried to the accompaniment of screams and curses as Cora gives free vent to the rage and grief she feels for a God who can take away so easily the life she has brought about. She consoles herself by nursing and rearing the youngest child of her employers, and gradually sinks back into her humble, uneventful routine. Years later, this girl, Jessie, becomes pregnant too, and Cora takes it upon herself to explain the facts to Mrs Studevant:

> So, humble and unashamed about life, one afternoon, she marched into Mrs. Art's sun-porch and announced quite simply, 'Jessie's going to have a baby'.
> Cora smiled, but Mrs. Art stiffened like a bolt. Her mouth went dry. She rose like a soldier. Sat down. Rose again. Walked straight towards the door, turned around, and whispered, "What?"
> 'Yes, ma'am, a baby. She told me. A little child. Its father is Willie Matsoulos, whose folks run the ice-cream stand on Main. She told me. They want to get married, but Willie aint here now. He don't know yet about the child'.
> Cora would have gone on humbly and shamelessly talking about the little unborn had not Mrs. Art fallen into uncontrollable hysterics.

The result is that Jessie is taken away for an abortion, and within a month dies herself, heart-broken. At the funeral, Cora, for the second time in her life, breaks through the ordered rituals of death, this time to expose the evil of the parents who took the life she had nurtured for so long:

> When the Reverend Doctor McElroy had finished his eulogy, and the senior class had read their memorials, and the songs had been sung, and they were about to allow the relatives and friends to pass around for one last look at Jessie Studevant, Cora got up from her seat by the dining-room door. She said, 'Honey, I want to say something.' She spoke as if she were addressing Jessie. She approached the coffin and held out her brown hands over the white girl's body. Her face moved in agitation. People sat stone-still and there was a long pause. Suddenly she screamed, 'They killed you! And for nothin' . . . They killed your child . . . They took you away from here in the Spring-time of your life, and now you'se gone, gone, gone!'
> Folks were paralysed in the their seats.
> Cora went on: 'They preaches you a pretty sermon and they don't say nothin'. They sings you a song, and they don't say nothin'. But Cora's here, honey, and she's gonna tell 'em what they done to you. She's gonna tell 'em why they took you to Kansas City.'

Crude and melodramatic as it is, 'Cora Unashamed' is also unaccommodating in its insistence on the emotional as well as the social realities of Negro life in the rural mid-west. It comes closer than anything else in this collection to realising the possibilities Hughes wrote about in his 1926 credo, 'The Negro Artist and the Racial Mountain.'

> Certainly there is, for the American Negro Artist who can escape the restrictions the more advanced among his own group would put upon him, a great field of unused material ready for his art. Without going outside his race, and even among the better classes with their 'white' culture and conscious American manners, but still Negro enough to be different, there is sufficient matter to furnish a black artist with a lifetime of creative work.

There are characters and episodes in Hughes's first novel *Not Without Laughter* (1930) that suggest his ability to create out of just such material a large, self-contained 'soul-world'. There are moments when his imagination escapes the restrictions of didacticism and irony, to affirm a positive, alternative life. In the characters of Jimboy and Harriett, Hughes is attempting to escape not only the White Protestant ethic, but also the black Protestant ethic, embodied in such characters as Aunt Hager and Tempy. The struggle is for the soul of the young hero Sandy, destined, if Aunt Hager has her way, to follow in the footsteps of Du Bois and Booker T. Washington; but who himself longs to share the warm spontaneous creativity of his father Jimboy and his Aunt Harriett. The best scenes in the book describe his childhood in the small Kansas town, fishing and playing in the yard, and his early experiences at school and work. But these are not organically related to his character and therefore tend to remain mere sketches for the novel Hughes might have written. As it is, the ideological structure drains the major characters of life, and Hughes has to depend on his large set pieces to provide most of the rich texture in the novel. These, the Revival Meeting, the Carnival, and the Dance, are beautifully observed and make concrete the specific myths and rituals of a vigorous provincial culture. Even here though, Hughes can't resist the opportunity to squeeze a little too much juice out of his materials. Like Ellison and Baldwin after him, he often uses the rhythms of Blues and Jazz to locate and focus the inarticulate emotions of his characters. But in Hughes's fiction the sharp shifts in point of view are too abrupt, and the rhetoric sounds forced, as in this piece from the climax of the Saturday night dance:

> The earth rolls relentlessly, and the sun blazes for ever on the earth, breeding, breeding. But why do you insist like the earth, music? Rolling and breeding, earth and sun for ever relentlessly. But why do you insist like the sun? Like the life of woman? Like the bodies of men, relentlessly?
> 'Aw, play it, Mister Benbow!'
> But why do you insist, music?
> Who understands the earth? Do you, Mingo? Who understands the sun? Do you, Harriett? Does anybody know—among you high yallers, you jelly-beans, you pinks and pretty daddies, among you sealskin browns, smooth blacks, and chocolates-to-the-bone—does anybody know the answer?
> 'Aw, play it, Benbow!'

Despite all its obvious weaknesses, *Not Without Laughter* largely succeeds in bringing to life the pressures and tensions *within* the Negro family. The final irony of the novel whereby

35

Harriett financially guarantees Sandy's education out of her earn-
ings as a Blues singer and sometime prostitute, crudely enforces
the rigid ethical scheme, it is true. But even this cannot seriously
undermine the dense actuality of Hughes's created world.

Hughes himself was more conscious of his failures in *Not Without Laughter* than of his successes, and wrote about the novel
apologetically in his autobiography, *The Big Sea*. Significantly, he
believed that he had in some way let down the characters by not
providing a convincing enough milieu for them, and for the rest of
his life he chose Harlem as the setting for his fiction. There was,
however, a second volume of short stories, *Laughing to Keep from
Crying*, published in 1952, which contained a good many items
dating back to the early thirties. Nothing in the collection is as
good as the fiction he had already published, except 'Big Meeting', which derives directly from the novel anyway; and most of it
demonstrates how bad Hughes can be when he loses sight of his
real subject. 'Something in Common' set in Hong Kong, 'Tain't
So' in California, and 'Tragedy at the Baths' in Mexico, all have
the clever mimicry and neat structures characteristic of the aver-
age *Esquire* and *Scribner's* fiction in the thirties.

In the latter part of his life Hughes's career as an artist suffered from his decision to devote so much of his time and energy
to the production of a wide variety of books championing the
cause of black Americans. He also wrote a series of introductory
books on Jazz, which, like the former, were designed for children.
So that, apart from occasional short stories, and the adaptation of
his play, *Tambourines to Glory*, Hughes's only important fiction
during this period was that first published in *The Chicago Defender*
and later collected as *Simple Speaks his Mind* (1950), *Simple
Takes a Wife* (1953), *Simple Stakes a Claim* (1957), and *Simple's
Uncle Sam* (1965).

In order to turn *Tambourines to Glory* into a novel, Hughes
added the bare minimum of descriptive writing, with the result
that it remains very much what it was—a morality play presented
as a folk ballad. Its relevance to this discussion, however, is
dependent, not on its fictional technique—or lack of it, so much
as on its manipulation of the values Hughes saw as central to the
identity crisis of the American Black. Throughout his entire career
Hughes reiterated his theoretical commitment to:

> The people who have their nip of gin on Saturday nights and are not too important to themselves or the community . . . they do not particularly care whether they are like white folks or anybody else. Their joy runs bang! into ecstasy. Their religion soars to a shout. Work maybe a little today, rest a little tomorrow. Play awhile. Sing awhile. O, let's dance!

But the commitment remained, for the most part, theoretical. If Jesse B. Simple is Hughes's most enduring character, it is just because he continually evades the retribution lying in wait for most of Hughes's characters who try to live their own unshackled lives. Laura, for example, in *Tambourines to Glory*, who, like Harriett in the earlier novel, stands at the book's emotional centre, free and spontaneous, ends up in prison as a murderer. But the man she kills is none other than the Devil, disguised as a Harlem 'numbers man'! The paradoxes in the plot make plain the ambivalence of Hughes's attitudes to his characters, and the novel's texture constantly undermines his intention of presenting 'a fictional exposé of certain ways in which religion is misused in large city communities today by various types of unscrupulous healers who might be called "gospel racketeers" preying upon the gullibility of simple people'.

In fact, the novel's main source of energy is the conflict between Essie and Laura, representing the Spirit and the Flesh, and, as in so many morality plays, it is the worldly who win all the battles, if not the war itself. The two women start a Revivalist movement that becomes successful and lucrative enough to attract the Harlem racketeers. But whilst Essie is on her knees praying to God, Laura is counting heads in the congregation and playing the numbers game. The exchanges between the two of them, based on Revivalist rhetoric give the novel whatever animation it has. The following are typical:

> ' "Surely goodness and mercy shall follow me all the days of my life" ', murmured Essie.
> 'And never catch up with you unless you get up and do something yourself,' said Laura.
> . . . .
> 'You have shook your tambourines to blessings', said Essie.
> 'I'm gonna shake it to a mink coat by Christmas', declared Laura.
> . . . .

37

'And neither my light nor my headlights will I hide under a
bushel. The Lord gimme these breasts and if they look like headlights on a Packard car, it is not my fault. "Let your light so
shine", is my belief.'

At least in the novel Hughes attempts to sustain Laura to the end,
and her final Runyanesque confession ('That little rat of a Birdie
Lee put the finger on me.') is comically appropriate, unlike the
equivalent song in the play:

> Mine was a sumptuous kind of sin
> Wrapped in diamonds and fur,
> Scattering money to the wind
> Like frankincense and myrrh.
> Mine was a giddy kind of sin,
> Laughing without care
> While others in this world I knew
> Found no happiness anywhere.
> Mine was a lustful kind of sin
> Close, close in lustful arms.
> Mine, was a hungry kind of sin,
> Hungry for a body's charms—
> Not stopping, no, not thinking
> Of another's harms—

But both versions are ultimately weakened by the demands of a
conventional plot, used to curb and confine the anarchic urge by
the imposition of law and order. Simple, on the other hand, is
never subjected to such restrictions. He embodies all the qualities
of the true Harlemite, and whatever tactics he employs to counter
the rational propositions of his middle-class, middle-of-the-road,
antagonist—fantasy, irony or his own brand of zany logic—he
always emerges triumphant with the last word. Simple is a licensed
Fool whose lucidity and wisdom illuminate the corruption and
sickness of his world; and the discovery of such a *persona* finally
enabled Hughes to express freely his most passionate convictions:

> 'It gives me great pleasure, Jim Crow, to close your funeral
> with these words—as the top is shut on your casket and the
> hearse pulls up outside the door—and Talmadge, Eastland, and
> Byrnes wipe their weeping eyes—and every coach on the
> Southern Railroad is draped in mourning—as the Confederate
> flag is at half-mast—and the D.A.R. has fainted—*Jim Crow, you
> go to hell!*

Here, of course, the fiction has been forgotten and Simple has walked right out of his character. But he can be equally direct while remaining himself, as in his diatribe on crime:

> 'Violence and crime are wrong', I said. 'Do you want the right to be wrong?'
>
> 'I want every right there is,' yelled Simple. 'Then I can pick out the right to be right. A man has to have the right to be *wrong* in order to have the right to be *right*, don't he?'
>
> 'Your logic defies reason', I said.
>
> 'Then you take reason, but give me right', said Simple. 'Meanwhile, I intends to grow younger.'

The real core of Simple, though, can only be approached indirectly, through the anarchic wildness of his comedy. Hughes himself calls Simple a *Chaplinesque* figure, but despite the similarities, the folk tradition he inhabits is a different one. It is a tradition that has been endangered by the urbanisation of black people, but which it is vital to maintain if Afro–American literature is not to become hopelessly entangled in mere polemics. Ralph Ellison spoke eloquently in defence of black folklore in his *Paris Review* interview: 'It describes those rites, manners, customs, and so forth, which insure the good life, or destroy it; and it describes those boundaries of feeling, thought and action which that particular group has found to be the limitation of the human condition. It projects this wisdom in symbols which express the group's will to survive; it embodies these values by which the group lives and dies'. This describes exactly the importance of Simple, and effectively distinguishes him from the characters who people the Harlem of Baldwin's fiction, or that of any of the 'Protest' writers who, as Ellison says, draw their blackness too tightly around themselves. For Simple, the good life is often—in a doubly alien environment—a matter of nostalgia, and the symbols by which he projects it, though elemental, are heavily charged with feeling. For Simple, the preservation of black culture in the cities is not only a political, or even a philosophical problem, but an all-embracing question affecting the texture of his existence. His dreams of the good life have a very earthy and tangible content:

> 'Greens make my mouth water. I have eaten so many in my life until I could write a book on greenology—and I still would

39

like to eat that many more. What I wouldn't give right now for a good old iron pot full! Mustard greens, collard greens, turnip greens, dandelions, dock, beet-tops, lamb's tongue, pepper grass, sheepcress, also poke. Good old mixed greens! Spinach or chard, refined greens! Any kind of fresh greens! I wonder why somebody don't open a restaurant for nothing but greens? I should think that would go right good up North.'

Even his wilder flights of fancy are rooted somewhere in the reality of his limited condition, and his mind always settles back in the contemplation of this:

'But there is one thing that I do not like in the morning—waking up to face the same old one-eyed egg Joyce has fried for breakfast. What I wish is that there was different kinds of eggs, not just white eggs with a yellow eye. There ought to be blue eggs with a brown eye, and brown eggs with a blue eye, also red eggs with green eyes.'

'If you ever woke up and saw a red egg with a green eye on your plate, you would think you had a hang-over.'

'I would,' said Simple. 'But eggs *is* monotonous! No matter which side you turn an egg on, daddy-o, it is still an egg—hard on one side and soft on the other. Or, if you turn it over, it's hard on both sides. Once an egg gets in the frying-pan, it has only two sides, too. And if you burn the bottom side, it comes out just like the race problem, black and white, black and white.'

Unlike nearly all his contemporaries in black American fiction, Simple wants neither to escape his condition, nor exalt it—merely to fulfil it. When asked why he always brings colours into every question he replies with disarming simplicity, 'Because I am colored. . . . If I was an elephant, I would bring in elephants.'

If his simplicity makes him appear a little old-fashioned, it also makes him more than a little sane.

3

Ann Petry:
The Novelist as Social Critic

by THEODORE L. GROSS

The most compelling feature of Afro-American fiction is its un-
embellished record of the physical conditions under which black
Americans have had to live. Influenced by early twentieth-century
naturalists, most black authors of the twenties and thirties discovered that the central notion of man dwarfed by a hostile environment and fated to exist hopelessly within that environment
coincided exactly with their own experiences; they did not have
to search further for a literary form and they drew the contours
of their fiction in absolute social terms. One thinks of Bigger
Thomas in *Native Son* as a social phenomenon before one thinks
of him as a character; one remembers that the autobiographies of
James Weldon Johnson and Saunders Redding, the stories and
novels of Rudolph Fisher, Claude McKay, and Langston Hughes
view man in a social matrix that constitutes his narrow and
dehumanizing destiny. Even writers like Ellison and Baldwin, whose
early development was in the forties and whose major achieve-
ments happened in the fifties, never freed themselves completely
from naturalistic constraints.

This tradition of naturalism, so evident in all of twentieth-
century American literature but particularly significant in black
literature, finds a late expression in the work of Ann Petry. Mrs.
Petry, who has been writing fiction for twenty-five years and who
has viewed racial affairs from a feminine point of view largely
absent in black literature, considers herself a novelist of social
criticism. Being a product of the twentieth century (Hitler, atomic
energy, Hiroshima, Buchenwald, Mussolini, USSR) she has

written, 'I find it difficult to subscribe to the idea that art exists for art's sake. It seems to me that all truly great art is propaganda, whether it be the Sistine Chapel, or La Gioconda, *Madame Bovary*, or *War and Peace*. The novel, like all other forms of art, will always reflect the political, economic, and social structure of the period in which it was created!

So compelled is she by the novel as an instrument of social criticism that the landscape of her fiction tends to be more memorable than the characters, the concepts, or the aesthetics. It is no accident that the titles of her three novels are *The Street* (1946), *Country Place* (1947), and *The Narrows* (1953). The reader's attention is riveted to the setting. People assume varying degrees of significance in these books, but the crippling conditions of black ghetto life in *The Street* and *The Narrows* and the perverse provinciality of a small town in *Country Place* are one's memories of the novels. Mrs. Petry has the heart of a naturalist and the head of a realist. Although she is interested in people, she is compelled by setting: by the look of a tenement, the smell of a bar, the bleakness of a country town, a dock at night, a darkened room, the streets of a ghetto.

Ann Petry's early life would seem to have provided little preparation for the events in *The Street*. Born in the small town of Old Saybrook, Connecticut, in 1911, she entered the Connecticut College of Pharmacy in New Haven with the intention of following in the tradition of her aunt, who had practised pharmacy for fifty-four years, and her father, who owned a drug store in which Ann worked as a child. But after her marriage to George Petry, a writer of mystery stories, Ann Petry moved to New York and lived there while he served in the United States Signal Corps. She worked as a journalist on *The Amsterdam News* and the defunct *People's Voice*, and served as a recreation field specialist and a sixth grade teacher in the elementary schools. These experiences provided much of the background to *The Street*; but the deepest experiences for the novel stemmed from her life in Harlem. 'It took me only a few days', she has remarked, 'to experience the shock and nightmare of Harlem'. When a story, 'On Saturday, the Siren Sounds at Noon', appeared in *Crisis*, the editors of Houghton Mifflin invited her to write a novel for them and in a short time she was awarded a Houghton Mifflin Literary Fellowship.

42

At the moment she conceived of *The Street*, she knew that her subjects would be violence and poverty.

> You don't have to work on a Harlem newspaper to get a picture of the violence and poverty there. Just go into some of the houses. You'll see rooms so small, and halls so narrow, it won't seem possible they were designed for humans to live in.
>
> Just live in one of those houses for a week. Any night you're liable to wake up and hear somebody screaming his head off—because he's sick, or because he's being beaten. You'll hear rats scratching around in the walls, see garbage piled in the halls and strewn in the backyards. Life will become a dismal, hopeless thing, and you'll want to write a novel, too.

The Street is a simple book, conveyed in straightforward language that traces the obvious yet powerful consequences of poverty. Mrs. Petry does not spare the reader any of the anguish of ghetto life. The street is 116th, between 7th and 8th avenues in Harlem, and the central figure is Lutie Johnson, who wants to free her son—psychologically, economically, and morally—from the attitudes of inferiority and low expectation that attend poverty.

The strength of the novel derives from its self-consciously narrow point of view. *The Street* is told through the eyes of a woman who is not, as in the traditional fiction of this type, a shadowy, heavy stereotype. Lutie Johnson is a beautiful, young black woman who refuses to trade on her beauty. Although her husband leaves her with a son, Lutie fights her poverty with simple dignity; she rejects prostitution, despite the existence of a brothel on the ground floor of her tenement. At the outset of the book, Lutie expresses an idealistic attitude that is in the traditional American manner. She thinks 'of Ben Franklin and his loaf of bread. And grinned thinking, you and Ben Franklin. You ought to take one out and start eating it as you walk along 116th Street. Only you ought to remember while you eat that you're in Harlem and he was in Philadelphia a pretty long number of years ago. Yet she couldn't get rid of the feeling of self-confidence and she went on thinking that if Ben Franklin could live on a little bit of money and could prosper, then so could she'. Her attitude is rendered absurd by her son, who acts on his own idealistic instincts and practises the only trade he knows—shining shoes. When his mother grows angry, he is only confused.

43

'It's the way you were trying to earn money that made me mad,' she began. Then leaned down until her face was on a level with his, still talking slowly, still picking her words thoughtfully. 'You see, colored people have been shining shoes and washing clothes and scrubbing floors for years and years. White people seem to think that's the only kind of work they're fit to do. The hard work. The dirty work. The work that pays the least. . . .

'I'm not going to let you begin at eight doing what white folks figure all eight-year-old colored boys ought to do. For if you're shining shoes at eight, you'll probably be doing the same thing when you're eighty. And I'm not going to have it.'

Although Ann Petry does not dwell overtly upon the conflicts between Whites and Blacks in American society—her concern is with the oppressive details of ghetto life—she does not permit the reader to forget that the white world has drawn the limitations and consequently caused the bitter despair of black people. Lutie, who speaks for the author, periodically expresses her hatred. New York, she thinks,

was any place where the women had to work to support the families because the men got bored and pulled out and the kids were left without proper homes because there was nobody around to put a heart into it. Yes. It was any place where people were so damned poor they didn't have time to do anything but work, and their bodies were the only source of relief from the pressure under which they lived; and where the crowding together made the young girls wise beyond their years.

It all added up to the same thing, she decided—white people. She hated them. She would always hate them. She forced herself to stop that train of thought. It led nowhere. It was unpleasant.

But inevitably she returns to these unpleasant reflections: 'In every direction, anywhere one turned, there was always the implacable figure of a white man blocking the way, so that it was impossible to escape. If she needed anything to spur her on, she thought, this fierce hatred, this deep contempt, for white people would do it!'

The white people frame *The Street* because they have created ghetto conditions, but dramatically they are the least convincing figures in the novel. In an attempt to support herself, after her husband has deserted her, Lutie Johnson works for a wealthy white Connecticut family whose misfortunes stem from a wanton materialism unattended by moral values of any sort: the wife is alcoholic and unfaithful, the husband a shadowy entrepreneur, the woman's brother a suicide, the child a coddled figure who lacks love and attention. But these people are abstracted images against the dark screen of Lutie's life—they and the other white characters in the novel are not real. White people are the cause of Lutie's suffering, but as individuals in a novel they are incredible because they are all types—Mrs. Petry has not succeeded in exploring their reactions to blacks, and her association of wealth and corruption is far too facile.

Ann Petry is most successful when she concentrates on the specific difficulties which confront Lutie Johnson and keeps the white world at a distance, as that final controlling force in the young woman's life, the fate that forbids her from emerging from her poverty. The most memorable quality of *The Street* is its direct, unsentimental, ruthless, bitter description of poverty: the black characters are caught in a suffering that fills them with meanness and hatred, that diminishes their humanity. The superintendent of the apartment house in which Lutie Johnson lives is little more than a scowling lecher, who abuses his mistress as he lusts after the young and attractive Lutie Johnson; a Mrs. Hedges, scarred by former burns and misshapen, is the madame of a brothel in the same house and peers out of her window constantly like some sort of omniscient, benevolent idol, trying to attract Lutie into a life of prostitution; and finally, most significantly, Lutie's child, Bub, watches her struggling against her poverty, and she watches him watching her:

> The women work because the white folks give them jobs— washing dishes and clothes and floors and windows. The women work because for years now the white folks haven't liked to give black men jobs that paid enough for them to support their families. And finally it gets to be too late for some of them. Even wars don't change it. The men get out of the habit of working and the houses are old and gloomy and the walls press in. And the men go off, move on, slip away, find new women. Find younger women.
>
> And what did it add up to? She pressed close to the wall, ignoring the gray dust, the fringes of cobwebs, heavy with grime

and soot. Add it up, Bub, your kid—flashing smile, round face, smooth skin—he ends up in reform school because the women work.

. . . . And while you were out working to pay the rent on this stinking, rotten place, why the street outside played nursemaid to your kid. The street did more than that. It became both mother and father and trained your kid for you, and it was an evil father and a vicious mother, and, of course, you helped the street along by talking to him about money.

The boy, in an attempt to earn money quickly, is imprisoned for naïvely becoming involved with the illegal machinations of his mother's landlord; the mother is driven to murder as she resists the landlord's attempt at rape. Both son and mother are presented as creatures with no control over their lives, the boy lost finally in a reform school, the mother leaving New York toward some large city that 'would swallow her up', wondering 'by what twists and turns of fate she had landed on this train thinking, "It was that street. It was that god-damned street" '.

In *Country Place* (1947), which appeared one year after *The Street*, Ann Petry attempts to adapt the successful descriptions of ghetto conditions in her first novel to those of a small town in Connecticut. But in *The Street*, the power of the novel stems from the depressed conditions of life in Harlem that were available for Mrs. Petry to record; in *Country Place*, the setting is a small town —any small town—that is burdened by its parochialism, its petty scandals, the stock types of the druggist, voyeuristic cab driver, cuckold, unfaithful wife, and the group of chattering old ladies. There is not the powerful social fact of ghetto life pressing down upon the young that is so congenial to Ann Petry's artistic sensibility.

The plot of *Country Place* is as banal as its setting. A soldier returns from the war—he is even called Johnnie—to discover that his fickle wife is sleeping with another man. It takes Johnnie Roans an unbelievably long time—two-thirds of the book—to discover this fact and when he does, the life he has hoped to create with his young wife disintegrates irreparably. Surrounding this thin and obvious story are stereotypical and curiously morbid caricatures who resemble grotesque figures from the fiction of Carson McCullers or Dostoevsky, without their redeeming humanity. Weasel is a misshapen cab driver who practises voyeurism, informing everyone of everyone else's misalliances and ultimately making a fifteen-year-old moronic girl pregnant; Ed Barrel is a bestial man who fascinates a variety of women but seems utterly unattractive; and a group of minor characters—Mrs. Granby, Mrs. Rowe, and Lilian—seem simply unpleasant and perverse. The country place in Connecticut is a carnal place, mean-spirited and oppressive. At some point in the conception of this novel, Mrs. Petry must have meant to concern herself with the death of idealism and the harsh readjustment of a returning soldier who finds his world irrecoverably altered and debased; this is the sense one has of the book in its opening pages. But this theme, however trite it might have been in itself, is not pursued seriously and the plot shoots off in too many different directions, encompassing too many minor figures and too many disparate scenes.

Mrs. Petry did not write another novel until 1953, when *The Narrows* was published. In the intervening seven years, she resettled in Old Saybrook, Connecticut, gave birth to a baby girl, Elizabeth, and wrote a children's book for her niece, entitled *The Drugstore Cat* (1949). During this period, her serious artistic concerns were devoted to her third and most ambitious novel, *The Narrows*, which concentrates once again on a small New England town, reworks the theme of cuckoldry, and, although less intensely than *Country Place*, creates a generally morbid atmosphere. Sex is a central ingredient, complicated by race and economics. A young black man encounters a lost and frightened married woman from a wealthy white family 'at the Dumble Street end of the river at two o'clock in the morning', in a slum area that is known as 'The Narrows'. The finest moments in this long and rambling novel take place in the slum, as Ann Petry dramatizes the oppressiveness of ghetto life and its effect on a young and sensitive black man, Link, who wastes himself as a bartender. Sex and race are inevitably heightened by economic differences until all these factors make the young man, like Bigger Thomas in *Native Son*, realize that he has been little more than the toy, the plaything, of a rich white woman, someone who has been tricked, used, played with. Minor figures spin around these two lovers—Hamie Powther, a sensualist who, like the wealthy white woman, has duped her husband in the past and is still unfaithful to him; Abbie, the

guardian aunt of Link; Jubine, a muckraking photographic journalist. Through the eyes of these characters develops the love
affair of Link, an attractive man who has been scarred by his
ghetto background, and Camilo Williams (whose actual name is
Camilo Treadway Sheffield), spoiled by her wealthy upbringing in
the Treadway household. After this love affair—really a rather
trite affair, with all the predictably 'tense' dialogue between the
rich white woman and the poor black man—has led to the death
of Link, Abbie expresses the author's view: 'It was all of us, in
one way or another, we all had a hand in it, we all reacted violently to these two people, to Link and that girl, because he was
colored and she was white.'

The Narrows (1953) is an interesting novel whose strongest
feature is the description of the enclosed ghetto that prevents the
talented Black from entering into the wealthy white world which
tempts him. The theme of cuckoldry, pursued on two levels simultaneously, is not quite convincing in terms of the present affair
between Link and Camilo Treadway; but in the remembered
romance of Mamie Powther, it is persuasive. As Wright Morris
points out, in a sensible review of the novel, 'The reader is caught
between an unreal present and a convincing past'; in that sense,
the novel is never completely coherent or convincing, despite
interesting scenes and a faithful picture of the black ghetto of a
small town.

In the decade after the publication of *The Narrows*, Ann Petry
expressed her concern about racial injustice through studies of
two black figures in American history, Harriet Tubman and
Tituba. Her intentions in these volumes are clear: 'It is my belief
that the majority of textbooks used in high schools do not give an
adequate or accurate picture of the history of slavery in the
United States.' As a consequence, in the first of these two works
—*Harriet Tubman, Conductor on the Underground Railroad*—
Ann Petry places Harriet Tubman's life story against the back-
ground of slavery and abolitionism. Chapters that deal with
Harriet Tubman's life are concluded by historical commentaries on
Thomas Jefferson, Henry Clay, Nat Turner, William Lloyd Gar-
rison, Thomas Garret, and others, as well as by sketches of his-
torical episodes that put into perspective the compelling story of
Harriet Tubman.

48

Harriet Tubman's life was long—she was born in 1820 and died in 1913—but her significance as an historical figure extended from 1849 until the Civil War, when she became a leader of the Underground railroad. Mrs. Petry traces Harriet's early life as one of ten children on a plantation in Maryland; her work in the fields as she loaded wood, split rails, hoed corn, and, consequently, developed great physical energy; her defiant nature, which manifested itself in a fierce loyalty to other slaves; her marriage to John Tubman in 1844 and their later separation when he refused to escape to the North with her and even threatened to report her to their master. But the main emphasis of this biography is naturally upon Harriet Tubman's adventures with the Underground Railroad, which, as Ann Petry points out, 'ran straight to the North' and 'was not a railroad at all. Neither did it run underground. It was composed of a loosely organized group of people who offered food and shelter or a place of concealment, to fugitives who had set out on the long road to the North and freedom.' Harriet Tubman led runaway slaves from Maryland to Pennsylvania and then, when that proved too dangerous, she guided them to Canada.

Mrs. Petry is not writing an analytical biography of Harriet Tubman but a tribute. Although her prose, for the most part, is restrained, her view of Harriet Tubman is purely poetic: she concentrates upon the messianic quality of Harriet Tubman—her religious nature, her visions, her role as a 'Moses' of her people who leads them from bondage to freedom, from darkness to light.

> She had always had the makings of a legend in her; the prodigious strength, the fearlessness, the religious ardor, the visions she had in which she experienced moments of prescience. Stories about her would be handed down from one generation to the next, embroidered, embellished, until it would be impossible to say which part was truth, which part was fiction. But each one who heard the stories, each one who told all of them or only parts of them, would feel stronger because of her existence. Pride in her would linger on in the teller of the story as well as the listener. Their faith in a living God would be strengthened, their faith in themselves would be renewed.

Mrs. Petry never really humanizes Harriet Tubman. 'Moses' or 'Molly Pitcher', as she was also called, is projected on the abstract, heroic level. The breakup of her marriage to John Tubman and her marriage after the Civil War to a man twenty years her junior are not seriously considered; her peddling of vegetables in Auburn, New York, as a woman reduced to penury, is briefly mentioned; her inner life is not explored. This sort of objective account is not the book Ann Petry is interested in creating. She is writing not analytic biography but tribute, in an attempt to redress the imbalance created by historians; and given this limited goal, she succeeds.

The same judgement may be made of *Tituba of Salem* (1964). This book deals with the Salem witch trials of 1692. Tituba was a black woman, one of three people convicted of witchcraft, and a slave from Barbados. Tituba was forced by a self-willed master to accompany him to New England. She was an intelligent and outspoken slave and, as a consequence, was accused of being a witch —Mrs. Petry draws an interesting portrait of the tension created between the intelligence of the slave and the condition of slavery that denies her intelligence. Although jailed, Tituba was released by a weaver and finally permitted to return to her husband, John Indian, in Boston.

During those years, Ann Petry was writing the short stories that appeared in *Miss Muriel and Other Stories* (1971). Her last published work, the volume is a good survey of her career, for it includes stories that were written as early as 1944 and pieces as recent as the title story, which was published in *Soon One Morning* (1963), and 'Mother Africa', which appears for the first time in this collection. All of these stories are concerned with race and most of them are set in the small upstate town of Wheeling, New York, a restrictive, provincial world.

Nowhere is provinciality more the theme than in 'Miss Muriel', a long story written from the point of view of a sensitive black adolescent girl who is first becoming aware of race. She knows that she objects to the relationship between the white shoemaker and her aunt because she has been 'trained in the subject' of race; but when a rival black man and her uncle arrange to have the shoemaker run out of town, the girl becomes aware of their brutality and their inverted prejudice. The story ends properly on an ambiguous note: the adolescent girl is torn between the staid traditional values of her parents—the only black family in this town—and the more militant views of young Blacks. Her own ambiguity, her honest confusion and doubt, are the direct signs of her compassion and humanity.

Ann Petry comments upon the many manifestations of racial prejudice in the subsequent stories of this collection. She never flinches before the brutality of prejudice, but she shuns easy formulations and simplistic judgements. In 'The New Mirror' for example, a trite situation—a druggist suddenly decides to replace his teeth—yields a considered response from the young narrator:

> perhaps the reason my father hadn't wanted to replace his teeth was that one of the images of the black man that the white man carries around with him is of white teeth flashing in a black grinning face. So my father went toothless to destroy that image. But then there is toothless old Uncle Tom, and my old black mammy with her head rag is toothless, too, and without teeth my father fitted *that* image of the black man, didn't he?
>
> So he was damned either way. Was he not? And so was I.
> And so was I.

The need for racial identity becomes the leitmotive that runs throughout these tales. In a successful story like 'Mother Africa', Mrs. Petry couches this need in totemic terms. A black junkman inherits a metal statue from a wealthy white woman and converts the image into a mythical Mother Africa, the sensuous and fabulous embodiment of his ancestry. He worships the totem until he discovers, as he looks more closely, that 'this alive-looking statue was of a white woman', although the metal was 'darkened with age'. His illusion shattered by the fate of white supremacy, he sells the statue so as to retain a modicum of personal freedom. In 'Olaf and His Girl Friend', a Barbadian man holds on to his girl because he recognizes their shared 'ancient, complicated African past'. In 'Like a Winding Sheet', the black man is humiliated by white women and tempted to hit them, but his frustration and bitterness are discharged upon his wife, instead. Other stories in the volume pursue the theme of a bigotry that leads to rape, race riots, and the cruelty of children to one another: all of them reveal Ann Petry's sensitivity to racial injustice.

Mrs. Petry is less effective as a short story writer than as a novelist, for she needs space in order to create the full credibility of her social setting. As she has remarked about herself, she 'set

out to be a writer of short stories and somehow ended up as a
novelist—possibly because there simply wasn't room enough
within the framework of a short story to do the sort of thing I
wanted to do'. But her theme in the sketches of *Miss Muriel and
Other Stories* is the same as it is in all of her work: the need
for men to recognize their dependence on one another. In 'The
Novel as Social Criticism', an essay which appeared in Helen
Hull's edition of *The Writer's Book*, Mrs. Petry underscores that
theme: 'In one way or another, the novelist who criticizes some
undesirable phase of the status quo is saying that man *is* his
brother's keeper and that unless a social evil (war or racial
prejudice or anti-Semitism or political corruption) is destroyed
man cannot survive but will become what Cain feared he would
become—a wanderer and a vagabond on the face of the earth. She
has little patience with the idea that art exists for art's sake and
views the great writers of the past as social critics. She places
herself as a novelist in this long tradition of social criticism that
ranges from *Othello* to *Native Son*, although she is keenly aware
of her own limitations and of the dangers implicit in the tradition:

> It offers the writer a convenient platform from which to set
> forth his pet theories and ideas. This is especially true of the
> books that deal with some phase of the relationship between
> whites and Negroes in the United States. Most of the talk in these
> books comes straight out of a never-never land existing in the
> author's mind. Anyone planning to write a book on this theme
> should re-read *Native Son* and compare the small talk which
> touches on race relations with that found in almost any novel
> published since then.

Mrs. Petry's fiction, published since *Native Son*, is an attempt
to continue in the tradition of Richard Wright; like Wright she
has created a fiction that remains most significant as social
criticism—rather than as the creation of memorable characters, or
as a style that is distinctive. She writes tradionally, fully conscious of the tradition in which she writes. 'The setting and the
characters vary in these books but the basic story line is derived
from *Uncle Tom's Cabin*; discrimination and/or segregation (substitute slavery for the one or the other) are evils which lead to
death—actual death or potential death. The characters either

conform to the local taboos and mores and live miserably; or refuse to conform and die.' In *The Street, Country Place, The Narrows*, and most of the stories in *Miss Muriel and Other Stories*, Ann Petry traces this conflict, and her characters achieve the latter result—they do indeed 'refuse to conform and die'. Her fiction is tragic because it is the criticism of a racist society. As a naturalist, she is compelled by the constraining effects of a hostile environment; as an artist she humanizes her characters so that they remain in the imagination as people who struggle against the fate of their blackness, who lose socially but who achieve the human triumph that is the essence of Ann Petry's memorable fiction.

4

Ellison in Black and White: Confession, Violence and Rhetoric in *Invisible Man*

by LAURENCE B. HOLLAND

It is possible that the vogue of 'the Black Aesthetic' in the United States which arose in the sixties could have pushed Ralph Ellison's *Invisible Man* deep into a limbo of inattention which it did not deserve, while throwing a lurid light on the announcement of Ellison's appointment to an Albert Schweitzer Professorship, which carried with it hugely visible amounts of prestige and of money for projects under his direction. Such academic prominence scarcely seemed healthy to Imamu Amiri Baraka (LeRoi Jones), at least, who already in 'Philistinism and the Negro Writer' complained that Ellison was 'fidgeting away in some college'. And Jones's concession then that *Invisible Man* was a 'most finely constructed archetypal, mythological novel' (or Larry Neal's, that *Invisible Man* is a 'profound piece of writing' though it 'has little bearing on the world as the "New Breed" see it') has not often been repeated by those black writers who claim, with Ishmael Reed, a 'marked independence from Western form'.[1]

To invoke archetypes and myths in Ellison's defence, however, may be no more to the point than to demonstrate their appearance in the writings of the same black writers who disown the traditions of English and Western literature that Ellison has been happy to acknowledge. What should engross our attention still is the way Ellison treats at once the matter of 'invisibility' and the form of his 'finely constructed novel'. Ellison's own criticism remains the most probing exploration of the fact that 'invisibility' is a complex and at least partly metaphorical reality, and that his novel is presented as what we may call a 'confessional form'.

'Confession, not concealment' is the tactic of his Protagonist, Ellison has written, but in declaring this and referring to *Invisible Man* as the Protagonist's 'memoir' Ellison is far from suggesting that the book is, on his or his protagonist's part, autobiographical in any literal sense. (Though of course Ellison has drawn upon his own experience, he has denied that the book is literally autobiographical in a well-known interview).[2] Neither is the mode of 'confession' to be defined simply as the explicit 'long, loud rant, howl and laugh' that Ellison declares the 'memoir' to be in the same breath,[3] for the usual formalization and reluctance or hesitation associated with confession consort oddly with naked ranting. Nevertheless, Ellison's term 'confession' is illuminating when considered in connection with his comments on the novel form and when we recognize that the Protagonist's account—his 'memoir', his novel—is intimately related to his concern about irresponsibility, his search for an identity, and to his 'invisibility'. The issues are puzzling but inescapably important for understanding Ellison's formal strategies, and they are brought into focus in the Prologue when the Protagonist speaks of his 'urge to make music of invisibility' while both comparing and contrasting the aim for music to the novelistic 'compulsion to put invisibility down in black and white' (11).[4] The 'music' of invisibility and the 'black and white' of its imprint are in problematic relation, and in Ellison's phrasing the 'black and white' of American racial identities are linked inseparably to the conventional black print on the conventionally white pages in our novels. Some attention to Ellison's critical comments on the novel form and on the problem of identities should clarify the Protagonist's position at the opening of the book.

Ellison's critical writings have made clear that the novel is 'a literary form which has time and social change as its special province' and that it takes precedence over archetypal and folklore traditions by absorbing or encompassing them,[5] and moreover he associates the adoption of the form closely with crises of personal transcendence. The 'restlessness' of his Protagonist, he has declared, is a function not of his particular social predicament as a Black nor of any despondency. Nor is it a function only of the fact that he is an American. It is a function more particularly of the fact that he 'appears' *in a novel*.[6] In the Prologue that restless Protagonist stands self-consciously on the threshold of committing himself to the institution of the novel as a literary form, and institutions serve the psychological function, according to Ellison, of providing 'bulwarks which men place between themselves and the constant threat of Chaos', protecting 'the citizen against the irrational, incalculable forces that hover about the edges of human life like cosmic destruction lurking in an atomic stockpile'. As a Black whom Ellison has called a 'displaced person' of American Democracy, without such 'institutions to give him direction', finding that 'his world and his personality are out of key',[7] the Protagonist is committing himself to the novel as a form of *activity* that is more 'intimate' than the techniques, important though they are, that he acquires to implement it. It is an activity through which 'he comes to possess and express the meaning of his life' but which more importantly entails the creation of the self: a writer did 'not so much create the novel', Ellison has written, 'as he was created *by* the novel'.[8] Accordingly the novel is a defensive protection, but it is also an activity that has a shaping impact on the self of the writer, and the form brings an increment of freedom, indeed it becomes the writer's 'greatest freedom'.[9]

The novel form makes possible the achievement for the self of something like the performance of jazz, as Ellison understands jazz, enforcing the recognition of one's limitations and his membership in the group, while nonetheless liberating the soloist's ingenuity and defining his 'identity', producing 'an art of individual assertion within and against the group'.[10] The problem for Ellison's protagonist, however, which complicates the confessional impulse behind his prose, is that the voice which seeks an outlet in music, and the 'compulsion' to get 'invisibility down' in the novel-memoir, are somewhat at odds—the novel seeks to encompass the tactics of music through emulation and rivalry—and that the identities of the Protagonist are not in complete harmony with the self that eludes, while seeking expression, recognition, and self-definition through those identities.

Ellison has made abundantly clear in his essays that the self can suffer from the identities it adopts or finds imposed on it but also that it needs and can indeed delight in the identities that are its labels, its roles, its 'names' as Ellison calls them, the forms which define its powers for growth and action and establish its relations with the society of other selves. The problem is that the fusion of self and identity or name is not given, and this problem is intensified painfully for the Black, whose labels are often stereotypes, whose roles are demeaning impositions, and whose names, even, were originally mere 'epithets' like 'Cato' assigned by European or American white owners as 'verbal evidence of a willed and ritualized discontinuity of blood and human intercourse'. So important is the matter of such identities to the self that Ellison celebrates the process by which a fusion of self and name is achieved, whether by Black Muslims who literally change their names, or by those who forge a unity of their selves and their given names through manipulative activity. 'Our names, being the gift of others, must be made our own', he has declared, and all must

> learn to wear our names . . ., make them the center of all our associations with the world. . . . We must charge them with all our emotions. . . . They must become our masks and our shields and the containers of all those values and traditions which we learn and/or imagine as being the meaning of our familial past.

Then 'we ourselves' can become 'our *true* names', and the self can transcend the mere 'epithets' that have been assigned it. The preacher's injunction, which Ellison quotes, to ' "Make Up Our Faces and Our Minds" ' under-scores the fact that the process of realizing one's self through the manipulation of names or identities derives from a decisive act of will and from deliberately constructive or creative effort.[11]

Ellison has made these assertions in the course of insisting that to begin with one no more selects his parents and his race than one chooses his name, and pointing out that by contrast 'we do become writers out of an act of will'.[12] Accordingly the act of writing is an activity that aims for the creation of the self and for its fusion with its names and identities, and that same activity inescapably involves the self with the names and identities that it manipulates, and with the 'intimate' form of the novel-memoir itself. The form of the novel becomes one of the self's 'masks' or

57

'shields' which, like names, must be used but which, like given names and identities, cannot be utterly equated with the self. And the masking game which Ellison, quoting Yeats, finds the necessary condition for the achievement of active virtue, and finds central to the American experience since the Boston Tea Party (when white rebel patriots were costumed as Indians), includes the masks of both blackness and whiteness that arbitrarily define American racial identities in actual fact and that are built arbitrarily into the 'black and white' of the literary form that Ellison and his Protagonist both use. Both 'aggression' and 'defense' may be motives for engaging in the masking game, Ellison has declared, and 'the motives hidden behind the mask are as numerous as the ambiguities the mask conceals'.[13] Through these masks and identities appears the mystery of the self that manipulates them in a process of self-creation.

For that mystery of the self, the label and defining identity that Ellison's novel makes central is the 'invisible man', the metaphor and fact of 'invisibility'. That invisibility is sharply particularized by the pigmentation of the skin of some Blacks, which tends to dissolve, on film for instance, in surrounding shadows. But in America, insofar as invisibility is defined by racial matters, the invisibility is a function of the interaction of both races.[14] Invisibility is located in the black person—or it is a blank space which comprises his immediate personal environment, not that of Whites who move in the visible glare of recognition—but it is created by the stereotyping bias, the ignorance and condescension, of blinded Whites, who relegate Blacks to a limbo of non-recognition, and by the masking identities which Blacks either contrive or find imposed on them. From the opening Prologue on, Ellison's novel never lets one forget that invisibility is both a fact of experience and a warping perspective generated by the interaction of Blacks and Whites in a racially mixed society.

But 'invisibility' is also a function of patterns in personal and social behaviour that have nothing directly to do with blackness or racial matters. The self, like that invoked by Whitman in 'Out from Behind This Mask', is a personal presence that can only be glimpsed fleetingly in the obscurity of its masks. Its emanations are revealed only through the shielding features of its masking face:

These burin'd eyes, flashing to you to pass to future time,
To launch and spin through space revolving sideling, from
these to emanate
To you who'er you are—a look.

The writer's self is like one of Edgar Allan Poe's white spooks, though Ellison's Protagonist strategically disowns them in his opening paragraph, for he undergoes an isolating crisis which he cannot understand but which adds a new dimension to his being. Poe's protagonist in 'MS Found in a Bottle' finds himself alone on a mysterious ship where the shipmates 'pass me by unnoticed'. He is invisible because 'the people *will not* see'. Walking undetected under the very 'eyes of his mate' into the captain's own cabin, he steals the pen and paper on which he inscribes his manuscript. Later in full view on deck he carelessly doodles with a black tar brush on a neatly folded white sail to find, when the sail is raised into position and filled with wind, that his daubs have spelled out the word 'discovery'.[15] Ellison's Protagonist likewise is embarked on a process of discovery through the task of writing. The actual writing is preceded by covert appropriations of the materials—an 'act of sabotage' (6) comparable to Poe's filching of pen and ink—and it produces an increment of articulate meaning in language beyond what was consciously intended. The self that is glimpsed in its struggle with its identities in *Invisible Man* is engaged in a complicated process that includes covert protection of the individual and an assault on the conditions that oppress him, and enables the will to assert its integrity, gain recognition, and forge a bond of 'agreement' on which recognition depends (11). With no name other than the identity which he has chosen to manipulate—the 'invisible man'—his invisibility becomes the otherwise indefinable correlation between an outward identity and an interior self, the mystery that his novel cannot so much describe as reveal in a ritual 'confession'.

Ellison's 'confessional form' has as much in common with the Confessions of Westminster or Augsburg as with pleas of guilty before a priest or bar of justice, because his aim is as much a declaration of faith (in brotherhood, in communion, in the novel) as it is a revelation of complicity. And 'to confess' is to occasion and to hear a declaration by someone else (as in the case of a priest or 'Father Confessor'), as well as to disclose information and feelings to a licensed listener (as in the case of a penitent sinner): the summons and listening, and the revealing response, are combined in an act of confession. Reluctance (whether to hear or to speak) and willingness (to listen or to utter) are conjoined in the confessional exchange, which can be as dependent in its formalization on tacit and implicit communication as on explicit statement. The very process rests, as the Latin roots of the term suggest, on mutual acknowledgement or shared recognitions. It is such a mutual engagement with his readers that Ellison's Protagonist initiates in the Prologue, where the 'ritual understructure' and the 'action' that Ellison has stressed in his commentary on his novel are launched. The ritual action is the confessional enactment that transforms the Protagonist 'from ranter to writer'.[16]

The brash and candid assurance of the Protagonist in the Prologue simply throws into relief the ambivalence of feeling to which he lays claim and the anxious concerns that agitate him when he boasts of the basement refuge he has improvised after escaping from the black nationalist orator, Ras the Exhorter, during the Harlem riot. He tells with undisguised relish of his brutal assault on a white man who is lost in the 'dream world' of the white power structure that excludes Blacks, who had called him an outrageously 'insulting name' (4, 11). But he discloses also that he was 'disgusted and ashamed', then 'amused' after realising that his verbal assailant, blinded by stereotypes, had not even seen him, and after holding back from murdering him with the knife the Protagonist had drawn for that purpose (4). But if he is ashamed for the brutality of his assault, he later confesses his cowardly 'irresponsibility' in not committing the murder that the white man's outrages called for. And he associates the irresponsibility with the 'invisibility' that he alternately acquiesces in, welcomes as a refuge, and boasts of (11–12). The temptation to murder and to self-definition through violent assault remain, even after his failure to carry through with them, and moreover the question of whether to act at all and whether to act in other ways is one he is reluctant to resolve. 'I believe in nothing if not in action' (11), he declares, but he fears the call to action that he hears in Louis Armstrong's blues, much though he envies that

rtist's power to make 'poetry out of invisibility' and enviously
wants himself to 'play the invisible music of my isolation' (10–11).
Particularly he fears the experience he knew once of hearing the
blues when under the influence of a reefer: he descended to
depths of 'unheard sounds' (7), an 'under-world of sound' where
he 'discovered unrecognised compulsions of my being' and could
not only '*see* around corners' of his mind but 'hear around them',
and the shattering experience appears dangerous because it both
demands action and 'inhibits action' (10–11). He fears both the
drug-induced trance that frustrates action and the blues whose
deeper rhythms embarrassingly demand it.

Nevertheless the Protagonist's account discloses a commitment
to a pattern of action that remains implicit in his definition of his
retreat as an hibernation, a 'covert preparation for a more overt
action' (11). The pattern is adumbrated in the hallucination he
has experienced under the influence of the reefer, when he heard
in the 'underworld of sound' a voice like his mother's and saw the
woman's 'ivory' (7) body on the auction block; he learned that
she both loved her white master, who had fathered her sons, and
had poisoned him, substituting the chemistry of poison for the
lacerating knives her sons had prepared for his murder. In the
hallucination one of the sons attacks the Protagonist but finally
releases his hold on his throat. Likewise the trumpet of Louis Armstrong that the Protagonist emulates translates violence into
sound, 'bends that military instrument into a beam of lyrical
sound' (6). The pattern is that of the Protagonist's own assault
on the white man, when he withheld the knife, then stared at the
figure he had mugged as 'the lights of a car', instead of knives,
'stabbed through the darkness' (4). The knives become poison; the
hands at the throat loosen; the military trumpet translates war
into melody; the assault occurs but the knife is withheld: the
asault of force is being translated into the piercing illumination of
light, into the high-powered illumination provided by the 1,369
klieg lights that the Protagonist has filched in an 'act of sabotage'
(6) from the white world's power plant. And as part of this process,
which reveals to him that there is a 'form' in his very invisibility
which thus validates his existence (5), he is adopting the form of
the novel, bringing his invisibility to light without diminishing it,
by getting it 'down in black and white'. The gestures of assault

61

are translated into the less violent verbal gestures of his novel just as his career as 'orator, a rabble rouser' (11), is being translated into that of writer, but that novel is nevertheless a mediating instrument preparing for action, and his commitment to it is the central fact confessed in his hibernation.

The effect of the Prologue—with its problematic connections among seeing, hearing, and writing, the racial identities of black and white, and the release and the moderation of violence—is to enforce the excitingly experimental but tentative, insubstantial basis of the main incidents of the memoir proper, including some of the most powerful and convincing as well as some of the less successful which deal with the Protagonist's career as orator in the Marxist Brotherhood. The reader is induced to respond to the succeeding incidents in their immediacy but also in the light of the fact often confessed only tangentially at the time, that they have only problematic validity. All the sections have indeed the 'expressionistic' and 'surrealistic' dimensions that Ellison claims only for later parts,[17] for, while the dreams and hallucinations invoked in the Prologue and later chapters deepen the significance of the novel their authority is not differentiated from that of the objective narration; they are parts of the same fictive context. The racist 'dream' of the Protagonist's white assailant in the Prologue, which stereotypes and excludes Blacks and provokes disclaimers of responsibility and mutual violence, has the same compelling but dubious force as the black farmer Trueblood's later dream, which he makes the basis for his disclaimer of responsibility for incest and which provokes the violence of his wife that he narrowly escapes. The drug-induced hallucination that probes beneath Louis Armstrong's blues to reveal mixtures of black and white, love and hate, erotic love and violence, leads into the Protagonist's accounts later of relations with white women and his eventual encounter with the black separatist, Ras the Exhorter. All of the dreams give point to the Veteran's declaration that Harlem, the Protagonist's destination, is 'not a place, it's a dream' (117). The self's struggles with its identities are conducted in arenas that are both social and psychic, and his dilemma is nowhere more dramatically rendered than in the episode following the explosion in the paint factory when he is subjected to electric shock therapy in the factory hospital. There is forged for him a fusion of identi-

es that is the culmination of his career up to that point and
that continues to agitate him for the rest of the novel.

In the nightmare of his treatment the patient is held not in
the glare of electric lights but in the pulsating grip of an electric
machine, the 'crushing electrical pressures' now 'stabbing' at him
with a power beyond that of auto headlights or klieg lights of his
own choosing.[18] He alternately dissolves 'into the blackness' where
the electric shocks thrust him, or stares at the whiteness of his
surroundings—his new white overalls, the 'cold white chair', the
dim white ceiling' of the 'crystal and white world' that engulfs
him. As if caught within the rhythms of Beethoven's fateful Fifth
symphony, he begins to hear snatches of remembered songs from
childhood and the sounds of a 'dark trumpeter' mingling his
sound with the 'live white cloud' of gnats that fill the air.

The machine is likened at one point to his mother, and at the
end of the treatment the staff congratulates him on being born
'new man', but the result of the treatment is something more
problematical than that phrase usually implies. For the treatment
culminates in the demand that the Protagonist recall his name and
identity—the demand is made by a figure in black writing the
request on a card—and the Protagonist dives first 'into' and then
below' the 'blackness' of his mind in a vain effort to retrieve the
answer. Not until the question is written in chalk, by a white
doctor writing on a child's black 'slate', does he recognize, 'with
the delight of self-discovery', an 'old identity' as defined by black
folklore, an identity as 'Buckeye' or 'Brer Rabbit' that he is
amused but ashamed to acknowledge. Recognizing that he is playing in some 'mysterious pantomime', a contestant in a weird
game', he resists the suicidal temptation to short circuit the
machine and is soon released. The self has been re-born in the
process of discovering that its identity has been defined and imposed by black folklore and by the dominant white culture that
provoked and still manipulates that folklore, and that the resulting fusion of black and white racial identities is both inescapable
and perplexing.

He feels that he had 'been talking beyond myself, had used
words and expressed attitudes not my own, that I was in the grip
of some alien personality lodged deep within me', but he feels
also that 'perhaps I was catching up with myself and had put into

63

words feelings which I had hitherto suppressed'. The precise rela
tion between the self and its identity, the 'alien personality'
remains unresolved and subject to change. But the self is strength
ened in its invisibility and the new fusion of its identities is subjec
to manipulation through language as the Protagonist demon
strates when leaving the hospital. He speaks with a new irony an
forced sophistication, defining both his blackness and his white
ness in his negotiations with the white world, saying 'It's bee
quite pleasant, our little palaver, sir'. His use of language soo
proves to be the basis of his career as orator, but his exhilaratio
as he enters that career is countered by the recognition which hi
novel-memoir has already confessed: that his exercise of powe
is dependent in part on an 'alien personality' implanted in him
and that in the catharsis of living out his career as orator he wil
deliberately abandon that role.

His new career is launched when he encounters an ageing coupl
being evicted from their tenement, with their belongings piled o
the sidewalk, and the buried memories and resentments that ris
up as he explores 'around a corner into the dark' are of 'remem
bered words, of linked verbal echoes, images, heard even whe
not listening at home', including the image of his mother hang
ing out laundry with her hands whitened by the raw cold (207)
The speech he improvises on that occasion—he later says he wa
seized by the words, 'I had uttered words that had possessed me
(268)—is the first of his own that is given in detail in his account
Earlier the florid and sentimental speech of blind Dr. Barbee
speaking with his white collar gleaming against his 'dark gar
ments' in the 'black rite of Horatio Alger' at the college chape
(91, 87), had been given in its virtual entirety while it worked o
the Protagonist's emotions 'as upon a loom' (93). But only
bare scrap of the speech the Protagonist had prepared as a bo
for the local smoker, when no one paid him attention, was give
in Chapter One. Such early indications of his verbal prowess a
the novel presents are enacted merely in fantasy and in memory
He only fancies lambasting Bledsoe as a 'shameless chitterlin
eater' (201); and he mocks after the fact his speeches as a studen
leader which voiced a challenge to the language of the school'
Establishment, those ostensibly 'innocent words' that were 'act
of violence to which we of the campus were hypersensitive'. The

64

Protagonist's fancies are gorgeously uninhibited but the novel's recapitulation of his flamboyant grandstanding presents his Claudius-like 'assault on the temples of the ear' as a mockery in its ineffectuality: it presents the *word-sounds* of a mere *bungling bugler of words*, evoking only *drowned passions*, *unachievable ambitions and stillborn revolts*, mere *counterfeit notes* (87–8).

By contrast, his speeches at the eviction and later for the Brotherhood are at once effective and controlled. Yet even the eviction speech, which protests the common 'dispossession' of all Blacks, does not escape from the rhetorical strategies that were displayed in Dr. Barbee's chapel speech and that have been shaped by decades of racial suppression and exploitation. The images of parents and grandparents that the orator evokes from the plight of the elderly couple are authentic but sentimental. Moreover the refrain he improvises by appealing to long-suffering black Americans as a 'law-abiding, slow-to-anger bunch of folks' is one of the 'shock-absorbing phrases' which he musters to moderate and channel the mounting violence which he fears from himself and from his listeners (210, 208). He does channel their protest into the gesture of returning the belongings to the flat, but the demonstration is ineffectual before the police who fire over the heads of the crowd and force the Protagonist to flee. His escape is supervised by white members of the Marxist Brotherhood who have been observing his performance, and soon the voices and designs of their white world have overcome his reluctance, enrolled him as a salaried member, and issued his 'new identity' in a 'white envelope' (235).

From then on the burden of the narrative is to acknowledge tacitly the tentative, preparatory, uncertain status of the Protagonist's career in the Brotherhood without utterly discrediting the career and the Protagonist's feats of oratory, over which the novel lingers. At his initiation into the organisation, the remoteness of his invisible selfhood from the role defined for him to play is underscored. The members welcome him as Booker T. Washington *redivivus*, 'as though they all knew the role I was to play' (236); white women dance with him and treat him as some 'natural resource'; they make him feel 'as though they had not seen me, as if I were here, and yet not here' (229–30). And his

c   65

first appearance on the speaking platform is presented as an agony like that of the shock therapy, producing at once a transformation of the self and a new identity that threatens his very being and frustrates his efforts to join in a community with his audience.

The naked light bulbs in the dressing room where the Brotherhood spokesmen wait their turn recall the glare of the lighted basement, the hibernation, in the Prologue, and the sheer experience of being 'the focal point of so many concentrating eyes' yields glimpses of his transformation into a new person, but the process demands that he suppress the 'dissenting' and 'observing' self watching from 'a point deep within me' and keep it at the remote distance in memory to which he relegates the crucial incidents of his earlier life—'the campus, the hospital machine, the battle royal' (253), which were so conspicuously subject to pressures from the white world. But the novel confesses that the significance of those early episodes cannot be obscured. Memories of abject blackness are displaced by those of spotted terrier dogs and shoes that mix black and white. As before in the hospital he feels 'an electric tingling along my spine' and feels as if he were in the midst of a symphony orchestra, indeed as if he again 'felt the hard, mechanic isolation of the hospital machine, and I didn't like it' (258). When finally he must deliver his speech he resorts to tried-and-true Southern political routines and under the careful surveillance of the Brotherhood he rises to the pitch of confessing his personal transformation and declaring that he and each of the others has been made 'new' in the community of the Brotherhood (261–2). But while he makes this peroration with the glare of their 'black and white eyes upon me', and feels the pressures of the hospital machine, he has been virtually blinded, like the Establishment's Dr. Barbee who was literally blind, by the glare of the spotlight; he stumbles afterward as if 'in a game of blindman's bluff' (263).

The flow of words has compelled him to confess things the Brotherhood's handbooks had not prescribed, that he had not intended to speak and knows he 'shouldn't reveal' (261), but beneath his plea that his inter-racial audience 'reclaim our sight . . . and spread our vision' (260), and beneath the applause that greets his triumph, is the fact that the experience renders his audience invisible *to him*. Before he takes the microphone he reports that the 'light was so strong that I could no longer see the audience, the howl of human faces' whose applause suggests that they respond 'without themselves being seen' (258). When he reflects on the experience afterward, exploring the meaning of his own words, lured by the prospect of sharing in the exercise of power and the 'possibility of being more than the member of a race' (268), he acknowledges that the people he is growing fond of comprise a 'blurred audience whose faces I had never clearly seen'. Moreover, phrases that the novel hurries over but presents none the less carefully confess the telling facts that he was not so much a member as an acquisition of the Brotherhood—'I belonged to them'—and that his audience recognised not himself but his language—'they had recognised my words' (267).

Accordingly, the novel reveals the occasion to have been a compound of rhetorical achievement, authentic commitment, and delusion that marks a crucial development in the Protagonist's career by defining more sharply, rather than resolving, his position in society and his facility with language. The experience prepares him to recognise the invisibility of others and to communicate with an audience that cannot be directly seen—the very condition he will face literally as a novelist—while suggesting that his new role in the inter-racial movement, and his oratory, are not as completely severed from the traditional patterns and exploitive manipulations of his society as he thinks at the time. The ground is prepared for his break with oratory when he discovers that the Blacks' predicament is callously exploited by the white leaders of the Brotherhood and that the explosive oratory in the speech of a black nationalist threatens the black community and the Protagonist himself with destruction.

The power of eloquence is polarised in the later part of the novel, divided between the Protagonist and the black nationalist, Ras the Exhorter. For all the Protagonist's commitment to 'climbing a mountain of words' and his faith in the 'magic in spoken words' (288), he records next to nothing in his novel of his own later speeches in the cause of black rights (or women's rights after his Brotherhood assignment is changed). He chronicles instead the tactical struggles within the Brotherhood bureaucracy and his relations with white women in the movement. Ras and his eloquence, by contrast, are first introduced in a stunning scene when the black nationalist attacks the Protagonist's favourite colleague in the Brotherhood, Tod Clifton, the handsome Black who eschews hair straighteners for an Afro hair style (277), and whose 'Afro-Anglo-Saxon' features testify to a heritage in which blacks and whites are as indistinguishable as 'the rifling of bullets fired from a common barrel' (274). Ras first attacks Tod with a knife, in a street brawl that reminds the Protagonist ominously of a bullfight and of the battle royal that had been his initiation into official race relations as a boy in the South, but the incident becomes precisely analogous to the Protagonist's own attack on the white man recounted in the Prologue, for Ras drops the 'still innocent knife' (282), then in tearful passion declares that he cannot kill a black man and denounces the black members of the Brotherhood for their collaboration with Whites. Though both Clifton and the Protagonist repudiate the Exhorter's impassioned argument, the Protagonist acknowledges being 'caught in the crude insane eloquence' of the Exhorter's proclamation of black separatism, and Clifton shows clear signs of being disturbed by it. Their reactions and their counter-attack with their fists are a portent of the explosive violence to come and of Clifton's subsequent defection from the Brotherhood, making a 'plunge outside history' himself to take abject refuge in the role of salesman of Sambo dolls, then attacking the policeman who tries to arrest him for street peddling (285).

The incident itself, and the entire sequence culminating in Clifton's murder by the police and the Protagonist's funeral oration, are crucial to the 'ritual understructure' of Ellison's novel because they define the perilous interconnections between the rhetoric of the antagonists and the strategic manœuvring and mounting violence that generate it. Although the Exhorter's eloquence is for this perilous moment a function of his abstention from violence with the knife, his 'magic in spoken words' is designed to produce violence in an environment whose habits and institutions are saturated with it. That violence consumes Clifton when in a striking exhibition of athletic dexterity, he attacks the white policeman who harrasses him, and is shot down by bullets whose sharp sounds 'blackjacked' even frightened pigeons on the scene (330).

The Protagonist's funeral oration for Clifton is a profoundly moving elegy—tender in its refrain which invokes repeatedly Tod Clifton's name, stirring in its impact on both white and black listeners, though the Protagonist cannot tell whether they were moved to 'tears or anger' (346). He notes after it is over that he has been able to see beyond the amorphous 'crowd' to the 'faces of individual men and women', though they had 'looked not at me but at the pattern of my voice upon the air' (347, 343). Yet his speech does not match the power of the duet of horn and voice that sounds out 'Many Thousand Gone' during the funeral procession, touching 'something deeper than protest, or religion', and drawing forth some deep communion beneath the traditional words 'for which the theory of the Brotherhood had given me no name' (342). That duet figures forth a communion through art and form that is the goal of language and music alike. Touching and resigned irony, rather than a covert exhortation to action, is the Protagonist's effect when he reminds his hearers that they in Harlem are locked in the same dark coffin as Clifton and that they 'should keep cool, stay safe away from the sun' (346). Indeed the Brotherhood defines the apt contrast to Anthony's provocative oration over Caesar's body when Brother Jack calls the Protagonist's speech 'an oration over the body of Brutus' (351). The Protagonist's original 'ruthless' intent of 'avenging [Clifton] and preventing other such deaths . . . and of attracting lost members back into the ranks' (338) is dissolved when he finds that he can do little more before the 'gray coffin' than remember Clifton's name (342); the crowd had got away from him, he recognizes, and he 'had been unable to bring in the political issues' (346). His eloquence is not as powerful as the music sounded in the procession though it is more in tune with its pathos than with the militant power of Ras the Exhorter which contratst so strikingly to it.

Nevertheless Ras remains a tempting challenge to the Protagonist after his discovery that the white leadership of the Brotherhood, as Ras had warned, had no genuine interest in black people and intends to sacrifice them to the ideology and historical mission of the revolutionary movement. And this challenge does not inhere simply in the fact that Ras himself instigates the self-consuming violence that the white world will exploit and that threatens the Protagonist with lynching, nor simply in the fact that the Protagonist discovers in the final crisis that he prefers 'the beautiful absurdity' of his 'American identity', which he shares even with the Whites who ignore and repress him (422), to the racial identity proclaimed by Ras. The ritual action that emerges in Ras's attack on the Protagonist during the Harlem riot, and culminates when the Protagonist strikes Ras in retaliation with Ras's own spear, reveals that there are bonds between the two as well as antagonism. Though their attitudes toward Whites and violence are different, both are genuinely interested in advancing the cause of black people, both are themselves black, and both are orators or spokesmen: as the Protagonist recognises, Ras's destructive fanaticism is but one step behind the insight he himself has gained since the 'stripping away of my illusionment' (422). The bizarre violence of the Protagonist's attack with the spear is intimately connected with his oratorical prowess and constitutes a ritual transformation, an act that appropriates and aims for a transformation of that power.

Just before ordering his supporters to seize and 'hang' the Protagonist, Ras hurled his spear into one of the white, 'Hairless, bald and sterilely feminine' department store mannequins hanging from a lamp-post (420–21). The spearing of the white female dummy is a nightmarish image both of Ras's intentions against the white world and of their futility, for he strikes not at Whites but at their possessions and at the mere simulacra or substitutes, the dummies or racist stereotypes, generated by his society. But the Protagonist's appropriation of Ras's weapon is even more significant. He reaches up in an 'oratorical gesture of disagreement and defiance' and it is thanks to this oratorical gesture that he accidentally seizes the spear. Then in the face of Ras's resistance to his argument he finds that he has 'no words and no eloquence' and he hurls the spear instead. His eloquence thus translated into action, he feels as if he has 'surrendered my life and begun to live again' while the spear cuts off Ras in the middle of a shout, 'ripping through both cheeks' to lock the orator's jaws (423). The Protagonist's act of violence—seizing the spear and hurling it— aims to extinguish the rhetoric of violence while appropriating its force, and to prepare for its transformation, its conversion into the rhetoric of fiction. Ras the Exhorter, in what is left of his

Abyssinian regalia, disappears into the riot, and the Protagonist soon falls into the coal pit that becomes his temporary refuge. He then suffers the fantasy of his castration by Establishment figures from the black and white worlds of his boyhood, and by the Brotherhood and Ras the Exhorter. But the 'ritual understructure' of the experience has prepared for the Protagonist's transformation from orator to novelist as Ellison described it in 'Change the Joke and Slip the Yoke': the creation of a 'voice issuing its little wisdom out of the substance of its own inwardness—after having undergone a transformation from ranter to writer'.[19]

The Epilogue simply confirms the significant features of the Prologue, and the main orientation of the fiction's movement that culminated in the attack on Ras the Destroyer, while bringing it to no completion other than that of an anticipatory and novelistic form. The effect of the form is to suggest that the action even at the end is mediatory and preparatory, not the consummation or fulfilment of the plot, and to define the ambiguities of the Protagonist's situation as well as his commitments.

He has rejected the tempting refuge of mere masking identities (the facades of a Rinehart behind a white hat and dark glasses), and he affirms, instead of that 'chaos', the 'infinite possibilities' of 'imagination' (435). Along with this commitment to the imagination he affirms the principles of American democracy. But the very movement of his progress toward creation of the self is compounded of incompletion and unresolved ambivalence. Hovering in the ambiance of possibilities, and anticipating emergence in a world where all are at best 'semi-visible' (434), he responds to the 'possibility of action' and he clearly thinks the writing of his novel a kind of 'action' as against relegating his experience to the files of forgetfulness (437). Yet while writing the novel has prepared for the resurgence of his desire to play a public role, enabling him decisively to will an end to his hibernation, the same job of writing—'trying to get it all down'—has 'disarmed' him (437–38).

Where earlier he associated 'invisibility' with 'irresponsibility', he now insists that he will be 'no less invisible' even while assuming the burden of responsibility for his fate, and his new birth leaves the self vulnerable as well as renewed. As he gratuitously assumes partial blame for his invisibility, standing 'naked and shivering before the millions of eyes that look through you un-seeingly', he acknowledges feeling like those black men who suffer 'that strange disease' which turns them from 'black to albino, their pigment disappearing as under the radiation of some cruel, invisible ray' (434). In these phrases he confesses at once his willingness to accept the responsibility and his shame in con-ceding the scarcely natural whiteness for which recent black critics have scorned Ellison. The Protagonist is ready as before to attack and 'denounce', but he confesses being also 'prepared to defend' because the very effort 'to get some of it down' in writ-ing has brought the discovery that 'I have to love' (437–38), re-vealing that the cost of 'infinite possibilities' is both involvement and unpredictability. The writing of the novel entails those vic-tories that the Protagonist claims at the end, which are his triumphs *qua* writer. Encountering white Mr. Norton in New York, long after the incidents at the Trueblood farm and the Golden Day, he can boast that he knows that white man because as novelist 'I made you' (437). As novelist he can echo Whitman's longing, at the end of 'Song of Myself', for communion as a 'dis-embodied voice' with his readers, voicing the closing sentence that asks: 'Who knows but that, in the lower frequencies, I speak for you?' (439). But the fiction that enables the Protagonist to create himself, prepare for an active role, and forge the bond of communion with his reader, provides no clear blueprints for his later conduct, and this discovery about the resources of his fiction—its mediating power and its disarming limitations—is confessed in black and white by Ellison in *Invisible Man*.

NOTES

1 Jones, *Anger and Beyond*, ed. Herbert Hill (New York, 1968), pp. 53, 59; Neal, 'Shine Swam On—An Afterword', *Black Fire*, ed. LeRoi Jones and Larry Neal (New York, 1968), p. 652; Reed, 'Introduction', *Nine-teen Necromancers from Now* (New York, 1970), p. xvi.
2 'Change the Joke and Slip the Yoke' (1958), and 'The Art of Fiction: An Interview' (1955), *Shadow and Act* (New York, 1964), pp. 57, 167.
3 *Ibid.*, p. 57.
4 References to *Invisible Man* are to the Random House Modern Library edition (New York, n.d.) and are enclosed in parentheses in the text.

5   *Shadow and Act*, pp. 46, 57–9.

6   *Ibid.*, pp. 57–8.

7   'Harlem is Nowhere', *ibid.*, pp. 299–300.

8   'Hidden Name and Complex Fate', *ibid.*, pp. 162–63.

9   'Change the Joke and Slip the Yoke', *ibid.*, p. 59.

10 'Living with Music' and 'The Charlie Christian Story', *ibid.*, pp. 189, 234.

11 'Hidden Name and Complex Fate', *ibid.*, pp. 149–49.

12 *Ibid.*, p. 146.

13 'Change the Joke and Slip the Yoke', *ibid.*, p. 55.

14 Todd Lieber finds that 'invisibility' is a metaphor defined by two traditions in black culture; one identifies the failure of society to recognize black humanity, while the other deals with the game of defensive masking by which the Black hides or shields the self and which may usurp, in the eyes of black and white alike, the integrity of the self. See 'Ralph Ellison and the Metaphor of Invisibility in Black Literary Tradition', *American Quarterly*, 24 (1972), pp. 86–100.

15 *The Complete Tales and Poems of Edgar Allan Poe*, ed. Hervey Allen, Modern Library Edition (New York, 1938), p. 23.

16 'The Art of Fiction', *Shadow and Act*, p. 180; 'Change the Joke and Slip the Yoke', *ibid.*, p. 57.

17 'The Art of Fiction', *Shadow and Act*, p. 178.

18 Quotations in this and the next two paragraphs are from Chapter 11.

19 *Shadow and Act*, p. 57.

5

James Baldwin:
Stepping Out on the Promise

by WILLIAM WASSERSTROM

To the Memory of George Wiley

Deliverance will come: It had not come for my mother and father, it had not come for Caleb, it had not come for me, it had not come for Christopher, it had not come for this nameless little girl, and it had not come for all these thousands who were listening to her song . . . Christopher did not believe that deliverance would ever come—he was going to drag it down from heaven or raise it up from hell—for Christopher, the party, that banquet at which we had been poisoned for so long, was over . . . I wanted deliverance—for others even more than myself: *my* party, *my* banquet . . . was over too . . . No song could be worth what this singing little girl had already paid for it, was paying, and would continue to pay. And yet—without a song?

James Baldwin: *Tell Me How Long the Train's Been Gone* (1968)

There is one theme I like above all others, and that is redemption.

Henry Roth: *Partisan Review* (1969)

Yes, the blacks are here to bear witness and to . . . make America more America, because more human.

Léopold S. Senghor: *New York Times* (11 September 1975)

1

Never, not once during a career now ending its third decade, has James Baldwin lapsed in public fealty to a single idea. Attaining

74

its crown and prosperity during the great age of tribulation in our time, the nineteen-sixties, Baldwin's credo—though by no means reducible to a code—might be said to have invested the arts of literature with Martin Luther King's preachments on the politics of race. Simultaneously, in what must be I suppose an improbable confluence of history and of temperament, fundamental features of Baldwin's ideology coincide with component traits of vanguard European sensibility in that era—with that anti-psychiatry of madness developed in Britain by R. D. Laing and a structuralism of sanity designed for France by Jacques Lacan. Although Jimmy Baldwin's loyalty to Martin—always Martin, not King, not Martin Luther King, just Martin—is unstinting, unfailing, still it's those other affiliations which disclose Baldwin's enduring claims on our vigilance, our esteem.

Extravagant though these associations may at first appear, it is an extraordinary accident of taste and interplay of motive which fifteen years ago impelled Laing and Baldwin not only to entertain the drama of apocalypse but also to choose nearly identical means for the salvation or damnation of souls. In their work and in their persons, both men reviled a widespread habit of propitiating that savage god whose feast is a provender of victims drawn from the ranks of 'Other,' says Laing, regardless of race, of colour. 'The common bond between Us,' according to *The Politics of Experience* (1967)—proto-typical text of the man who tied himself into knots trying to measure and close the gap between persons, between 'Us and Them,' as well as between person and persona—'may be the Other'. Because inexorably 'We are They to Them as They are They to Us,' it's no trivial fantasy but powerful presences mankind conjures up and is captivated by, phantasms that summon us to 'die, kill, devour, tear and [be] torn apart'. Maybe so, Baldwin says. But in fact 'the situation of the black male is a microcosm of the situation of the Christian world.' One whose ability to love has been utterly eroded, he is left with 'absolutely no floor on which to dance, no room in which to move, no way to get from one day to the next'. It's difficult enough to be born, to learn to walk, to grow old and to die, difficult 'for everybody, everywhere, forever. But no one has the right to put on top of that another burden, another price which nobody can pay, and a burden which really nobody can bear.' Like Laing, then, who rejected that conventional wisdom which said it's impossible to get inside the skin of another human being, Baldwin is unique among American writers for concentrating his whole purpose, his immense talent and prestige, on diverse demonstrations that skin itself, black skin in its hue and its history, is the measure of distance separating a man from his inner life, each of us from one another, humanity itself from deliverance. 'The only reason I'm here', he concluded his conversation with Margaret Mead in August 1970 (*A Rap on Race*, 1971), 'is to bear witness.'

Reading Baldwin's fiction, seeing the plays, considering the pamphlets and the criticism and the film script and the interviews, the 'dialogues', we find ourselves in an embrace so tight, an encapsulation so snug, a febrility so hot that the taste and smell of his ferocity and sensuality exclude, expel all other flavours, odours, ties. Even if it were untrue that Baldwin set himself to conquer or seduce or invade us, even if we are able to hear in his tone now and then a resonance of black cool, what we hear is thin insulation against the white heat of will, whatever his tone of voice or choice of genre, to make himself visible, palpable, penetrable. In materializing himself by way of literature, he has meant to induce us to alter our lives. Once Baldwin's blackness, unalloyed, has corrupted us then we'll be liberated, purified, purged of vileness in an America whose archaic taste for delusion and deceit has made 'real companionship, honest art and purposeful politics impossible'. Like Baldwin, furthermore, who knows that it's easier to pass through the eye of a needle than to circumvent the natural barriers and unnatural guardians of the self Laing, in that final wild Gnomic section of his book notifies us that he too won't quit until he's truly got to us. Indeed in the final segment, 'The Bird of Paradise', he engages in exactly the kind of exhortation which marks one traditional way of American imagination, a way adopted by Baldwin in order to infuse all readers with the experience of blackness. 'I want you to taste and smell me, want to be palpable,' Laing says as if in paraphrase of Baldwin's intent, 'to be an itch in your brain and your guts that you can't scratch out and that you can't allay, that will corrupt you and destroy you and drive you mad.' Evoking Lacan's theory of psycho-analysis as a language 'close to poetry, close to delirium', Laing's practice—

'the great intellectual Rorschach Blot of the latter Sixties', Peter Sedgwick says in valediction—and Baldwin's art converge in a common will to find means whereby interpenetration hence salvation can occur.

Whether or not 'the case of R. D. Laing is', as Sedgwick presents it in *Salmagundi* (Spring–Summer, 1979) 'less a part of any intellectual history than of the social history of stunts', none the less he did invent a peculiarly psychiatric and British way of bearing witness. Stressing disjunction and distance even as he celebrated communion, he maintained that nature intransigently shells us round quite as culture—class and colour and region and accent—thrusts us apart. 'Well,' said Baldwin in *A Dialogue* (1973) with Nikki Giovanni, 'as a black man I've paid too much for America to abandon it.' 'I don't think it's a question of abandoning it,' Giovanni remarked, 'where else would we go? I mean, nobody wants us.' More to the point of abandonment, however, is not Baldwin's flight to France at the start of the seventies but Laing's contention that the time is past for saints to be kissing lepers: 'it's high time that the leper kissed the saint'. Are you coming home soon Jimmy, people asked in 1977. 'I say yes, soon.' When the new novel is done—as it is now done and due out in fall, 1979—'maybe it'll be the end of more than the novel—a long apprenticeship, I sometimes think.'

It may well be of course that Baldwin and Laing bear witness to the end of a whole era of apprenticeship—professional, national, global. I venture no prophecy in matter of Laing. But if one were to draw up a short list of American writers whose biographies may be said to parallel the history of a culture and an epoch, who embody in an oeuvre the shame and splendour, the force to create and to destroy which disfigure and dignify our leprous time, Baldwin would stand very near the top. A writer unembarrassed to say 'I am the history of America,' whatever else he does from here on out, whatever honours are won or favor is lost, the period of his apprenticeship is inexorably pegged to so long a season of triumph and gall, of hurt and heal—twenty-five years of damage and recovery assure that neither health nor harm in either the man or the nation will in this generation be final or whole. An era that began for him 'in Paris at the first African Writers Congress held at the Sorbonne in September, 1956' and concluded with the death of Martin Luther King, the catastrophe which 'brought me back to Europe again—the most embattled years of this apprenticeship, chronicled in *No Name in the Street* (1971), disclose why he was desperate for distance enough from 'the American Negro Problem' to enable him to 'write with a half clear head' about a demented people. Softly at first, Baldwin told Angela Davis in a famed open letter to *The New York Review of Books* (7 January, 1971), then louder and louder, insistently, stridently, making 'as much noise as I can, here in Europe, on radio and television,' I have been saying that American whites, demonstrably 'unable to contend with their own leaders for the redemption of their own honour and the lives of their children,' are unlikely to come to the aid of Blacks, 'the most rejected of Western children'. We must therefore be prepared to 'fight for your life as though it were our own' and 'render impassable with our bodies the corridors to the gas chamber. For if they take you in the morning, they will be coming for us that night.' Following Davis's acquittal on charges of assisting in an attempted prison break, he entered into a state of truce but not accommodation with a society about which as he said in 1973 he'd always felt 'hopelessly ambivalent'. Through the seventies he's been 'a kind of commuter' rather than an expatriate: 'I can't live in exile, but I can't work here.'

'If I hadn't become famous,' he said just before publication of *If Beale Street Could Talk* (1973), 'I might not have survived.' Four years later in an eclipse of fame but again ignited by an-incandescent black American energy, by a 'certain sense of life' which it is the 'assignment of the artist' to liberate—'and the key is love'—in 1977 Baldwin vowed to end his state of semi-truancy and to resume a course whose pursuit had been too long stalled. I'm going to do what Andy Young does, he remarked to Robert Coles. I look at Andy on the screen and see 'the frustration and hurt in his eyes'. But 'there's a glow in his eyes too—a smile that says he's going to keep taking a chance, one more and then one more after that.' So too does Jimmy Baldwin, welcoming 'the tension, the drama, the struggle for a handle on life' in America, in the world, relying on that black energy which sanctions faith in the arts of revelation, prepare once again to 'step out on the promise' not of reform or reconciliation merely but of deliverance.

One or two words more of prologue are in order before we carry on, proceed to recapitulate the history of this illustrious man's struggle to compose a classic black literature of liberation in an authentic American grain. Not least among instigations to this rehearsal, to a revival of interest in Baldwin's lustrous art, is the need to set a stage for his reappearance in mid autumn 1979 with a fiction treating a figure of lofty place, a subject of exemplary merit in any hierarchy of American persons and values.[1] More's at stake therefore than a book only, a reputation alone. For in announcing a novel about a gospeller, a singer whose genius crystallizes the very soul of race, Baldwin reconfirms beyond rhetoric the solemnity of his ambition to step out on the promise—a promise, furthermore, that transcends 'Us and Them', black and white politics of madness. Ten years ago in that conversation with Nikki Giovanni, timed to coincide with his removal to St. Paul du Vence, Baldwin insisted on the ineffability of black music, the intimacy of music and culture, the indivisibility of song and story and, strikingly, on a sort of mythic or sociologic or psychologic inefficiency of white response to black being in America. Almost as if in paraphrase and confirmation of Laing's series of axioms on the same theme ('I cannot experience your experience. We are both invisible men. All men are invisible to one another. Experience is man's invisibility to man. Experience used to be called the Soul.') Baldwin insisted that this century is lost, virtually damned, until whites begin 'to apprehend the experience out of which a Lena Horne comes, for example, or an Ethel Waters'. Or Paul Robeson or Bessie Smith or Billie Holiday or Aretha Franklin or, above all others, Ray Charles. And if 'white people don't know what they come out of', the reason is not a matter of eugenics or metabolism. Rather 'there's no metaphor in their experience for it—or the metaphor in their experience is so deeply buried and so frightening' it's been banished. '*If our experience is destroyed,*' Laing said as if with Baldwin in mind '*our behaviour will be destructive*' (Laing's emphasis).

Herself unable to follow Baldwin's effort to encircle and capture that black 'sense of life' which finds its way into song, Giovanni ('I tend to be slow sometimes') changed the subject and instantly, inadvertently, snared the sense of Baldwin's notion. 'Do you think you would ever write a work of fiction or maybe even a work of nonfiction that did not include white people?' she asked. Yes, he said. 'I'm working on something now in which there are no white people.' Though he didn't identify the book it must be surely *If Beale Street Could Talk*, a virtuoso tale recounted from a woman's point of view. A story with a large cast of black characters, its plot requires just two Whites, a cop who scarcely speaks and a shopkeeper who says very few words, plays a role in cameo. Though both are pivotal in the action, Baldwin allots neither more than a stroke or two of portraiture, just enough for a contrast of portrayal—stereotypical Whites vis-à-vis archetypal Blacks, star-crossed lovers. The young man, an artist in wood, jailed though innocent, from the prison side of 'glass and stone and steel' says to his pregnant wife-to-be: 'I'm coming home, can you dig that?' ' "Yes," I said.'

> *Now.* I'm an artisan . . . like a cat who makes—tables. I don't like the words artist. Maybe I never did. I sure the fuck don't know what it means. I'm a cat who works from his balls, with his hand. I know what it's about now. I think I really do. Even if I go under. But I don't think I will. Now.

Straining for a way to render in ordinary white speech an ambiance of negritude, Baldwin told Giovanni that 'it takes a long time before you realise that there is a connection between *Tell Me How Long the Train's Been Gone*' (his last novel published before their conversation) 'and "Swing Low, Sweet Chariot" or what Ray Charles does with dreary little anthems one wouldn't dream of hearing until he got his hands on them and put our experience into them . . . that's what I mean by energy.' And that's what he tried to convey more or less unsuccessfully to Margaret Mead too, on that other occasion of talk in 1970. 'I've never learned anything through my mind. I learned whatever I've learned through my heart and guts.' But that won't do, Mead said, you need a controlling brain. 'But without a certain passion, and passion has no mind, without a certain love that—how can I put it baby? Something has happened here and you have to feel a discipline to build that pipeline that brings it up to your mind.' How taxing this discipline is, how enveloping this passion to conscript energy —a flow in the pipeline linking guts and hand and brain—in behalf of black constancy, durability, perpetuity, is apparent in still another of his efforts to transmit, in plain white talk about black art, the buried meaning of metaphor. In the narrative and dramatic setting written for a concert Charles gave at the Newport Jazz Festival in 1973, Baldwin sought 'to reflect what Ray's music expresses', an 'affirmation that has come out of depths that most Americans find difficult to imagine'. Nothing less than 'one of the keys to black survival' in the United States, music is the central trope of Baldwin's art even as art itself is invariably his recurring conceit of affliction and deliverance.

2

Having established connections between gospel song and narrative art, between Charles and Baldwin, between *If Beale Street Could Talk* and *Tell Me How Long the Train's Been Gone*, and also between other stations and texts which mark Baldwin's progress both as an ideologue and an artist, let us without more ado recount the record of his apprenticeship as a black singer of American gospel. Hit or miss my aim is not at all to reproduce still another temperature chart of a fretful and liverish flux, prophetic book to visionary sermon. This exercise has been done uncommonly well by a number of critics, notably Robert A. Bone and Colin MacInness, less well by others in what is now a long and lengthening queue. A line that runs among Whites from F. W. Dupee and Alfred Kazin and Irving Howe to Benjamin DeMott, among Blacks it contains at least two collections of papers in assessment, the most recent being *James Baldwin: A Critical Evaluation*, edited by Therman O'Daniel (1977). What none of these essays does address or measure, however, is the cumulative weight of conversation—not TV blague and gabble but colloquy both sober and light, soaring and lowdown. Stepping in and out of his books, Baldwin has transformed the edited transcript of talk into a vehicle of autobiography. A genre given to the uses of self-evasion and self advertisement, in Baldwin's instance it serves as a means of self-disclosure, self-composition, and therefore divulges the character and pulse of the man distinct from contrivance or

mask. Unmasked, Baldwin turns out to be not in the least like the
effigy invented by Eldridge Cleaver for *Soul On Ice* (1968). Perhaps the earliest rival for black power in literature during the
sixties, Cleaver devoted nearly as much space to the effort of over-
mastering Baldwin as Baldwin himself had once devoted to the
work of disestablishing Richard Wright. In his own way of course
also a survivor, now no longer a rebel voice and revolutionist
leader but instead an evangel-entrepreneur awaiting the dock—
about a decade ago in an essay called 'Notes On a Native Son'
Cleaver accused Baldwin of ethnic self-hatred and traced its cause
to a desire, common among black homosexuals, to submit to
white men. Unimaginable: less than a dozen years have passed
since Cleaver denounced Baldwin for 'embodying in his art the
self-flagellating policy of Martin Luther King' and damned him
for being as timid and perverse as Wright had been manly and
brave.

Like Wright during his last years, like other colleagues in militancy in the early and mid-sixties, Cleaver defied blackness,
exalted negritude and envisioned an alliance with the Third
World. Contradicting Baldwin's views on the value of that 1956
conference of black African writers, Cleaver rejected Baldwin's
argument attributing the psychology and temper of Africans and
West Indians to their having been invaded and overrun and as a
result left 'with no recourse against oppression except to over-
throw the machinery of the oppressor'. Given this circumstance,
colour alone Baldwin had taken to be insufficient grounds on
which to declare or justify common cause. Even though Blacks
everywhere shared a painful relation to the white world, a necessity to remake the world in their own image and, most acutely, an
'ache to come into the world as men', nevertheless American
Blacks and American Whites 'made and mangled' by the same
machinery were irretrievably linked in a resolve not to destroy but
to compel the machinery of politics, of government, to work for
their common benefit.

In recalling the main points of divergence between Baldwin
and Cleaver in the sixties, we return to the first dawn of that era
which for James Baldwin ended with the murder of King. At its
start Baldwin took up a position, sketched above, identical to
that of Cleaver's hero, Frantz Fanon, and set down in Fanon's

sacred text, *The Wretched of the Earth* (1965). Indeed it was at the famed congress in Paris that conferees had agreed on fundamental differences between 'problems which kept Richard Wright and Langston Hughes on the alert' and 'those which might confront Léopold Senghor or Jomo Kenyatta'. In truth those test cases of civil liberty in America with which both Whites and Blacks try to force society to end racial discrimination, Fanon said, have very little in common with 'the heroic fight of the Angolan people against the detestable Portuguese colonialism'. What Africans and American Blacks do indeed share is a resemblance based on the fact that all are 'defined in relation to the whites'. Beyond that single crucial fact, little else.

Admiring Fanon, Cleaver picked his way through ideas which enabled him to play the role of Antony to Baldwin's Brutus and Wright's Caesar. Richard Wright 'had the ability, like Dreiser, of harnessing the gigantic, overwhelming environmental forces and focusing them, with pinpoint sharpness, on individuals and their acts as they are caught up in the whirlwind of the savage anarchistic sweep of life, love, death, and hate, pain, hope, pleasure, and despair across the face of a nation and the world'. Baldwin lacks this power, Cleaver insisted. At his worst he creates black eunuchs unmanned by self-violation. But at his best he is, unlike Wright peculiarly skilled in examining the nuances of unconscious motive animating his people. This much Cleaver allowed him, a 'superb touch when he speaks of human beings, when he is inside them—especially his homesexuals'. Though enlivened by a surcharged love of flesh, intoxicated by lusts, his work is not driven by a revulsion against the white world, by a politics of revolt. When 'he looks beyond the skin', therefore, he founders.

Cleaver's opinion, not at all disinterested, was intended to advance a specific programme of revolutionary change in the American life of race. Only a few years of age separate them but whole continents and oceans span the distance between Eldridge Cleaver, Californian and adoptive African, and James Baldwin, New Yorker and quondam European. Had not the genetics of colour and the perturbations of culture accidentally joined them there would be no longer any reason to speak of either in connection with the other. Unpredictable child of an unbolted nation, a guerrilla of the ghetto fated for war, rape, loot, jail, at this moment Cleaver is a born-again Christian preaching a Pentecost not of the stark Seaboard storefront church but of the gold Coast. In contrast Baldwin, first and last a man of letters, in another time and place would write books and collect honours. And in viewing him as larger than life-size Cleaver not only vented a taste for melo- drama but in addition confirmed the charge which black writers address at those white critics who somehow imagine black Ameri- can artists to be cast in titanic mould.

A just accusation and honest complaint from which neither Cleaver nor Baldwin are exempt, it may represent one of the last barriers of segregation as yet unbreached. Without question, however, it demonstrates intent no less than internecine: in the war between black generations, as in the current battles between black women and men, much sympathy but no quarter is given. And if fratricide was Cleaver's aim, nothing less than patricide led Baldwin to present Wright not as a writer with virtues and vices, good at this and bad at that, but as a failed Prometheus. Given the kind of man Wright was—recalled by Chester Himes in *The Quality of Hurt* (1972) as 'condescending', 'cruel', 'lordly'— given, too, Himes's view of the American literary establishment as prepared to admit only 'one black at a time, to the arena of fame', there's a full measure and stop of social history in the sight of Wright and Baldwin (Paris, midnight, spring, 1953) at a dead heat of venom in debate, 'The last I remember before I left', Himes said twenty years later, is Baldwin repeating ' "the sons must slay their fathers." And I realised suddenly that he was right.' It may well be true that so long as black writers are or imagine themselves to be confined in a literary ghetto, only one at a time can assume the heroic mode. Beginning in the mid- fifties, in any event, lordly and Promethean in his turn, Baldwin acquired Wright's international following, a public unmatched by writers of larger accomplishment though by no means of greater distinction. Culture hero though he is today, it's indisputable that he hasn't yet written everybody's protest black novel. It's equally plain, as MacInness observed, that the 'bardic voice' of this 'pre- monitory prophet' unquestionably rang true in everybody's pro- test essay, *The Fire Next Time* (1962), composed in counterpoint to a rising anxiety about black insurrection. Finding in his ser- mons an authentic rhetoric of conscience society promptly gave him most of its awards. This is not to say that radical chic alone conferred fame or that Baldwin's reputation was the fruit of fad or that his fiction is lame. But now that he's well advanced in middle life, at peace with himself and at an interval of lull in his battle for survival, there's time for calmer appreciation of a career taken more nearly whole rather than in pieces. Having performed Herculean feats of discourse in uniting Harlem and Concord, mission church and Transcendentalist pulpit, having exploded great glissades of shamanistic chant which exposed the psychic origins, historic affects and social causes of white idiocy and guilt—from the mid-fifties until the late-seventies Baldwin has sought to create out of raw and redneck wilderness a whole nation.

3

Quickly exhuming main facts of biography in order to understand how he got from South to North, from Harlem to Paris and back, from Richard Wright to Henry James, James to Gide, Gide to Mead and Giovanni and Ray Charles and whole new cohorts of writers on race—returning to a point of origin, we ought to know that Baldwin was born in 1924 in New York City and lived there, in Harlem, until 1942. Eldest of nine children, he and his family exhibit both the most remarkable and the most conventional effects of the great Southern migration in our century—his father having come North to work in a factory and serve as a preacher, his mother having emigrated from the state of Maryland. In 1942, upon graduation from a leading New York City high school, De Witt Clinton, Baldwin tried various jobs, both war- and peace-time. Simultaneously, with the help of two fellowships, he undertook to begin a literary career. In 1948, following the lead of his first mentor Wright, he went to Paris. Ten years in France were interrupted by what is described as a sort of breakdown spent in Switzerland where, 'armed with two Bessie Smith records and a typewriter, I tried to re-create the life that I had first known as a child and from which I had spent so many years in flight', Go Tell It on the Mountain (1953) and The Amen Corner, a play first produced in 1955, Notes of a Native Son (1955) represent both the accomplishment of those years and the resolution, at least for a time, of conflict and torture of mind. Even twenty years ago it was obvious that these first works heralded a major career. It may indeed turn out to be *Go Tell It on the Mountain* which is Baldwin's unsurpassable fiction, quite as his essays may well reserve for him a central place in the history of ideas, the cultural history of our era. What is stunning about that novel is precisely the most compelling thing about those fabled collections of essays, *Notes* (1955), *Nobody Knows My Name* (1961) and *The Fire Next Time* (1963), which established Baldwin, who had returned to the United States in 1957, as the chief spokesman and most eloquent voice of mediation between black want and white neglect. These texts—and predictably the forthcoming fiction too, in that it is said to take up 'where *Go Tell It on the Mountain* left off'—habitually refer to an ideal America, both the discovered country and a region located inside Baldwin's head. The first is a Deep South, old and strong and strange. Heard in residues of speech and rooted in the lore of section and in the nature of place it is manifest, according to a specialist in these subjects and modes, Richard M. Dorson, an academic collector of black oral tradition and tale—it is incarnate in the figure of those Alabama grandmothers who have seen ghosts and know signs, auguries, omens. They bestow on their literary heirs certain particular 'deep responses of mind and imagination and tongue'. Listen to a black intellectual chatting with white colleagues, Dorson remarks. However masterful his white talk, he has a deeper vein. Tap it and you discover how fast he can switch to that other realm—'what you might call Negro *soul*', said Malcolm X and Himes in autobiography before the word became cant.

Baldwin is indisputably a son of the South, though a wayward one. Alongside that legacy he inherits another, incorporates a third and imports, domesticates, a fourth. Deep South and ghetto North, Old World and native land—these unite inside Baldwin's imagination and surface in Baldwin's prose. This teller of tales in New York and Paris and St. Paul du Vence, this city slicker is surely the most vagrant of wayfaring grandsons and his literary powers ebb and flow in confluence with the play of these currents in his mind. Perhaps the most economical and accurate way to identify his range and flow of mind is to recall his choice of masters, the one he inherited and the ones he adopted. Possessing powers of a grandmotherly kind, following Wright, he at first those black fable and fact as the most natural and appropriate means to launch himself. What stirred his imagination was not just a jungle tooth and claw struggle of black men to survive in a white world but also a ferocity of more personal and intricate kind—of the will to triumph over complexities of fate common to all American writers but especially acute in a writer whose diffusion of identity is the more pronounced due to aspersions of colour.

Baldwin himself believes that his mind was in considerable degree cramped during the period of his affiliation with Wright and that his art first flourished under the auspices of Henry James. But whatever the reason, whatever the cause—cause and reason which may be quite detached from Wright and James—his first work continues until now to express his genius at its keenest. *Go Tell It on the Mountain*, the stories of *Going to Meet the Man* (1965) and his five collections of criticism, display a writer whose merit does not rest on intricacy of invention or originality of analysis in examining the relations of race in America. Rather, a coincidence of race and rage brought Baldwin to literature and brought his page to a boil. In fiction, long and short, in literary, cultural and film criticism, Baldwin developed permutations on one paramount, single, overriding belief which refined his art and stabilised his mind. For all the experiment and expertise of genre represented in this work, for all his apparent range of interests, there is a persistent set of recurring images and passions, an obsessive pattern of thought and pattern of plot which Baldwin has chosen in order to dramatize crisis. At the very point in a story or essay when radical change is shown, when the action or argument requires an analogue or emblem of a shift in direction, a new plan of attack, Baldwin's imagination has almost invariably resorted to the experience of conversion, either undisguised or cunningly hid.

It is impossible to overstate the power of this habit in determining the character of his intelligence or the quality of his art. For it identifies so unquenchable and intense a will that its use as a literary tactic is all but instinctive. Obsession with religious experience is surely in part an accident of race in America, a country in which displaced Southern Blacks who were originally compelled to manœuvre within the narrowest negotiable notions

87

of redemption and were later trapped in Northern ghettos, there suffered still fiercer constraint. The instrument of survival, a strait-jacket they called salvation, reduced the principle of grace to the simplest conceivable idea of virtue. No wonder then that Baldwin (who calls himself a 'much-scarred man') in 'Down at the Cross' recalls his first sexual adventure with the holy girls of his church as 'grim, guilty, tormented experiments . . . at once as chill and joyless as the Russian steppes and hotter, by far, than all the fires of hell'. It cannot on balance matter that white American sensibility is tainted in similar ways. In the ruins of Harlem the taint is nastier and the scar goes deeper. 'They understood that they must act as God's decoys, saving the souls of the boys in marriage.'

This distorted legacy of Harriet Beecher Stowe ('*Uncle Tom's Cabin* meant a lot to me'), subtilised beyond its merit as a moral idea, reappears in Baldwin's pamphlets, novels, plays, stories—even in the film treatment of Malcolm X's *Autobiography*, *One Day, When I Was Lost* (1973)—to both triumphant and disastrous effect. Having inspired *Go Tell It on the Mountain*, a work endowed with riches of suffering and relief unavailable to writers less deeply scarred, it has served Baldwin ill on those occasions when the language of apocalypse is unwarranted or unearned. No question about its authenticity in this novel, a story in which religious conversion serves as the quintessence of plot and the essence of need—quite as it does, incidentally, in Malcolm's exchange of a satanic Christianity for a messianic Muslimism, a conversion which occurs during a sequence of scenes by far the most fearful and telling in the script as a whole. The point of course is not that the works are equivalent. More to the point is a habit of equivalence in which, according to Baldwin's praxis, rebirth is somehow indispensible as a reagent of progress in the drama of growth. Unlike the extraordinary instance of that first novel, the results are not invariably blessed. There, however, the boy John, tyrannized by an overbearing but weak father, arrested by terror, is an easy victim of a man mobilised by crimes, guilts, shames, sins carried to a phantasmagoric North from a South which is itself an exquisite symbol of social and sexual hallucination. Himself torn by phantasmagoria and hallucination, in his very person John summons up the father's shameful past and evokes an unendurable present. An unnatural man who is not even John's natural parent, obviously he must be outwitted or overborne if the boy is not to succumb. If John is indeed to outlast the elder man he must seize one of the two opportunities of choice available in their world: the church racket or the street hustle. Leading John first into a soul-shattering breakdown, then to the temptations of conversion and finally through a process of self-re-constitution beyond both racket and hustle, Baldwin devises splendid means of plot to enable the young man to negotiate rites of passage in Harlem.

The impetus of these first years carried Baldwin from book to book in which the resolution of an action or an idea turned on one or another rite of salvation. Consider 'Sonny's Blues', for example, that widely reprinted but not highly polished story from *Going to Meet the Man* (1965). In surrendering this story to the dogma of transformation Baldwin sacrificed his earliest effort to exploit that black sense of life which finds its way into song. Today of course it's possible to redeem the impulse which underlies a fiction in which two brothers learn that they must love each other or die. Discovering that pure hate will consume their lives in a society which doesn't care whether they live or die, they learn too that the very society which threatens to extinguish them, which they despise, which at its most benign finds them to be neither worthy of interest nor worthy of care—this benighted America has endowed them with a tradition and an energy which can save them. Like Ray Charles they find in music a means of access to the very heart of their instinctive and communal lives. 'Then they all gathered around Sonny and Sonny played. Every now and again, one of them seemed to say, amen.' Making music Sonny re-makes himself and in behalf of his people converts grief into grace.

Whatever the subject, however lavish his material, Baldwin resorted almost exclusively to this certain ground of motive, this sure mode and sanction of fulfilment. Even the two main texts of *Nobody Knows My Name*, 'The Discovery of What It Means to Be an American' and 'Notes for a Hypothetical Novel'—essays treating the most familiar of temptations for an American writer, the lure of Europe—portray the process of analysis and judgement as a long dark night of the soul. Disdaining to present a balanced tally of profits and losses which led him to return to the United States that first time, he cast the whole enterprise of expatriation into the discourse of spiritual exercise, of trans-figuration. In appraising the value of exile, he said, the day came round at last when in a great burst of clarity he perceived that Europe could never be a culmination only an overture. If an ex-patriate black writer 'has been preparing himself for anything in Europe, he has been preparing himself for America'. Brought full circle 'from the vantage point of Europe, he discovers his own country. And this is a discovery which not only brings an end to the alienation of the American from himself, but also makes clear to him, for the first time, the extent of his involvement in Europe.' Self-possessed at long last, this convert found himself prepared to take up his burden, accept his calling, assume his vocation: an American life in art.

Especially dazzling was the flamboyance with which he elabor-ated his special subject. Contrasting 'the vision of the Old World with that of the New', a vision of the Old expressed as constraint, a sense of the inexorable limits of life, and of the New as en-largement, a 'sense of life's possibilities'—resolving classic ques-tions of antithesis in culture, Baldwin orchestrated a dialectic in which alienation, at odds with involvement, predictably leads to transcendence. Oedipal exchange of Wright for James, replace-ment of Fanon by Martin Luther King, transmutation of Pente-costal talk into the music of gospel and blues, conversion of heterosexual into bisexual or homosexual love—all conflict of attitude, allegiance, appetite, ambition were stylized by a system of interlocution which Baldwin brought to bear on literature, politics, sex and race in the sixties.

4

These grand thoughts and big themes coalesce, in fiction, first in *Giovanni's Room* (1956) and not long thereafter in *Another Country* (1962). The former work, useful in documenting Bald-win's habit of thrust and counterthrust as a kind of foreplay of fusion, is a more accurate map of the novelist's mind than it is an appreciable novel. Map it is surely. Polemic it is too in behalf of a notion of civilization incarnate in males, a union of men in love: David and Giovanni. David's disquietude—the result of his inability to decide whether to marry American fiancée, Hella, or to commit himself irrevocably to his Italian male lover—is conceived not as a straightforward problem in sexual taste or national morals but of clerical duty. Unwilling to marry the girl he decides that heterosexuality at its merriest is at best a meagre semblance of rapture. If he were to pretend to love women he would commit fraud. And in turning fraud into a sovereign principle of behavior, he would increase the power of sham and sanctimony in America, already controlling modes of intercourse. In contrast the relationship with Giovanni, glorifying high passion, enacted a benediction of malehood. To his torment, however, he realises that he is too timid, too much unmanned to advertise so heretical a case for the disguises of love, not gypsy enough to insist on this form of devotion as a true rite of love and fit sanction of masculine being. 'The burden of his salvation seemed to be on me and I could not endure it,' David says, speaking in behalf of Baldwin's effort to impose on gender and sex an honorific splendour.

Sanction is Baldwin's profane term for sanctification of manhood, the unadorned theme of *Giovanni's Room*. A rather old-fashioned contrast between the stringencies of sex in a straight country and the resiliences, combinations and elasticities of the life of passion in the Old World, in its interpenetration of eros and ananke this novel lofts itself to heights of aspiration undreamt of in San Francisco. And though the plot is an account, at bottom, of the brutalisation of an Italian male whore, its drama is centered in the mind of a man who finds himself to be unworthy of the holy office thrust upon him, a high priesthood of love. In contrast to *Giovanni's Room*, which charts a series of complications stemming from David's craven spirit, *Another Country*, immeasurably grander in design, moves by way of a series of deaths and transfigurations toward a transformation of race in this native land. 'Don't get me wrong,' he was quoted as saying in *Ebony*, 'I love America'—loved it, he preferred not to add, in the fashion set by a most eminent mentor, Henry James, on whom he relied to modulate and calibrate a missionary ardour 'to tell as much of the truth as one can bear, and then a little more'. An American writer works under hazards uncommon elsewhere, Baldwin wrote in the *New York Times* (14 January, 1962) shortly

91

before *Another Country* appeared, in that he lives 'in a country in which words are mostly used to cover the sleeper, not to wake him up'. A writer must therefore find a way of language which won't pander to somnolence but will arouse his people, put them 'in touch with reality'.

The most impressive example of a writer who served his people well is Balzac, but as a model for his own purposes Baldwin, anointing James, turned to *The Ambassadors*. In all James's oeuvre it is this work, written in tribute to 'masculine sensibility', which most resourcefully portrays the 'moral dilemma of American malehood'. Not that its 'erotic activity' is especially instructive. But 'the responsibility that men must take on themselves of facing and re-ordering reality'—James's engagement with this theme leads him to confront Strether with the very question which 'torments us now. The question is this: how is an American to become a man? And this is precisely the same thing as asking: How is America to become a nation?' With James's guidance, therefore, in *Another Country* Baldwin set out to resolve the twin torment of that intertwined pair. Following the lead of this best of modern Virgils, he undertook to pierce the 'air of this time and place', heavy and 'thick with soothing lies', in a voice assertive enough for everyone to hear. We work in the dark, Baldwin rounds off his conclusion in James's words, 'we do what we can, our doubt is our passion and our passion is our task. The rest is the madness of art.'

Unfortunately the novel itself, *Another Country*, turned out to be a touch shrill. A work of almost sheer will rather than passion, mind not guts, it comes off less as an exfoliation of art and energy than as a programmatic text planted on the same high ground to which not James but Lawrence long ago staked vast claims. Like Lawrence indeed, Baldwin argues that a condition of manliness is not attained, the fullest aspiration of moral life is unrealized until the deepest human intimacy imaginable is sealed in a blood brotherhood from which Lawrence pretended to exclude sexual attachment but in which Baldwin, without pretence, finds erotic transport. Even as *Another Country* thus shares in the great tradition of the Anglo–American novel—Baldwin, like James a déraciné, traces his lineage to those writers who, as F. R. Leavis says, invent grandeurs of civility and civilization that are 'found in no country'—so too is Baldwin's drift anticipated in Leslie Fiedler's *Love and Death in the American Novel* (1960). Consistent with Fiedler's account of a 'Holy Marriage of Males,' *Another Country* as well as the novel that followed it, *Tell Me How Long the Train's Been Gone* (1968), postulates an immersion in homoerotic love to be the principal precondition of a 'natural renewal of the soul', of the body politic.

If in the fifties Baldwin staked his career on a conversion of Oedipal rage into apocalyptic frenzy, in the sixties he raised his own ante by attempting to transmute frenzy into a phallic shamanism empowered to redeem a retrograde people that duplicitiously honours only those men who are to women wed. Intimated in *Another Country*, phallicism is framed in the person of Christopher, the hero's paramour in *Tell Me How Long the Train's Been Gone*. Amalgamating a paganism of sex with the politics of revolution, Christopher—simulacrum of Huey Newton perhaps and countless others—joins forces with Leo Proudhammer, a man unmistakably kin to Baldwin himself or the actor Sidney Poitier or Ray Charles. Ironically named, the anti-Christ Christopher, created as a foil to Leo's Christly brother Caleb, embodies segments of an idea Baldwin discovered in Gide and dilated in an essay called 'The Male Prison'. In arguing that Gide sought to reconcile the paganism of his lusts, his homosexuality, with the rigours and austerities of his Protestant past, Baldwin proposed that marriage was in Gide's mind a symbol of 'Heaven'. Installed there, Madelaine 'would forgive him for his hell and help him to endure it'.

Whether or not Baldwin found his own real Madelaine, in this novel he duplicates Gide's feat by imagining one, a white-Kentucky-heiress-actress-mother-wife-sister, and installing her in a New York City slum called Paradise Alley. Found there by the novice actor Leo, Barbara, apotheosis of Woman, willingly serves as Proudhammer's lifeline out of an American hell.

> Barbara had done something very hard and rare. As though she had known I would need it, and would always need it, she had arranged her life so that my place in it would never be jeopardized . . . The incestuous brother and sister would now never have any children. But perhaps we had . . . helped to open the world to one child. Luckier lovers hadn't managed so much. The sun-

light filled the room . . . For some reason, I thought of Paradise Alley.

Harboured in her life, at home in her body—in the flesh of an exhilarating white girl in whom there was 'a black woman moaning, struggling to be free'—moored so, Leo conquers the nation. But conquest nearly kills him, as we learn with the first words of a long book that opens with Leo's heart attack. Reduced henceforth to a diminished state of health, every act performed on pain of death, he shifts the ground of conquest. Conducting Proudhammer through a process of renewal usually transcribed in the discourse of theology Baldwin, who alters his trope but not his tone, here inscribes conversion in the language of physiology. Once Leo has sloughed off his old skin the effect of convulsion, of metamorphosis, is a quickening of the sort Baldwin described in the letter written to Angela Davis. 'The enormous revolution in black consciousness', he was to say, 'means the beginning or the end of America.' White and black, some of us 'know how great a price has already been paid to bring into existence a new consciousness', an 'unprecedented nation'.

As the novel ends Leo is prepared to pay the price. Having all but lost himself in reaping rewards bestowed by people who applaud his talent but villify his race and despise his colour, having feasted at this poisoned banquet, Proudhammer knows what he must do to be saved. For if art cannot work the miracle of redemption, this novel concludes, then revolution must do the work. Life in a free society is dear, Baldwin has said repeatedly: in America its fee is the total liberation of black men and women before the law and in the mind. 'To me,' he told Margaret Mead, echoing and paraphrasing Laing on lepers and saints, 'the key to the salvation of America lies in whether or not it is able to embrace a black face. If it cannot do that, I do not think the country has a future. Until the darkness of my skin stops panicking my countrymen, they risk chaos.''

'Violent sex and sexual violence,' according to Winthrop Jordan's study, *White Over Black* (1968), a richly ornamented study of racialism from Colonial times to the present day—'creation and destruction, life and death': these thoughts locate a spectre deep inside the American mind. And it's there not in the South, not in

94

our surface anxieties about the despoliation of cities, about vandalism and homicide in streets and subways—it is in the swampy depths of imagination that the bestiality of race roots itself, discloses itself to be a terror of private beastliness not much mitigated by the diffusion of a black bourgoisie in the suburbs. So loathsome and perverse are its powers indeed that at this moment it has set Black against Black, as Robert Staples comments in *The Black Scholar* (March–April, 1979). Wondering why the most gifted contemporary women writers, Ntozake Shange in *For Coloured Girls. . . .* (1976) and Michele Wallace in *Black Macho and the Myth of the Superwoman* (1979) currently vent a collective black female 'appetite for black male blood', Staples makes a stab but misses his target, ends about where Nikki Giovanni began. 'I don't like white people,' she told Baldwin in their conversation nearly a decade ago, 'and I'm afraid of black men. So what do you do? It's a sad condition.'

White self-distrust and black self-loathing—self-revulsion so pitiless, so pestilential, is an experience which blots out colour and stretches beyond the cover of skin. But if self-hatred, both white and black, is not immune to exorcism then the end of Baldwin's apprenticeship as our foremost practitioner of that redemptive art may perhaps coincide with a climax of American faith in, enslavement to the phantasm of 'Other'. He is fashionable now, it was said of him many years ago in the *New Republic* (15 June, 1963), 'and how extraordinary is his difference from the Negro who used to be fashionable. Walter White was all executive competence. Marion Anderson was endurance and calm. Baldwin is exhaustion and tension, a rag doll pulled to one side by a child who loves and the other side by a child who hates. He is a waif, an outcast, living in a waiting room between Harlem and our America; yet he is on the cover of *Time* and the Attorney General calls him for counsel.' In those days Baldwin's least whisper was overheard not just by Robert Kennedy but also by journalists, reviewers, critics, editors far and wide. Those best of times were also of course the worst of times, and times have changed. By 1968 according to an annual survey of writing in America, 'interest in James Baldwin [had] momentarily subsided'. By 1974 he was in fact a missing person. Reinstated the following year, he now appears annually as the third personage of a black trinity:

'Wright, Ellison, Baldwin.' Amid pioneers, progenitors, precursors he is today an ancestral presence, not fashionable at all but formidable above all, the writer whose fervour has left its ineradicable mark on American literature in our time.

Whether or not he will ever again serve as a counsellor of state—Minister of Culture in Andy Young's administration?—he casts an exceedingly long shadow. A writer whose art glorifies the principle of diversity in love, he has embodied in himself chief causes of our national addiction to perversity in love. An expatriate who was unable to weep for two years after Martin Luther King's death—who couldn't abide his own reflection in the eyes of those who saw in him the very likeness of dread—Baldwin finds decided benefit and promise, he said last fall, in the fact that Vietnam made us all niggers, fell and fallen, in the eyes of the world. That we in the United States today are among the most 'rejected children' of the Western world, events do most plausibly show. How fortunate we are therefore to have among us a man of letters whose distinguishing trait of genius, as Alfred Kazin observed in *The Bright Book of Life* (1973), is found in the ingenuity and force with which he has transformed 'every recital of his own life into the most urgent symbol of American crisis'. It is indeed in this epic Whitmanesque union of self and society that James Baldwin's career is lodged, this ichor of energies in which his art is moored—a life's blood, nobly spilled and spent, to which his being bears witness.

NOTE

1   *Just Above My Head* (New York, 1979).

6

Towards the Alternative: The Prose of LeRoi Jones

by ERIC MOTTRAM

October 1965 carried LeRoi Jones into public life as a figure newly emerged into visible politics and therefore enviously attacked and vituperatively loathed by both Blacks and Whites in New York and in America. A demonstration against Livingstone L. Wingate and the administration of Haryou-Act finances was led by a man carrying the banner of the Black Arts Repertory Theatre School, an HA summer project. Jones, director of the School, exhorted the crowd to 'lock arms against these white beasts', according to the *New York Times* of 15 October. Kenneth B. Clark, founder and former director of HA, author of *Dark Ghetto* (1965), and psychologist of NYCC, denounced Wingate as a black McCarthy, but Wingate was clearly no such traitor to the scheme, nor to the Harlem community as a whole. Jones and five of his staff were still on the payroll for undisclosed amounts, and planned to produce, on 29 October, Jones's play *Experimental Death Unit*. But about this time, it became hard for him to believe in the efficacy of art to make significant local changes in the black condition. Eloquence in rhetoric might well have to be replaced with physical revolutionary attack, a form of action prefigured in his poem 'Black Dada Nihilismus' in the 1964 volume, *The Dead Lecturer*, and recorded in 1965 with the New York Art Quartet, which then represented the most advanced forms of jazz.

Part of his liberation from what he took to be white liberal mockery of the revolutionary changes required for the deliverance of American Blacks took the form of sounding off against liberals on various platforms. The Whites masochistically enjoyed it as

D
97

part of their protest-meetings syndrome. Reviewing Negro poetry in *Poetry (Chicago)* in 1964, he had already given it as his opinion that 'where what we are faced with is the *act* of protest, certainly picket sign, or pistol, would do much more good'. The hippie—Left—a curiously impotent American phenomenon of the early Sixties—weighed in with an unsigned article in *The Realist* (May 1965), presumably by the editor, Paul Krassner, reporting a meeting at the Village Gate, in downtown New York—'You Don't Have to be Jewish to Love LeRoi Jones.' A drawing depicted Jones's bifurcated black-and-white head, a characteristic piece of petty revenge for what was taken as the black poet's betrayal of Village liberalism. The issue was Jones's statement that the two white civil rights workers murdered in Mississippi were 'artefacts' who were 'assuaging their leaking consciences', and would not receive his mourning: 'I have my own dead to mourn for'. He admitted his own paranoia: 'because I do not trust America as far as I can throw it'. If these remarks, crude though they may seem, are less inflammatory today, it is a measure of the revulsion generally conceived for American official policies. Jones had had the experience of newspapers refusing advertisements for his plays and of the police stopping the sale of theatre seats after obscenity charges filed against *The Toilet* (1964) were rejected by the city attorney's office. The same issue of *The Realist* carried a cartoon called *The Adventures of Superiorman* featuring Leroi Baldose, 'savage apologizer for his people, that ruthless crybaby for his rights, that real credit to his race'. It was a vicious personal attack on Jones, who at that time was going through the crisis of his life, having to choose between his white literary and family environment, developed through the fifties and sixties, and a Harlem and Newark, New Jersey, black environment suspicious of what it took to be a newly vocal recruit to black liberation politics. At the same time Stanley Kaufmann delivered an attack on him in *Dissent*, the Trotskyite politico-literary organ of the New York intellectuals, entitled *LeRoi Jones and the Tradition of the Fake*. This scurrilous abuse recreates the writer as a preacher of violence and revolution against a society in which he lives 'cosily'. What Kaufmann hated was simply Jones's outspoken revulsion and thoroughgoing warnings against violence to come—which, of course, continued into the seventies. In *Shadow and Act* (1964),

Ralph Ellison, while subjecting Jones's *Blues People* (1963) to to decent scrutiny (but entirely underestimating the political protest content of blues and jazz), attacked him as 'a dangerous nuisance' for the development of civil rights, 'providing pseudo-orgasmic thrills as distraction for energy that might otherwise be usefully employed'.

The fact is that a close reading of his plays and the poems in *The Dead Lecturer* reveals, rather than an advocacy of bald violence, profound distress and desperate irony in a writer deeply needing to dramatize the emotions within the increasingly tepid civil rights movement. The personal anguish and self-therapy, as well as the social conscience, are obvious; they take place in a body of work which once again exemplifies in America the imagination of catastrophe. Who would now disagree completely with Jones's statement at the New School conference in April 1965, sponsored by the Harlem Writers Guild, that 'the role of the black artist in America is to help in the destruction of America as it now exists. If what he does—whether it's polemical or lyrical or however it functions—if it contributes to that destruction, it is valid and beautiful'? Nat Hentoff, reporting the conference in *Evergreen Review 38* (November 1965) added that Jones read his poems 'as if he were a hornman . . . fiercely lyrical . . . each had to be coped with in exhilarating, dangerous recognition of a particular universal or coped with in stiff resistance to parts of one-self that had been so private for so long that one feared to find out what had become of them'. On this occasion—and it is part of the crisis of this year—he spoke of a universal society in which:

> just being born—that fact alone—would qualify everyone for everything of value in that world . . . it would be a society which could admit to any man's beauty. But at *this* point in history, we're still in the equivalent of prehistoric times in terms of *that* society . . . But you can't speak of simply 'changing' it. How can you change a model T Ford into a jet plane? The Form would have to be destroyed first.

Later in the conference he spoke on 'The Revolutionary Theatre' (reading a paper commissioned by the *New York Times* but unprinted there):

a theatre of victims . . . ethics and aesthetics are one . . . All men in live in the world and the world should be a place for them to live in . . . The revolutionary theatre will soon be peopled by new heroes rather than victims. We are the witch doctors and the assassins, but we will make a place for the true scientist. This is a theatre of assault . . . Our heroes are Crazy Horse, Denmark Vesey, Patrice Lumumba. These are the true heroes and the enemies are most of you who are listening to this. . . . It is futile and stupid to talk to any white man on this subject. You reach an abyss where you're finally using the language that's been forced on you. You can't really say anything to the man. He talks about universality, about aesthetics that are durable. Where? In *this* society? . . . As Sartre said of Fanon, he was only trying to talk to his *brothers*, not to the white man. We must bring the black vision where it belongs—back to the people we're supposed to be writing for. It doesn't *matter* if they call you a polemicist or a racist.

Exactly what Jones is exposing had appeared in exemplary form in an article by George Dennison in *Commentary*, February 1965, entitled *The Demagogy of LeRoi Jones*. Dennison writes of 'desperately over-determined feelings' becoming 'policy', and attacks Jones for speaking, he believes, 'to the private and fragmentary wishes of individuals, and . . . assuring the fragmentary person that he is in reality a thundering herd'. He does not analyse the plays he accuses of racism and personal demands for power, and is completely ignorant of how these plays enact familiar black attitudes and experiences. It was not the theatre which 'swarmed with the hatreds of racism' but America. Jones, says Dennison, 'needs to frighten people and succeeds: his *frisson* is part of contemporary American response to guilt'. But, as Jones has stated explicitly, revolutionary theatre assaults prior to political action. *Commentary* has never worked towards revolution, of course, and one does not expect it to understand the need for it. But without revolution, the black condition cannot change in America, and this is the point of Jones's writing from the plays of 1964 onwards. As Jones observed in a Channel 11 TV discussion with Norman Mailer and David Susskind in January 1966, 'Like Burroughs in *The Naked Lunch*, the Black is not innarested in your horrible condition.'

As he came of age and moved from Newark, where he was born

in 1934, to New York, LeRoi Jones moved into a literary scene predicated by poets associated, however loosely, with *Black Mountain Review* (edited by Robert Creeley and containing poets, including Charles Olson, already known from their appearance in Cid Corman's *Origin*), the Beat Generation magazines and readings (Ginsberg, Kerouac, Corso and others), and, to a lesser extent, the New York Poets (although only O'Hara seems to have been active at all strongly for this downtown action). When Jones founded *Yugen* in 1958 it was to these writers that he turned for contributions. His highly important editing continued with *Kulchur*, with which he was strongly associated from its first appearance in 1960 till its penultimate issue in 1965. In his interview in David Ossman's *The Sullen Art* (1963), he discusses, in 1960, his work on *Yugen* and his poetic influences from Lorca and Pound to Olson, Creeley and Williams, and then speaks of his particular position:

> I'm fully conscious all the time that I am an American Negro, because it's part of my life. But I know that if I want to say, 'I see a bus full of people', I don't have to say, 'I am a Negro seeing a bus full of people' . . . I'm always aware, in anything I say, of the 'sociological configuration'—what it *means* sociologically. But it doesn't have anything to do with what I'm writing at the time.

During the run of *Yugen* and *Kulchur*, Jones taught at the New School, at Buffalo and at Columbia, published two volumes of poetry, the plays *Dutchman* and *The Slave*, several articles on the Negro writer, and *Blues People: Negro Music in White America*. This body of work shows him steadily articulating his development from white-orientated post-war American literature towards his founding of the Black Arts Repertory Theatre School in 1965, his shift from Greenwich to Harlem and Newark, and his attempt to become both a literary and a political black leader, with a black audience of a predominantly classless 'liberation' character. Where *Dutchman* won its Obie at the Cherry Lane theatre on the lower West Side in 1964, *Great Goodness of Life* was performed at the Spirit House, Newark, by the Spirit House Movers, and *Madheart* at San Francisco State College by the Black Arts Alliance—both in 1967. 'Philistinism and the Negro Writer' (1966)

101

traces the stages of his increasingly black writer's consciousness. It appeared in *Anger and Beyond*, edited by the labour secretary of the National Association for the Advancement of Colored People, a book which disclosed a middle ground where intellectuals discussed racial and non-racial functions of writing in order to come to grips with that 'two-ness—an American, a Negro' which DuBois had exposed in 1897. Jones recalls his Newark high school and its mainly Italian ethnic orientation, the crass inverted racism of Howard University (and its characteristic spurning of black jazz), the racist fantasies he encountered in the Army (through which he learned indelibly that white society intended death for him), and his position as an American artist (a condition which makes his experience typical in a non-black sense):

> The denial of reality has been institutionalized in America, and any honest man, especially an artist, suffers because of it. That is how the institution perpetuates itself, through the suffering of the honest and the naïve. For myself, I aspire to the craziness of all honest men, that is, the craziness that will make a man keep talking even after everyone else says he shouldn't. Perhaps one way Negros could force institutionalized dishonesty to crumble, and its apologizers to break and run, would be to turn crazy, to bring out a little American Dada, Ornette Coleman style, and chase these perverts into the ocean where they belong.

Black Dada and the radically disruptive music of Coleman are subversive equally to the white and the black bourgeois: they do not repeat and reassure but dislocate and reassemble in new forms, always politically dangerous and psychologically abhorrent to the liberal, the gradualist.

> The Negro writer is in a peculiar position, because if he is honest most of what he has seen and experienced in America will not flatter it. His vision and experience cannot be translated honestly into art by euphemism, and while this is true of any good writer in America, black or white, it is a little weirder for the Negro. Since if he is writing about his own life and his own experience, his writing must be separate, not only because of the intellectual gulf that causes any serious man to be estranged from the mainstream of American life but because of the social and cultural estrangement from that mainstream that has characterized Negro life in America.

The black writer has to resist the urge to be in the mainstream of the culture—'the way people live . . . reinforced by memory'— and say: 'I am a Negro, I am black' and 'All my writing is done by a black man.' He refuses to be middle class in order to survive; he must obtain a vision beyond the white vision of America: 'and this is not necessarily racial. It's scientific, in a certain sense'.

The role of *Yugen* included the publication of Allen Ginsberg's refusal to be merely a Jewish dissenter within that official cultural pattern which 'asks all immigrants to strip themselves of the very things that would make their own culture valuable'. The black American must likewise refuse to be stripped and integrated. The black writer's role is like the Irish in British twentieth century literature—its main strength. The problems of style and content are therefore primary and formidable. Jones began to tackle them in *The Moderns* (1963) and *The System of Dante's Hell* (1965). The writers in the former included Douglas Woolf, Paul Metcalf, Michael Rumaker, Fielding Dawson, Hubert Selby, Robert Creeley, Jack Kerouac and William Burroughs—that is, the major prose stylists of the decade. Jones's contributions were 'The Screamers' (1963, reprinted in *Tales* (1967), and two sections from *The System of Dante's Hell*; they represent his effort to articulate his complex experience within the sophisticated white European–American prose of the twentieth century, and at the same time to move away from it and into an area where he could speak to a black audience as a leader of the cultural politicisation of the black masses. In his introduction to *The Moderns*, Jones accepts his inheritance—along with Kerouac, Creeley and his other contributors—of the mainstream, the equivalent of his poetry being in the mainstream of the poets he published in *Yugen*. 'The formal frustrations of urban America' and the 'common national futilities' in the Ike–Nixon era required, he says, styles which renewed active value rather than complacent torpor. If '*all* of America is desolated' these writers show their resistant lives in personal aesthetic which relates them to those 'whom Spengler called Fellaheen, people living on the ruins of a civilization'. Therefore the active forms of Joyce and Burroughs are not simply linguistic innovations but ways of projecting the socio-cultural nature of desolation and ruin. Burroughs is necessarily as central for Jones as for any intelligent writer in the sixties:

Naked Lunch is Burroughs spinning a parable in which all existence can participate. He merely names it as it shows up, i.e., he is not necessarily 'pulling for anything'. Guilt in this sense, as the modern philosophers posit it, becomes anonymous. There is no one good person or one bad person, living out their lives under the auspices of the reluctantly mortal Augustan christianity; there is only the idea of good and the idea of bad and 'characters' wander into these categories as they relate to the central logic of the writer's intent.

Kerouac's writing, on the other hand, keep prose 'as personal as it ought to be. To keep even the rhythms and awkwardness of its creator as a part of its final "story": the writing as part of what is being said.' These two positions are major determinants of Jones's own prose in so far as it exemplifies Creeley's aphorism: 'form is never more than an extension of content'. The content is the condition of being black. So that at the personal level *The System of Dante's Hell* is an exorcism of that heresy which consigns a man to the deepest hell:

> against one's own sources, running in terror, from one's deepest responses and insights . . . the denial of feeling . . . that I see no baser evil.

This leads to violence against self, others, God, nature and art: the penalty within the book's structuring from Dante is the seventh Circle. But heretics in Hell is the structure of articulation of autobiographical materials taken from the Fifties. The style lies between Burroughs and Kerouac; the writer's voice sounds from his own peculiar experience:

> From blues reflection, through the fence to the railroad. No trains. The walks there and back to where I was. Night queens in winter dusk. Drowning city of silence. Ishmael back, up through the thin winter smells . . . For the different ideas of the world. We would turn slowly and look. Or continue eating near the juke box. Theories sketch each abstraction. Later in his old face ideas were ugly.

With the black American Ishmael, and prose which inherits Melville as much as Joyce and Burroughs, appears his Melvillean familiar:

The black Job. Mind gone. Head lost. Fingers stretch beyond his flesh. Eyes. Their voices' black lust. The fog. Each to the other moves in itself. He loves nothing he knows yet love is on him like a sickness.

The first Circle section recalls the procedures of poems in *The Dead Lecturer*:

You've done everything you said you wouldn't. Everything you said you despised. A fat mind lying to itself . . . What do you want anymore? Nothing. Not poetry or that purity of feeling you had . . . Whatever clarity left, a green rot, a mud, a stifling at the base of the skull. No air gets in . . .

Diane disintegrated into black notes beneath my inelegant hand . . .

Circle 7 recalls Jones's play *The Toilet* (1964):

The brown naked bodies. They turned and hurt or walked or pronounced my name. Does the word 'foots' mean anything to you? She would say. Before she got skinny and died . . .

Circle 4 recalls the days of *Yugen*, the Village, *Howl*, 'Olson broke, Allen losing his hair'—'Did John Holmes really jump off Warren St. bridge?'—'I was erudite and talked to light-skinned women'. So the artist tours his own life as Hell, a Dante in the Hell of his times, lifted through and out by no Virgil, but reaching through the impetus of his self-knowledge a certain wholeness without guilt and waste which would precede the removal to Harlem and Newark. Hell is also America's racist and capitalist system—from its origins to the present day:

> The Dead,
> are indians. White bones dust
> in their jelly. Dead in the world, to
> white dust bones.
>   And Riders,
>   coming towards us . . .

Being American means, therefore, that the self cannot distinguish sharply between violence within and without the body:

>   My name, like
> Indians. Dead hard ground.

Violence
against others,
against one's self,
against
God, Nature and Art.

In Circle 8:

> Violence to my body. To my mind. Closed in. To begin at the
> limit. Work to the core. Centre. At which there is—nothing. The
> surface of thought . . .

In Circle 9, treachery breaks loose in scenes which are abominable
and well-known:

> The car rolled its banging stones against the dark. Ugly fiend
> screaming in the fire boiling your bones. Your cock, cunt, what-
> ever in your head you think to be, is burning. Tied against a
> rock, straw packed tight into your eyes. POUR GASOLINE,
> SPREAD IT ON HIS TONGUE. NOW LIGHT THE STINKING
> MESS.

*   *   *

> Shadow of a man (Tied in a ditch, my own flesh burning my
> nostrils. My body goes, simple death, but what of my mind? Who
> created me to this pain?)

The bottom of Hell is the segregated South where Blacks are Whites'
examples of lust ('their insensible animal eyes') and bus-drivers
have the power of their employing society to behave brutally. But
the black Dante himself betrays his black fellows to the South.
Dressed in Army uniform he 'passes':

> He liked the wings, had a son who flew. 'You gon pay for that
> ol coon?'
> 'No,' I said. 'No. Fuck, man, I hate coons.' He laughed. I saw
> the night around his head warped with blood. The bus, moon
> & trees floated heavily in blood. It washed down the side of the
> hill & the negroes ran from it . . .

In Chicago such impotence becomes overtly sexual. The black US
Army Airforce boy is tormented by a whore for his 'fairy' impotence with her. He remembers his homo-erotic experiences, and
tries to insist on identity with Joyce's Stephen Dedalus as an alibi
for his romantic cultured worth. He runs from male assault, 'win-

ning in new time and leaping in the air like I saw heroes do in flicks'. But Hell is at least a threat to a falsely integrated self whose value he had assumed: 'I am myself after all. The dead are what move me. The various dead.' Excessive self-making is madness—'do you really think you were sane always?'. He recalls those—the white poet John Wieners among them—who were themselves and still yielded. So the writer talks to himself, about his book, about his memories, about people trapped in the fifties as he was. The pain is sometimes overwhelming, and, structurally, the point of extreme pain mark the shifts in scene. Self-criticism becomes masochism especially when he recalls physical violence as part of group action in which he took part or how he repeatedly made 'the queer scene' in Chicago and elsewhere. But as a whole *The System of Dante's Hell* is a drama of purgatorial initiation through such violence and sexual ambivalence. *Ulysses* is recurrent model, especially the nighttown scenes, for this reason, as well as for the stylistic inheritance. The book's tonal centre is a bitterness generated by being vulnerable at the centre of a power structure, as a Black, as an uncertainly sexual man and an intellectual of uncertain direction. The only limitedly stable role is that of soldier and that, ironically, is a drafted performance.

Circle 8 is crucial, therefore, since the Army is the over-riding instance of manipulation by the State, where men are numbers, where sex is indiscriminate, and pretention to intelligence and culture—ironically, even to knowledge of the blues and jazz—signifies homosexuality to the majority. Fear of the de-sensitised mass of men in this Circle fuses with fear of groups and gangs in general, as tests of ability to be other than solitary and forced into isolation by differentiating education and experience. He envies the group he can never fully enter, in spite of 'that civil strife our bodies screamed for'. Hell pulsates between isolation by individuation and 'the second phase of our lives. Totalitarianism. Sheep performing in silence'. Dante's 'system' is envied for at least containing a Heaven. In Jones's America, violence and power complete a world of social and sexual assault in which it is impossible to realise what Christmas or Gods whose world sat wet in the morning with our own could potentially mean. If this world has a system it is an entropic arena of anarchy. Circle 8 concludes in a complex structure of rape and dead Gods:

> The sun moved . . . Our Gods, I said, had died. We weren't
> ready for anarchy . . . but it walked into us like morning.

The black American has slipped from slavery to 'smart clothes
our fathers' masters wore'; in Circle 9, betrayal of the enslaved
past is identical with living as white and middle-class: 'Ran on
what I was, to kill the arc, the lovely pattern of our lives.' The
shift at this point to the South brings the masturbating would-be
writer in his white elegances, the Airforce boy in his impotence,
first to self-criticism of his 'foppery' and then to self-mockery,
self-betrayal, and the beginning of a measure of self-redemption.
The role-playing fakes are resolved within a powerful prose, some
of Jones's finest writing. As the old selves are destroyed he begins
to see the meaninglessness of his postures and his bookishness, and
to see the 'huge city melting', the possibility of softening, of
being loved, of not being forever imprisoned in 'Negro'. It is the
turning point; a Virgil appears:

> My fear of my own death's insanity, and an actual longing for
> men that brooded in each finger of my memory.
> He laughed at the sign. And we stood, for the moment (he
> made me warm with his laughing), huge white men who knew
> the world (our wings) and would give it to whoever showed as
> beautiful or in our sad lone smiles, at least willing to love us.
> He pointed, like Odysseus wd. Like Virgil, the weary shade, at
> some circle. For Dante, me, the yng wild virgin of the universe to
> look. To see what terror. What illusion. What sudden shame,
> the world is made. Of what death and lust I fondled and that
> to make beautiful or escape, at least, into some other light,
> where each death was abstract & intimate . . .
> Of course the men didn't dig the two imitation white boys
> come in on their leisure. And when I spoke someone wd. turn
> and stare, or laugh, and point one out. The quick new jersey
> speech, full of italian idiom, and the invention of the jews.
> Quick to describe. Quicker to condemn . . .

But the transformation cannot last because the scene of its lasting is beyond the scene of the book, beyond Hell. The black Dante
is still choked with history and stifled by the present. After release
into imitation white he becomes African black and returns to the
horror of the continuous present: 'Nobody. Another secret nigger.
No one the white world wanted or would look at.' A white soul

is encased in black skin and a 'Negro' history. The ex-fairy 'Peaches', makes it with the whore. They become friends. He is contented, eating watermelon:

> It seems that things had come to an order . . . Things moved naturally for us. And what bliss we took. At our words. And slumped together in anonymous houses I thought of black men sitting on their beds this saturday of my life listening quietly to their wives' soft talk. And felt the world grown together as I hadn't known it . All this before, I thought . . .

But 'ugliness' returns to end the healed condition in the form of 'cowardice', 'despair', 'alien grace', a return to the individuation process which forces a man to 'find sweet grace alone'. He is beaten up by Blacks who dance around him, and he comes to his senses two days later with white men, 'screaming for God to help me'. The 1965 epilogue, 'Sound and Image' speaks of the recovery through undestructive blackness:

> I am and was and will be a social animal. Hell is definable only in those terms. I can get no place else; it wdn't exist.

The book's Hell is offered as a 'fast narrative' vision, a 'fix' on and an interpretation of the discovery years of his life. The fire of Hell is 'the flame of social dichotomy' felt as 'the early legacy of the black man unfocussed on blackness'. A white God controls Hell as a white 'idea' and will continue to do so unless a stronger image 'delivers us from the salvation of our enemies'. Neither the tormenting Blacks nor the white Army men are community. The original pain of Africans brought to America is to be felt again, and 'the propaganda of devils that they are not devils' resisted and defeated. Hell's function is therefore to be the *agon* which may lead to peace, defined as 'things bathed in soft black light'. Hell is a war of consciousness and definition. *The System of Dante's Hell* is nothing less than a redefinition of cultural inheritance which insists on blackness as satanic lust and evil animality, an action away from the evil western religious, philosophical and economic tradition, nurtured by Christians and exploited by all authoritarian systems. Jones is defining a possible home, a yearning for limits in which to develop, and not only for Blacks but for all minorities and proletariats for whom Hell is an inferno of frustration. This considerable achievement met with scorn and subsequent neglect from the body of American critics unprepared for any but the most superficial and impersonal statements of position in the Civil Rights civil war.

Tales, which appeared two years later, covers the development towards accepting blackness in a different way, and shows LeRoi Jones's prose moving from 'A Chase (Alighieri's Dream)', which was first published in *Pa'lante* in 1962 and reads like a section of *The System of Dante's Hell*, toward a less white-literary and more locally black vernacular style in 'Answers in Progress' (*Umbra Anthology, 1967–68*). In 'A Chase' men are 'cages of decay'; the author replaces Satie and 'the manicured past' with 'a black suit'. 'The Alternative' shows a black leader in development from college to adult organisation, Ray McGhee (who reappears in the tales) being the persona for that part of Jones's life which leads to his position in Newark in the sixties. Black vitality is shown assimilating and freeing itself from white cultural controls; the struggle to be black begins with the struggle to be a leader without the tyranny of cultural elitism and yet still lead 'because he said some words no one had heard of before'. He will always suffer the loss of being separate, of being dubbed a 'crippled fag' for his intellectual ability even in his triumph (Jones constantly uses 'faggot' as a word of abuse for a man who gives in to the mainstream of cultural assimilation—which for him means impotence): 'Nights they kick you against the buildings. Communist homosexual nigger.' The 'elegant performance' of the black intellectual has to be renounced, with its 'tinkle of European teacups'. But the struggle is exhausting:

> To want. And that always . . . to want. Always, more than is given. The dead scramble up each side . . . words or drunkenness. Praise, to the flesh. Rousseau, Hobbes, and their betters. All men, from flesh to love. From love to flesh. At that point under the static light. It could be Shostakovitch in Charleston, South Carolina. Or in the dull windows of Chicago, an unread volume of Joyce. Some black woman who will never hear the word *Negress* or remember your name. Or a thin preacher who thinks your name is Stephen. A wall. Oh, Lucasta . .
> . . . Again. 'Verde que te quiero verde.' Green. Read it again Il Duce. Make it build some light here . . . where there is only

darkness. Tell them. 'Verde, que te quiero verde.' I want you Green. Leader, the paratroopers will come for you at noon. A helicopter low over the monastery. To get you out. But my country, My people. These dead souls, I call my people. Flesh of my flesh . . .

. . . The 3rd floor of Park Hall, an old 19th-century philanthropy, gone to seed. The missionaries' words dead & hung useless in the air . . .

Physical conflict with his fellow men is inevitable, and comes in this story as he attempts to defend two homosexuals from a cruel student raid. The leader looks back on the violence of language and his body:

And their voices, all these other selves screaming for blood. For blood, or whatever it is fills their noble lives.

In 'The Largest Ocean in the World', the alternative to such bloody conflict is a too easy peace:

There are men who live in themselves so they think their minds will create a different place of ecstasy. That it will love them.

But 'Uncle Tom's Cabin: Alternate Ending' shows black origins and training pressing against such quiescence. The inculcation of the American dream of endless promises, which is the process of school, is the basic fake. It is the black Ishmael once again who survives, not the pathetic conformers to America's 'apocalyptic profile of itself as it had urged swiftly its own death since the Civil War'. The disinherited, both white and black, 'would die when the rest of the dream died not even understanding that they, like Ishmael, should have been the sole survivors. But now they were being tricked.' In 'The Death of Horatio Alger' LeRoi Jones is working in his own rearing-ground of Newark—'Negroes and Italians beat and shaped me, and my allegiance is there'. The young black poet finally resists 'the glamorous world' which seduces a man into belief that 'thinking could be gotten from books'. But the boy in the story breaks down within the strains of gaining direction within white America's ambition, and the Melville epigraph to 'Going Down Slow' (1966) emphasises the horror: 'Ah, miserable, thou, to whom Truth, in her first tides, bears nothing but wrecks.' The story which follows records the sense of personal futility within 'national futilities' with murder and heroin as ends to insane misery. The end in 'Heroes are Gang Leaders' is hospital:

> So no more from Tarzan to Christopher Tietjens, but the concerns are still heroism. And what to do to make the wildest, brightest dispersal of our energies.

Writing for the *Yugen* circle which includes white poets like Joel Oppenheimer and Paul Blackburn, with whom Jones worked and read in the Village of the early Sixties, is not 'serious': the end would be a rubbed out black poet. A major source of return to black society is presented in 'The Screamers' (1963)—the bebop breakthrough effect on local Newark musicians, with the excitement moving from musical to civic and political—jazz against the rest, self and group definition through an aural and visible style against levelling desolation in a ruinous city:

> America had choked the rest, who could sit still for hours under popular songs, or readied for citizenship by slightly bohemian social workers.

The release of jazz is erotic and civic, and for once this placing of music is not avoided:

> Any meat you clung to was yours those few minutes without interruption. The length of the music was the only form. And the idea was to press against each other hard, to rub, to shove the hips tight, and grasp at whatever passion. Professionals wore jocks against embarrassment. Amateurs, like myself, after the music stopped, put our hands quickly into our pockets, and retreated into the shadows. It was as meaningful as anything else we knew.
>
> All extremes were popular with that crowd. The singers shouted, the musicians stomped and howled. The dancers ground each other past passion and moved so fast it blurred intelligence. We hated the popular song, and any freedman could tell you if you asked that white people danced jerkily, and were slower than our champions.

Parker's 'Ornithology' is accurately placed, therefore, as social awakening, as well as great music, and the politics of ecstasy is to bring the magic controls of jazz into the civic streets:

112

Ecstatic, completed, involved as a secret communal expression. It would be the sweetest form of revolution to hucklebuck into the fallen capital, and let oppression lindy hop out . . .

Then the Nabs came, and with them, the fire engines. What was it, a labour riot? Anarchists? A nigger strike?

The police do their violent work—'America's responsible immigrants were doing her light work again'. The Blacks respond with knives, razors, coke bottles and aerials: but retreat is inevitable—'to save whatever it was each of us thought we loved'. The final seven episodes of *Tales* plunge into Harlem and Newark, during the period from 1965 onward, of which this early event is a presage.

The black artist–intellectual up from the Village has it rough at first:

To be always under so many things' gaze, the pressure of such attention. I wanted something, want it now . . . To have the thing I left and found. To be older than I am, and with the young animals marching through the trees. To want what is natural and strong.

Ray—'a name I'd already saved for myself'—is in danger of stupidly 'dying from his education': can he find work and love in the black proletariat world? The model of heroism in both Hemingway and the Rolling Stones is sheer hedonism; Hamlet is mere burden of ego—'white bullshit, to always be weighing and measuring and analysing, and reflecting. . . . Mahler vs. The Vandellas. It's not even an interesting battle.' 'Unfinished' recalls the uptown New York scene of summer 1965, the turning point in Jones's career, when decisions for revolutionary action against white society and the black bourgeois managers they employed were firmly taken. 'New Spirit' repudiates the Village–Beat image of the 'christ–jew a beatnik in sandals with a psychedelic twitch', but the language here still lies uncertainly between white hip and black vernacular. The intermediate condition is painful:

This is the silhouette of the man. The flashes of light. Signals from the future evolutions, the future worlds, that we will be there. What we make and are, we long for our strength, as a completion of the energy we project.

113

A measure of that completion is projected, at least as an artist, by Jones in the final two episodes, some of the most important writing he has achieved. 'Now and Then' is a hilarious and serious work in a fine new, hard-earned black style, and as so often in his career it is from jazz that he draws his strength—jazz musicians as brothers voicing spirits through their skills:

> But when they stopped, the brothers, they were not that strong. Like any of us, the music, their perfection, was their perfect projection of themselves, past any bullshit walking around tied up unspiritual shit. . . .
> I am all the not being that my limit has set, not knowing yet my whole. Yet I do and can not speak with my entire spirit. Can not fly. Though I understand the need. The way . . . Like I write to keep from talking, and try by that to see clear to where I must go. Chakra. Enlightenment. The seven lives. The many planetary adventures . . .

The writer's function is to tell tales of the brothers, and not primarily of personalities and the self but, like jazz, to achieve group style. The prose gives what the brothers can do:

> I loved them in sound. They loved women tho. Like Amos and Andy in the Harem of Butchers. It was a conquest they thought about winning shit. Like boys. The tall one was all boy, a kid, really. Raw, like they say, of a new kinda gunfighters type. The other rooted in a cleaner rhythm than the world around him, though he created things that could weaken him. Responded. There are invisible allegiances in our bones. Things we must look at. . . .
> Wrestling a killer humility. A egogod, telling the shadow of what you claim you never had. Or left, the older ones claim to have gained knowledge through error. And how much of that is really true. . . .
> A dazzle, a stink glow of the source, the possibility of being kings and loved men of a strong people.

John Tchichai makes a ghost appearance playing to what Jones takes to be impossible Danish audiences, and there is a racist jab at Ornette Coleman's 'jewish bass stealers', which reminds us of one of Jones's hang-ups: even he cannot deny that David Izenson is one of the great bassists in jazz. But he is out to demolish

114

the threat to black music of 'yr *avant-garde* shit' as some kind of fascist theft:

> Ya Wohl, marches out the plank splashes into the little rich lady section of universal attention. A vibration in the yellow pages. Pussy for sale!

But 'Now and Then', for all its minor disasters of intelligence, is a firm satire on how blacks, black jazzmen and 'Muslim chicks' have inevitably been part of 'a photomontage of success', a mix of sex and competitiveness which potentially threatens to be engulfed in show-biz. The style takes Kerouac's rush of detailed impressions and Burroughs' montage and places them within a local vitality:

> Then everybody unfreezes and a loud cackle of success in America rises from this not really humble abode. Lil brother is happy, and puts on his newest record. Hostess titters walks around touching her guests on the arm. Tall brother, finally comes out of the bedroom sez, 'Shit, that cat cdn't seen me anyway, even if he'd come in there, I was really a ghost'.

The humour continues into the last episode, 'Answers in Progress' (1967), written in a projective form with a variety of linear and spatial devices to contain the tale of spacemen landing in Newark looking for Jazz Messengers records, on the day after the initial slaughters of the Black Revolution. The spacemen dig Albert Ayler while 'dead blancos all over and a cat from Sigma Veda, and his brothers, hopping up and down asking us what was happening—and in the streets the victors sing: 'now, it's/ ours, take is slow / we've long time, a long way / to go'. The blue space cats offer something better to smoke than 'bush'—'tastes like carrots'—and everyone talks about Ben Caldwell's painting and feels like Bird, 'the old altosaxophonist . . . but the limits opened out into pure lyric tone of powerful being'. The alliance with spacemen confirms the confidence of the Blacks that their turn has come, but the story is not heavy with rhetoric. It has a good euphoria within its black humour, and a serious fantasy which projects a confidence far beyond the despair of *The Slave*, written three years earlier, and a restraint beyond the loudness of In Search of Revolutionary Theatre, which appeared in *Negro Digest* in April 1966.

115

Looking back in 1971—in an interview in the *New York Times*, 27 June—Jones respects his painful struggle to create a career and survival as a black American and a writer:

> I was working my way through things that I didn't really understand—for instance, the ending of 'The Toilet', where there is a sort of coming together of the black boy and the white boy . . . the kind of social milieu that I was in dictated that kind of rapprochement. It actually didn't evolve from the pure spirit of the play.

But of *The System of Dante's Hell*, in spite of its address to European form, he believes the content is firmer:

> the content of *Dante,* however screwed up it is, still concerns a young black man—in many senses a schizophrenic one at that time—trying to clarify himself. What I was doing was trying to break away from European influences and the strong influences of many white poets who had affected my work. I did it consciously, but I didn't know that I was specifically breaking away from white forms at the time. I did know the forms weren't mine. I was trying to find a voice, my own, and I needed to oppose myself to the European influence.

Blues People and *Black Music* (1967) extend the process of definition and the key lies in 'What Does Non-Violence Mean?', written for *Midstream* in 1964:

> a political rebellion within the existing social structure is impossible. Any energy seen to exist within the superstructure of American society is almost immediately harnessed within acceptable motifs, and shaped for use by the mainstream, whether the results of this process are called Swing music or CORE. The interest is the same: *white music*. There is no way the black man can be heard, or seen, clearly in the existing system.

The chapters in *Blues People* on 'Afro-Christian Music and Religion', on the position of jazz within the middle class, and on 'The Modern Scene' are uniquely detailed and penetrating, and it is clear that one of the impulses towards this exemplary understanding is the fact that in 1964 no black writer had reached the quality of John Coltrane, Cecil Taylor, Ornette Coleman, Sun-Ra —to whom, in 1967, would be added Archie Shepp, Marion

Brown, Sonny Murray and Pharoah Sanders: the very richness of the development of jazz challenged the black writer. *Blues People* sharply makes the point that the Black had to understand that the liability of his blackness was a *social* deformity and not one inherent in his self, but that this was very understanding leads to increased alienation from that society. Further, 'the idea of the Negro's having "roots" and that they are a valuable possession, rather than a source of ineradicable shame, is perhaps the profoundest change within the Negro consciousness since the early part of the century'. Out of the 'weirdness' of 1940s jazz, a value was generated, and 'the step from *cool* to *soul* is a form of social aggression'. An Afro–American culture now 'had to be reinterpreted in terms of the most profound influences in the open field of all *existing* cultures, or it would retreat to the conditional meaningfulness of the folk or the final meaninglessness of the popular'.

Black Music extends Jones's insights into the intersections of aesthetics, politics and culture, and his radical criticism of the borrowed inauthenticities of Beatles, Rolling Stones and other manifestations of the popular. The yellow submarine 'shoots nuclear weapons': 'chances are it will never come up', but it hoarded big money. Jones tends to underestimate the absence of black audiences for later sixties jazz, a potential audience narrowed to the limits exemplified in the abortive awakening of Clay, the hero of *Dutchman*, to his blackness. But the dates attached to each section of *Black Music* correspond to those for the essays in *Home*, since the jazz changes between 1959 and 1967 are those of Jones himself, 'secret as for the rest of America was concerned'. Paul Desmond and John Coltrane are 'different ways of viewing the world' (1961). Marion Brown and Archie Shepp develop 'largely in semi-private due to the stupidity of the commercial record and night club industry' while English pop groups make 'large doses of loot' while taking 'the style (energy construct, general form, etc.) of black blues, country or city, and combining it with the visual image of white American non-conformity, i.e., the beatnik, and score very heavily' (1965). In 1966, Jones writes:

> Sun-Ra wants a music that will reflect a life-sense lost in the West, a music full or Africa . . . (his) Arkestra is really a black family . . . convinced that music is a priestly concern and a vitally significant aspect of black culture.

In 1965 he quotes Shepp saying the purpose of the black musician 'ought to be to liberate America aesthetically and socially from its inhumanity', and Jones's key linking essay, 'The Changing Same (R & B and New Black Music)' shows how the *avant-garde* is not esoteric but politically central, 'a central body of cultural experience' which equally rejects middle-class black and white taste and its social compromises. The central impulse of black music, from the black church onwards, has been towards deliverance from the white system and its dominating culture. Its style is historically an 'all inclusive . . . wild joy—deep hurt' felt by a whole people. This is the 'black spirit', a religious legacy felt right through to Coltrane, Sanders, Sun-Ra and perhaps most obviously in Albert Ayler. Compared with this process, white pop and folk-rock is superficial, and Jones sneers at its operatives openly, forgetting that deliverance for one section of a complex society cannot be morally had at the expense of *any* other.

Apart from this deep involvement in jazz, the major understanding of the possibility of revolutionary deliverance came during a visit to Cuba in 1960, registered in *Home: Social Essays* (1966) as the beginning of that process, between 1960 and 1965, of learning that overt political action would have to be the context of the black writer's active life in the period from 1965 onwards: 'the sense of movement—the struggle in myself, to understand where and who I am, and to move with that movement'. But the conclusion of that movement is that black Americans 'cannot transcend their social history' and that integration would be 'merely whitening to fit the white soul's image'. White sexuality in violence and killing is differentiated from black by the white's homosexual racial conditioning, an idea drawn from his Army experience as well as the history of the South (and used in *The System of Dante's Hell*, of course). For both social and sexual reasons, therefore, the black American is 'weakened' by any contacts with whites: influences may shift what should be his essential concerns. Raw black survival problems will be replaced by 'unwhite hallucinations'. Black is in any case genetically dominant and perhaps one way out of racial conflict would be to turn the whole world 'black' by orgy. Cuba was Jones's example of the possibility of an alternative to a society crumbling through 'lack of direction or purpose'. Cuba enabled him to take action against

118

'the void of being killed by what is in this country and not know-ing what is outside of it'. In 1960 he could still say to Cubans: 'I am a poet . . . what can I do? I write, that's all, I'm not even interested in politics.' But 'ecstatic' and frightened he saw a people on the move. His hero becomes Robert Williams, the black leader hounded by white America for his advocacy of blacks returning the KKK's violence in kind. Jones began to use 'Afro–American' instead of the white-invented term 'Negro', the lin-guistic parallel on his attack on 'tokenism', 'one hundred years of "legal" freedom' which barely concealed the hypocrisy of Amer-ica, and within which black writers and jazzmen tended to groom themselves to meet white anticipations of excellence. He con-cludes that the black writer as artist and leader may not imitate Martin Luther King and seek to involve 'the most oppressed people in this country in a sham ethic that only has value for the middle class power structure', 'the industrial-liberal née mission-ary element'. The Black loses his identity as a 'carrier of possible dissent'.

LeRoi Jones has always known his own vulnerability; like every black American he knows what John A. Williams in *This is My Country Too*, knows: that 'the strength of the contemporary Negro is in being ready to die'. This is no crude death wish. The dissenter, the drop-out and the hipster pursue strategies of sur-vival within the structure of capitalist racist democracy. Jones chooses the cunning 'fight without quarter', the act of the revo-lutionary; any man who separates himself from the official Ameri-can programme is a mad target for murder. The Black has known this earlier than anyone. Therefore his plays of the Sixties— *Dutchman*, *The Toilet*, *The Slave* and *The Baptism*, all per-formed in 1964—begin with the essential: how to become a man in America, and stay a man: difficult as a white, impossible as a black:

> in fact you will find very few white American males with the slightest knowledge of what manhood involves. They are busy running the world, or running from it.

The violence planned against the Whites is an extension of the continuous violence of American class conflict, with the difference that it is directed towards black deliverance:

119

they'll cut your throats, and drag you to the edge of your cities so the flesh can fall away from your bones, in sanitary isolation.

The words could be those of any white reactionary, but they come from Clay in *Dutchman*.

To always strike and know, from the blood's noise, that you're right! . . . No social protest—right in the act!

The words of the black ex-poet and new revolutionary leader in *The Slave* have a long antecedent history in western revolutionary action, even if they are in fact delivered in the play by a man broken by his new life, drunken and hysterical under the pressing emotions of the revolutionary occasion. These plays are very much part of that period of distress and dichotomy registered in *The Dead Lecturer*, a bitter self-therapy projected through a double action of belief in necessary violence and necessary refusal of the bourgeois writer's illusory safety within Village limitations, that 'intellectually liberated' area, of which he writes in a 1965 essay in *Home* as a danger to the black male because it drains off 'the strongest emotional reference in his life, his blackness'.

The next stage for Jones was neither the Muslims' closed bourgeois self-reliance nor Malcolm X's incipient socialism. (And the first issue of *The Cricket* [1969], edited, as Imamu Amiri Baraka, with Larry Neal and A. B. Spellman, contains this remark from his hand: 'It is said that Bobby Seale digs Bobby Dylan. We think they should make an album together. It's a "natural" '). After the Harlem 'riots' of '65, he envisaged some kind of black organization yet to emerge—the statement is from an interview in *Literary Times*, Spring 1967:

This kind of disorganized violence will soon find some kind of organizations—some kind of structure. Farmer and King and Rustin and all those cats do not have the ear of the ghetto Negroes. Essentially theirs is a dialogue with white America.

Of the hero of *The Slave* he says:

He's hung up in his own ego-syndrome, his individualism. . . He is supposed to be leading his brothers. He is supposed to be fighting, he's not supposed to be sitting there bullshitting with white people.

Of Allen Ginsberg, the pacifist who has consistently fought with America, his old collaborator in *Yugen* days:

> even where I find a man that I once was aligned with and still feel close to, I find that we are at opposite poles now, because I know no amount of pacificism is going to break Charlie's back.

Four Black Revolutionary Plays (1969) and *Black Magic: Poetry 1961–67* (1969) are the work of a man addressing potential black audience in a spirit of revolutionary change. As Peter Schjeldahl wrote in 'LeRoi Jones: Poet Laureate of the Black Revolt' (*Avant Garde* No. 4, September 1968), 'his poems, once the chronicles of private events, now are pronunciamentos of a collective consciousness being born . . . they are absolutely his best work—crisp, funny, subtle, and exploding with energy'. His two most recent works show Baraka continuing his development, and the writer is never sacrificed to the now successful political activist. The first essay in *Raise Race Rays Raze* (1971), 'Newark Courthouse—66 Wreck (Nigger Rec Room)', uses the new style developed in *Tales* and in the final section of *Black Music* to document with great care white accusers and judges locked in primary conflict with black victims, 'the anonymous banal boring horror of slavery' taking its course in the 'false Greek' courthouse of Baraka's home town. The trial characters are far more cogently portrayed than anything he has written till now, and the following essays on poetry, the arts, a black cosmology and a black value system stem from the need to place this documentary evidence in a context which will hopefully enable the sons and daughters of the trials to envisage a new society. The rapid notation is a new imaginative realism:

> Now Turner trails in the Addonizio jetstream by default with pictures shaking hands with NoNeck and LBJ.

The Lessons of Burroughs, Kerouac and *The System of Dante's Hell* are fused into a notation of the political intersections of the pre-revolutionary action—image of the ghetto and the white historical presence. The action of the people of Newark is exemplary and epic, and Huey Newton, Eldridge Cleaver and Sidney Poitier receive equally short shrift in the collective emphasis: 'our theories must be made of real action'. The artist LeRoi Jones at last stands at the primary intersection of political action. Having come through his own trials at white judges' hands, he writes as a man who has come through; the viable intellectual has the right to use Newark vernacular to create himself within his people's society, and may exemplify Trotsky's famous definition in *Literature and Revolution*:

> Individuality is a welding together of tribal, national, class, temporary and institutional elements, and, in fact, it is in the uniqueness of this welding together, in the proportions of this psychochemical mixture that individuality is expressed.

As Baraka says in the *New York Times* interview, the Blacks 'struggle to exist . . . to ensure that our definitions of the world can exist'. *In Our Terribleness* (1970) is directed explicitly at a black audience, as it comes to consciousness: 'a kind of revelation of identity and an investigation of the style of blackness', through both his prose and poetry and Fundi's (Billy Abernathy's) photographs. The idiom is intensely ironic. Each pasage, virtually, is a black intersection:

> Terribleness—Our beauty is BAD cause we bad. Bad things. Some bad bad ass niggers . . .
> Since there is a "good" we know is bullshit, corny as Lawrence Welk On Venus, we will not be that harmony shit. We will be, definitely, bad, bad, as a mother-fucker . . .
> To be bad is one level
> But to be terrible, is to be
> badder dan nat

The book embodies also the myths of black magic and black sense developed under the kingdom of the Sun; it accepts the black body in the Sun as a globally powerful instance of a tyrannized life about to leap to power. The example of Egyptian pyramid societies of Mao and Nkrumah, as viable and humane systems is depressingly blind in its sentimental rewriting of history and evaluation, but generally the work is a penetrating praise of the young blacks of American cities, and are fully presented understanding of the role of writer as priestly 'conductor of the energy, no a secret gos hisself', and an emotional instance of those ideas of black separateness Baraka has now inherited from Ron Karenga, 'the master teacher'. The message is clear:

Draw away from the diseased body . . . STEP 1
Embrace the blackness, the alternative . . . STEP 2
          . . . and the creation of the nation
          where we stand.

The white stereotype of the black artist is left far behind. Baraka
is the artist not only of his community but an artist within a
body of doctrine, the concepts of which he writes in 'The Pan-
African Party and the Black Nation' (*The Black Scholar*, March
1971). He writes as the man present at the 1967 Newark rebellion, the man who helped elect the first black mayor in Newark,
and the disciple of Maulana Ron Karenga. 'The black man of
responsibility' must be accountable to black people, 'constantly
expose the white system as corrupt and unworkable', and 'support
Nationalism and Pan-Africanism'. The Party provides a value
system, 'a way of living that will ensure *predictability of beha-
vious, ultimate authority, and a means of security . . .*'. The aim is
to 'move *together* as a people conscious that we are a people,
struggling for national liberation'. The arts' function is ideological
but the programme has unfamiliar elements:

> we must not be coopted by talk of instant revolution, into being
> the peasant army, the first slaughtered wave, for *another people's*
> rise to political power . . . . you can talk about black mayors to
> more black people, with some credibility than you can about
> nations, which is the problem . . . you must build where you
> are . . . 'Murder mouthing' will only get you murdered . . . we
> must train to live, we must study and work to *live*.

The artist is therefore an activist who shapes resistance to anonymous recession for the masses under manipulation. At this latest
stage in the development of one of the most important careers in
American culture, the 1963 essay in *Kulchur*—on James Baldwin
and Peter Abrahams—is a measure of what does not change in
LeRoi Jones–Imamu Amiri Baraka:

> Individuality is not merely the cross one select number willfully
> bears among the broken heads and lives of the oppressed. We
> need not call to each other through the flames if we have nothing
> to say, or are merely diminishing the history of the world with
> descriptions of it that will show we are intelligent. . . . An idea
> must be specific and useful, and must function in the world; it

must be, even, an interpretation of that world that permits a man to use himself. The singular man uses, first, himself. That is why he is singular. Because few do.

As Baraka writes in *In Our Terribleness*:

> I hear and see you too brother jones
> from the year 1968 talking to me . . .

Since the above was written Baraka has certainly behaved and composed as the singular man who uses himself: the 1970s have proved to be a decade of radical change in his analysis of America and the condition of the Blacks. It is therefore worthwhile to consider the gist of *Raise Race Rays Raze* to ascertain the distance travelled since 1971. To a socialist that book almost negated its own anger and energy by a neglect of political–economic analysis to the point of impotence. In so far as change took place after black revolt, it was to give Blacks more token appearance on TV and to enable them to vote for self-interest, a larger share of the capitalist pie. In the opening essay of his 1971 book Baraka referred to 'the beauty of our own necessity' as against 'apathy and sensual compensation', 'revolutionary insights' against 'problems'. And elsewhere: 'we, black people, are the spiritual people, yes, caught here among sinister materialists; there are no mists over the African empire'; 'the Panthers turned left on Black people. And the love of Beverly Axelrod has left terrible Marx on the dirty Lenin Black people have been given by some dudes with dead 1930s white ideology as a freedom suit.' The racist onslaught against marxist diagnosis in the 1969–70 essay is absurd in its scope and in its detail:

> It will be a Black ideology of Change, as perhaps an aggregate of world information, that will free us. Lenin, Marx and Trotsky, or O'Neil, Beckett, and the Marat–Sade dude, are just the names of some more great white men. There are other dudes who will give you other lists like Washington, Jefferson, Adams, or Paul McCartney, Cream, Grateful Dead, or Mozart, Pinky Lee and the fag with the health tv show. They are just lists of white people.

The year before he writes: 'Do not talk Marx or Lenin or Trotsky when you speak of political thinkers. . . . Why do you think Mao split off with Stalin. The Russians are European. Dig it!' In 'Nationalism Vs. Pimp Art' (1969–70):

The great deluge of nakedness and homosexuality, is a 'revolution' within the Euro–Am meaning world. The great dope 'revolution' . . . We 'support' the white revolution of dope and nakedness because it weakens the hand that holds the chain that binds Black People. But we must not confuse the cry of young white boys to be in charge of the pseudo-destruction of America (with a leisure made possible by the same colonialism) with our own necessity.

Raise Race Rays Raze contains a good deal of accurate analysis and inventive perceptions about what passes for change within American capitalist democracy. But the term 'black' is so loaded to mean 'human' that diagnosis cannot move into praxis. Baraka terminates movement by 'a Black value system' and fails to understand that Malcolm X's final incipient socialism was a main criticism of black bourgeois nationalism and the conservative anarchism of Afro-reversions. 'Black' has to equal 'justice', 'post American', 'afterwhiteness', 'health', and 'spiritualism'. The black artist is 'the vessel of God', as the Bantu claim, and nationalism is 'the power to control our lives ourselves' in a world reduced to evil–versus–god surrogates. Black has to be a total category, an 'entity'. The confusion is clear: black consciousness is said to be both existent and in need of creation. Thoreau's anarchism is given in Olsonian notation, but remains inert (1967):

> The Power and will to shape, ourselves. To move, our selves.
> From the involution
> > the involve
> > to the evolve = (Change to)
> > the revolution = change
> Nationalism as forming of nation, and the idea, and will to do that.
> Regroup. Rebuild so to speak.

The basis is bio-metaphysical in the fashionable alibi jargon of the late 1960s—with curiously Emersonian overtones—black is universal energy transforming itself'. The angry diagnosis of American urban–political power in the 'Newark Courthouse' essay quoted earlier—an attack on the combined force of police, mafia, gangsterism and Roman Catholic church—proved prophetic: the blacks, with Baraka's help, changed the city to a state of pre-revolt colonialism. But the next stage is said to be a separate black state:

> We are foreigners, aliens, sons and daughters of slaves, people taken forcibly from the lands. Now we wish to establish our new land just where we are, in these cities or on that southern dirt. Nothing can stop us from doing this.

Presumably Marx's diagnosis had to be excluded because of his race, just as Cleaver in 1970 is cited as a jew-orientated revolter and as Baraka admits to being himself 'jew-hypnotized and white committed'. In the 1969 essay for *Black Scholar*, '7 Principles of US /Maulana Karenga & The Need for a Black Value System', the black man is 'the balance of East and West, completer of this cycle', and the racial core is 'kawaida', Karenga's doctrine of a black value structure, an undefined entity poised in imagination between existent and created, an 'African socialism' or ancient pre-European 'cooperative economics'. The 'super rational' aspect of Nationalism is 'imani' or 'faith in your leaders, teachers, parents —but first faith in *Blackness*—and that it will win'. Malcolm had no 'doctrine', 'no real organization', unlike Elijah—the Black Muslim leader—who had 'a formal teaching . . . but made some other decisions'. Karenga is doctrine, a sort of African Power of Positive Thinking. Malcolm's gestures towards socialism at the end of his life are ignored.

The Panthers criticized nationalists like Karenga and Baraka for superficial cultural Africanism, and explicitly stated in 1969 that 'the main problem in the United States is not the race contradictions but the class contradictions'. The details of black groups policies are usefully exposed in Thomas L. Blair's *Retreat from the Ghetto* (London, 1977). Blair also critically describes Baraka' founding of the Congress of Afrikan Peoples and the Temple of Kawaida in Newark—the New Ark of *Raise Race Rays Raze* (*Black New Ark* was also the title of the Congress journal). In view of 1970s revelations from the FBI's files, one passage in Blair has a peculiar significance. Karenga's followers were, he states:

> astonished at his involvement with the Los Angeles police in quelling the Watts riots in 1968 following the assassination of Martin Luther King, Jr., and the way he curried favour with the

arch-conservative politicians like California Governor Ronald Reagan and Los Angeles Mayor Sam Yorty. Furthermore, Karenga has never overcome the stigma of involvement with US gunmen in the grudge killings of two Black Panther Party members John Huggins and Alprentice "Bunchy" Carter, in 1969 at the University of California, Los Angeles, campus.

In Blair's own conservative language, Karenga and Baraka in 975 'embraced the class war dogma of the twenties, proclaiming 1at Marxist–Leninist scientific socialism is the solution to the 1ack man's problems', partly influenced by what Blair oddly 1lls the 'Socialist experiments' in Cuba, Vietnam, Tanzania and 1uinea. In fact, Baraka's Marxist analysis of American imperial-1m has nothing to do with whatever 'dogma of the twenties' may 1ean. It is part of a growing augmentation of socialist diagnosis 1 America following the scandals of war and defeat in South-1st Asia and in the light of continuing poverty and unemploy-1ent, among American Blacks and Whites alike. Baraka's moves 1wards Marxism in the 1970s are far more important than 1air's insistence on their 'Communism' implies.

In *Unity and Struggle*, the revolutionary socialist journal of the 1ongress dedicated to 'the concrete struggles of oppressed people 1gainst imperialism' and 'various ideological positions being taken 1 the revolutionary movement today', Baraka wrote in 1975:

> In order to liberate black people or any other oppressed people, capitalism must be smashed and replaced with a system of public control of the means of producing wealth . . . such a change can only be brought about by socialist revolution. . . . Our principle enemies are the Ruling Class, the big capitalists, and not all whites.

1is support for 'the entire multi-national working class' is, con-1ary to Blair's belief, specifically anti-Communist. The 1972 con-1ention at Gary, Indiana, which Baraka co-sponsored, manifested 1ecessary changes in black strategy, based on community, peace, 1ustice and ecology against war, profits, domestic conflicts, and 1xploitation. The resulting agenda included National Health In-1urance, the end of the FBI–CIA–Justice Department surveil-1ance of Blacks, a guaranteed income, and 'free academic and tech-1ical education for all Blacks up to their highest attainable level'. The main tyranny would appear to be 'Black control of the mass

media'.) At the second convention in 1974, at Little Rock, a
independent black political party to unite all views was propose
and defeated. The reasons are clear in Baraka's later 1970s writ
ings—the black bourgeoisie would not relinquish power. Fightin
for Kenneth Gibson in the 1968 Newark elections taught Barak
that his place was on the Left. Mayor Gibson became for hin
'just another bourgeois nigger with a gig he thinks is hip'. (I
fact, the situation is not as bad as he makes out—see Danie
Gaby, 'Newark: The Promise of Survival', *The Nation*, 14 Decem
ber 1974.)

Baraka featured prominently in government plans against a
Civil Rights and Anti-War groups and leaders in the 1965-7
decade. In a talk in the Gray Chair series at the State Universit
of New York at Buffalo in 1978 Allen Ginsberg drew on officia
agency files—to which Americans now have partial and uncertai
access—to speak of CIA and FBI falsifying documents which pre
cipitated Baraka's denunciation of Tom Hayden's actions i
Newark in the 1960s, and which show Karenga receiving mone
from the agencies for his violently anti-white programme of non
cooperation with liberals and leftists. Black nationalism and th
promotion of university Black Studies, Ginsberg alleged, wer
the official agencies' line.

But Baraka emerged from the 1960s civil war—perpetuated b
the agencies—with a reinforced basis for action. Where Cleave
became a protegé of Giscard d'Estaing and was born again, lik
President Carter and the followers of Jim Jones, when Stron
Thurmond picked up almost 20 per cent of the black vote i
South Carolina in 1978, and when black leaders came out of th
White House at the end of 1978 to denounce Carter's anti-blac
programme, clearly Baraka's socialism is nothing more or less tha
the way ahead for Blacks. Carey McWilliams' 1940s statement ha
to be quoted again to a stupefied nation in 1978 (in *The Nation*
12 December):

> Race relations are not based on prejudice; prejudice is a by
> product of race relations . . . Psychological theories of prejudice
> offered as theories of race relations do not explain the strategie
> by which certain groups maintain their dominance over othe
> groups. . . . With subtle but unmistakable emphasis, Negroe
> have been offered a bargain: civil rights for a repudiation o

radical protest . . . Yet civil rights does not guarantee full equality when the basis of inequality is to be found in unequal competitive power.

From the limited papers circulating out from FBI and other agency files after the Freedom of Information act, the disastrous pattern of Baraka's 1960s control by the state is clear. In 1967 the FBI established a secret 'Counter-Intelligence Program' whose aim was 'to expose, disrupt, misdirect, discredit, or otherwise neutralize the activities of black nationalists, hate-type organizations and groupings, their leadership, spokesmen, membership, and supporters, and to counter their propensity for violence and civil disorder' (a directive dated 25 August 1967). An FBI document dated November 1970 gives 'LeRoi Jones, a black extremist, poet and playwright who helped to elect Kenneth Gibson, the black mayor of New Jersey', as a main target. The FBI planned to fake a Black Panther Party letter denouncing Jones as 'an Uncle Tom who is using the black people of Newark for his own purposes', which would be circulated to main black organizations and to newspapers in order to disrupt the movement:

> LeRoi Jones, the poet who calls himself Ameri (sic) Baraka, is Tom Pig pretending to be a true Black Revolutionary. He ask people not to buy the Black Panther newspaper because, he want the people's money for himself, Jones use the people's money for liberation soul power to line his pockets. . . . Now Jones try to put himself on a throne, like maybe you saw his picture. He fancies himself the reason Ken Gibson got elected mayor of Newark. . . . Jones shove his Congress of African People down the throats of Brothers and sisters on High St. . He hustles his 'religion' to make them his slave. He think he's black Jesus, and he should be put on his own cross. . . .

In 1968 the FBI's Newark branch proposed to discredit Tom Hayden as informer or Government 'fink' (document dated 27 May) and to use government money to undermine the black cause there. Agency infiltration reached a scale where it appears to have been designed—in the admitted absence of any Communist threat—to undermine the confidence of the nation. It is pointless to sneer at the naïvety of civil rights and black leaders when the whole nation was duped. In fact Baraka comes through remarkably fit.

His 1978 one-act play *What Was the Relationship of the Lone Ranger to the Means of Production* ends, like Odets' *Waiting for Lefty* in 1936, with a call to strike. But the core of Baraka's play is not a Thirties living-newspaper naturalism but the analysis of a major myth within the American manufactured mythology of power and racism: the masked figure of comics and movies. The 'Masked Man' character subsumes Lone Ranger, Spider Man, Batman and Robin, Captain America, and the rest, and appropriately he claims that he wears a mask, like the other 'superheroes', to 'hide my identity from evil doers'. So he is the type of capitalist lies—that behind the masks of power lies good. Lone Ranger's 'deep love' for Tonto is the form of white ruling class control over Indians and Blacks, and by extension class control of white workers, since the majority of the play's characters are black car factory workers. Lone Ranger embodies the Paternalist and divine myth which the bourgeois West perpetuates to reinforce class and racist society with heavy wealth at the apex of the social pyramid.

Masked Man is trying once again to con the workers to agree to 'the new age. Post strike post strife, post worker post revolutionary post angry post nastyshit', the era of 'Marcuse, CPUSA, Jesse Jackson, NAACP, all who urge righteous moderation'. His myth barely veils the threat of unemployment—'Lucky you are is to have has a job gig slave' in the classless USA, 'undoubtedly the best system in the world'. But some of the workers in this agitprop drama know better and see through this 'metaphysical claptrap', the equivalent of 'whiskey and dope' to keep their minds off wage demands. Masked Man or Money Master has come to raise the spirit of the workers, with the help of his union agent, the union rep, Taffy, who stands for 'the rule of the cool'. Their joint threat climaxes in the myth of 'no more jobs anywhere . . . Not in Russia china or greasball coon fantasies of everybody bein equal bullshit'. But the workers know that Russia is not a socialist state but a worker-bullied tyranny, a system similar to the United States. Masked Men and Taffy chant the names of American union leaders—Meany, Woodcock, Miller, Reuther, Lewis, Gompers—as 'the great bribereenies' tradition the workers can join,' lucky to be amuricans . . . .lucky as shit lucky as pizza pie eatin lucky luciano'.

Baraka hits at the centre of competitive philosophy: that luck

130

rules—'Luck–keee that's the name of our game. Lucky to be in this great country. Lucky to be allowed in here some of us . . .'—especially the Blacks at Colonel Motors: 'you cullid guys you cullid people MM brought you from where? Africa! Geez, think of it, the freakin dark continent, savages and shit'. The alternative is to accede to 'the New Agrees', 'new point of unity, a whole new contract for labour and management'—'Buy it buy it buy it! It's real! Peace in our time!'

Baraka has mastered the agitprop play form—the action and language are direct, exuberant and politically clear. And his verve is contained by a firm and accurate political diagnosis. The language combines natural speech and poetic forms into an explosive vehicle to expose a sick society, crazed with money controls and their myths: 'Dracula runs this country and that's frankenstein bullshitting us right now.' Within Baraka's career as a writer it marks a clear advance on the anger in 'Look for you Yesterday, Here you come Today', the poem in *Preface to a Twenty Volume Suicide Note* (1961) which handles similar materials, not so much in formal invention as in social direction. At the end of the play the dead worker, Felipe, whom MM and Tuffy have trundled in as a warning—he has allegedly committed suicide—speaks out as Tonto for all the oppressed in American history who are potentially a proto-revolutionary nucleus for the destruction of the American system. There is no other alternative to the mythical praxis of MM.

That the play is ahead of his black nationalism, Baraka acknowledges in *Hard Facts: 1973–75* (*People's War*, Newark, n.d.), a book of revolutionary Marxist poems, some in prose-poem form, in the introduction to which he raises the main issue for a revolutionary writer:

> We want to raise the level of the people, but to do that we must start where they are which is on a much higher level than the majority of intellectuals and artists. We also want to popularize, to make popular, to make a popular mass art. To take the popular and combine it with the advanced. Not to compromise, but to synthesize. To raise and popularize . . . The work and study should be work toward making revolution.

Otherwise poetry becomes:

131

Old American academics reflecting on our gardens . . . . world exercizes in smartness, compromise. It all becomes celebration of the power of the world's rulers. . . . Earlier our own poems came from an enraptured patriotism that screamed against whites as the eternal enemies of Black people, as the sole cause of our disorder, oppression. The same subjective mystification led to mysticism, metaphysics, spookism, &c., rather than dealing with reality, as well as an ultimately reactionary nationalism that served no interests but our newly emerging Black bureau-cratic elite and petit bourgeois, so that they would have control over their Black market. . . . Our nationalism was reactionary when it focussed on White people as the cause of our oppression rather than the system of monopoly capitalism.

The poems therefore organize a new mode of attack—against the white supremacist multinational corporation, but also against 'crazy ass Abernathy', Jesse Jackson, the Jesus-orientated black world (spookism'), 'rich blackies', 'niggers . . . left in the middle / of the panafrikan highway, babbling about / eternal racism', 'chas rangel, in drag, the new statue of liberty, he, and Shirl / our lady of constant backwardness', 'niggers who think they revolutionaries —cause they hair aint combed', and 'Black studies pimps in interesting tweed jackets'.

The indictment is controlled by marxist analysis playing over the experiences of the 1960s and early 1970s. For example, the sexuality of power displayed by cops is given with accurate vio-lence in 'Stop Killer Cops':

> His uniform soaked wet to his skin, fly hung open, and
> the blue flash weapon whipped in freakish frenzy
> to come in the blood from the youth's ripped head.
> How sick is the killer cop? How sick is
> this government? how sick is capitalism?

Kissinger, Nixon and Rockefeller are part of the overall disease, and so are the black bourgeoisie:

> They have taken the niggers out to lunch, for a minute, made us partners (nigger charlie) or surrogates (boss nigger) for their horror. But just as superafrikan mobutu cannot leopardskin his way out of responsibility for lumumba's death, nor even with his incredible billions rockefeller cannot save his pale ho's titties in the crushing weight of things as they really are.

132

The only alternative is 'the total control of society by the majority, the multi-national working class. The proletariat in modern dress'. In many ways, 'Class Struggle' is the key to what this book represents in Baraka's strenuous career. It opens:

> Years ago we both swore oaths, with another,
> of revolution. You, malcolm & I, one night
> in a room at the waldorf. . . .
>   . . . . it was just a little after cuba
> and the fumes of revolution were blasting open
> our nose. We had still not made the motion toward
> science, had not yet tracked the long distance to
> reality. Close then, we had yet to make a march away
> from the most liberal wing of the bourgeoisie, that wing
> which paints and poets and snorts cocaine and laughs.
> We had yet to make the frantic dash towards our black selves
> nor opened up wholly into our afrikan selves, to ready that
> strong long striding for distanced arrival at our whole
> selves. Malcolm was murdered a month after the three of us
>   met.
> We disappeared into islam and kawaida, into sections of truth
>   that each
> veered away toward fantasy. Not grasping the fundamental
>   political truths
> that the rulers had murdered malcolm behind, nor seeing the
>   cold blooded split
> between the black bourgeois preachers of religion and crypto
>   culture and the prophet of fire.

The sense that 'islam and kawaida' were fantasy—the sleep of consciousness—is carefully asserted, as if it were a necessity now to be learned from. The aim is to confront reality—'no where to go / but to consider what actually / exists' in order to move revolt out of evolution into revolution ('For the Revolutionary Outburst by Black People'), a direct reconsideration of the 1967 notation of anarchism quoted earlier. The change is radical:

> The freeing of America from bourgeois rule
> Not just an outburst, but the steel burning fire of
>   The Peoples' War
>   The violent birth process
>   of Socialism!

133

Baraka is explicit in his replies to Kimberly W. Benston, the author of the best study of his work to date, *Baraka: The Renegade and the Mask* (Yale, 1976). The interview is in *Boundary 2* (Vol. VI, No. 2, Winter, 1978). He begins by reconsidering 'The Myth of a Negro Literature' (1962):

> What I did not look at was the *class* structure operating behind black writing. So then I said that the reason that black *music* is strong is because it was directly black . . . . the incorrect thing in the essay was not clearly making a class analysis all the way through . . .

Speaking of his association with the writers of *Yugen* and *Kulchur*:

> The people I worked with all the time were all Creeley–Olson types, people who took an antipolitical or apolitical line (the Creeley types more than Olson's followers—Olson's thing was always more political). I was coming out saying that I thought that their political line was wrong. A lot of the poetry in *The Dead Lecturer* is speaking out against the political line of the whole Black Mountain group, to which I was very close. . . . I was consciously striving for a post-bourgeois / Western form, even before the cultural nationalism period. Now, Creeley, Olson, *et al*, were themselves post-bourgeois / academic poets, and that was valuable for me. But they were also, in some ways, an *extension* of Western art, so I tried to get away from them in *System*. . . .

His radical change is given as a rejection of 'the bourgeois worldview' which 'perceives things as static, unchanging, eternal', and can therefore assert that 'it's human nature to have classes, somebody must be on top', the equivalent of MM's 'luck'. The alternative is 'the world in a constant state of change—that is the one constant, change', but not as the metaphysical principle which, for instance, Olson inherited from German idealistic philosophy, but as a Marxist interpretation of change which relegates nationalism to 'bourgeois ideology just turned inside out—black instead of white':

> The bourgeois nationalist poet would react against Greek mythology and praise Yoruba myth, for example, but if you analyze their economic bases you find they come out of the

same thing: slave society and feudal society. What the bourgeois nationalist doesn't understand is that African slave society
is no better than European slave society. The masses are slaves
in both. . . . The one added fact in the United States was racism,
which did not exist with black versus black or white versus white
slavery, a fact created by capitalism. . . . I tried to make African
culture an absolute, a static absolute to which Afro-American
culture related at all points in a static way. . . . The static, a
historical worldview that cultural nationalists take tends to ele-
vate ritual as a form that defies time, space, economic conditions,
etc . . . . it tries to make African culture a static, unchanging
artifact . . . We have not evolved from some static paradise. Life
then was like life today: continual and progressive struggle.

The least one can say in conclusion is that Baraka has earned
the right to self-criticism. His Marxism is at present relatively
simplified. The projected book on John Coltrane will show what
he has learned meanwhile to bring to his unmatched experience
of jazz. The urge to change has always been there, though. The
distance travelled from 'Footnote to a Pretentious Book' (*The
Dead Lecturer*) is fundamental and exemplary:

> 'Changed my life?' As the dead man
> paced at the edge of the sea. As
> the lips, closed
> for so long, at the sight
> of motionless
> birds.
>
> There is no one to entrust with
> meaning.

7

Ishmael Reed's Fiction:
Da Hoodoo is Put on America

by FRANK McCONNELL

Well, and keep in mind where those Masonic Mysteries came from in
the first place. (Check out Ishmael Reed. He knows more about it
than you'll ever find here).

Thomas Pynchon: *Gravity's Rainbow*

The history of American fiction is cluttered with talented black
writers—Frederick Douglass, James Weldon Johnson, Richard
Wright, Ralph Ellison, James Baldwin, James Alan McPherson—
who had to wait for their recognition until they were officially
acknowledged, patted on the head, by an influential-enough
member of the white literary establishment. Every twenty or so
years, it seems, white America discovers with amazement and
sighs of delight a new—the first—true black genius, the one who
will finally articulate the sufferings of his people in an undeni-
able, inescapable voice and who will make that most native American experience, the Blues, into that most venerated American
shibboleth, Art. (There is an analogy here, as Ishmael Reed would
be quick to point out, to the birth of the 'swing era', when a
talented clarinettist and a canny recording executive created a
national fad by buying the arrangements of a brilliant but down
on his luck black arranger named Fletcher Henderson.)

These observations are by way of apology for introducing an
essay on Ishmael Reed's fiction with a reference from a novel by
a white writer, and one accepted, however grudgingly, as a major
writer by the Establishment. But Reed (as Pynchon would insist)
doesn't need such puffs. And there is nothing condescending or
patronizing about the passage I have quoted. Reed does 'know

136

more about it' than you'll find in *Gravity's Rainbow*: and it, in this case, is the whole world of occult, pre-or anti-Christian religion, of the hip American underground, and of that special with-it, outside-it-all sensibility that he has made distinctively his own.

Ishmael Reed has written five novels—*The Free-Lance Pallbearers* (1967), *Yellow Back Radio Broke-Down* (1969), *Mumbo Jumbo* (1972), *The Last Days of Louisiana Red* (1974) and *Flight to Canada* (1977)—as well as two volumes of poetry and numerous essays, reviews, and interview articles with other artists. In the Introduction to his recent collection of essays, *Shrovetide in Old New Orleans* (1978), he speaks as frankly as he ever has about the business of writing:

> Writing is hard work, don't let anybody fool you. . . . I'd say I get the most kicks out of writing poetry; fiction is the second most fun; the essay is the ditch-digging occupation of writing. I spend a lot of time running up and down the stairs for Facts!

This is an important passage for understanding Reed, I think. Fiction, the craft of the novel, lies somewhere between the kick of lyric poetry and the drudgery, the fact-bound plodding, of the essay. But that is to say, also, that fiction—if it works—can include the best powers of both the other two kinds of writing, the sheer sweep of poetry and the urgency, the argumentative power of the essay. From his first novel to his most recent one, Reed has kept close to this distinction. And while his poetry may sometimes be too private to understand, and his essays sometimes too complex to follow, his fiction has remained the clearest and best expression of his vision, and by the way one of the most brilliant and funniest bodies of storytelling of the last twenty years.

Sometime after the publication of his first novel, *The Free-Lance Pallbearers*, Reed came to take VooDoo seriously. Or, maybe, VooDoo came to take him seriously, since Reed is fond of insisting that some of his best writing is simply a matter of taking dictation from the loas, or gods, of that complex and fascinating religion. By 1970, in his anthology of contemporary writers, *Nineteen Necromancers from Now*, he was describing his work as 'Neo-Hoodooism', and had published one of his wittiest prose pieces, the 'Neo-Hoodooist Manifesto' (reprinted in *Conjure*,

1972). Some scattered assertions from the Manifesto will give its flavour:

> Neo-HooDoos would rather 'shake that thing' than be stiff and erect. . . . All so-called 'Store Front Churches' and 'Rock Festivals' receive their matrix in the HooDoo rites of Marie Laveau conducted at New Orleans' Lake Pontchartrain, and Bayou St John in the 1880s. . . . Neo-HooDoo ain't Negritude. Neo-HooDoo never been to France. Neo-HooDoo is 'your Mama' as Larry Neal said. . . . Neo-HooDoos are detectives of the metaphysical about to make a pinch. We have issued warrants for a god arrest. . . . Neo-HooDoo is a litany seeking its text.

Many of Reed's main influences, and much of his distinctive brilliance, are apparent in these telegraphic sentences. Among the influences: Richard Wright, Ralph Ellison, and LeRoi Jones in the confident observation that Black American street culture, *without embellishment,* is a full and rich cultural heritage, the stuff of major myth ('Neo-HooDoo never been to France'); William S. Burroughs and Thomas Pynchon in the surreal transformation of history into nightmare, and nightmare into pop-melodrama ('Neo-HooDoos are detectives of the metaphysical'); and the whole tradition of comparative religious thought from Fraser to Eliade in the swift, sure discoveries of the elemental and archetypal under the quotidian ('Neo-HooDoo is a litany seeking its text').

But there is something more than a mere catalogue of influences at work in the Manifesto. Reed's tone, a combination of high intelligence, carefully academic terms and citations, jive talk and stand-up comic one-liners, seems at first not only confusing but confused. Here as in his fiction, he shifts voices as quickly and as disconcertingly as anyone writing in America, except perhaps Pynchon. But Pynchon's jumps at least are within the extremes of a given cultural context: high to low culture, scentific to humanistic, tragic to comic. Reed's jumps of tone are on that axis, too, but also on another, scarier one: from everything we have been trained to take as 'culture' to its opposite, which is not 'low' or 'pop' culture but deliberately corrosive anti-culture. Here is an example, from *Yellow Back Radio Broke-Down.* A group of cowboys who work for the evil genius Drag Gibson are discussing the

ook's hero, the Loop Garoo Kid, who is an outlaw cowboy, a
rickster HooDoo, and Satan himself:

> You see the Kid ride off last night? It was as if he were light-
> ning taking a hiatus from nature. Looked like two ghosts were
> waiting for him. I could see only their outlines in the moonlight.
> What you say we pick up our gear and make it, Skinny?
> The other cowpokes needed no encouragement and began to
> get their stuff together. Suddenly Drag's voice boomed through
> the intercom:
> Men come on up here a minute. Something big is cooking on
> the range.

The speech of the cowpokes ranges, in this short passage, from
he lyrical and metaphysical to street slang (and what is the inter-
com doing in this Gene Autrey scene?) to a groaner of a pun at
he end. Examples of this technique could be multiplied from
Reed's books, though one of the best is the moment in *Mumbo
Jumbo* when he explains the personality of the VooDoo goddess
Erzulie, whore and virgin, remarking that she is known among
Americans as the girl with the red dress on (but among the
Egyptians as Isis and among the Greeks Aphrodite).

The point is that these leaps, outrageous as they are, work. But
they do not work the way associations usually work in novels, even
n so-called 'post-modern' novels. To understand how funny and
how profoundly right is the combination of Erzulie, Aphrodite,
and the girl with the red dress on you have to know a little about
VooDoo (Reed tells you that), a little about Greek mythology, a
little about Ray Charles. But more than that, you have to know
how to let all those associations merge instantaneously one into
another, while still retaining their individuality, their historical
specificity. The same is true of the outrageous pun, 'Something big
is cooking on the range.'

One way—the best way, I want to suggest—to understand Ishmael Reed's fiction is precisely in terms of these fast, jagged
changes of tone and context; 'as if he were lightning taking a
hiatus from nature', as the cowpoke in *Yellow Back* puts it. But
lightning, however flashy, doesn't really take a hiatus from nature.
Rather, it reveals in its sudden violence the possibilities of disaster
and illumination that are part of the otherwise hidden nature of
things.

139

Reed's narrative voice, at its best, has this kind of effect. And it is exactly the effect, more than of anything else, of a *voice*. One important source for this kind of storytelling is that distinctively modern American narrative tradition, the stand-up monologue. In cheap bars and expensive clubs for the last thirty years, from Lenny Bruce to Richard Pryor, the most manic and creative of American underground men have had their own back at the expense of the Establishment in free-form, improvisational 'bits'—instant short stories and novels, actually—whose illogical scenarios mock our official expectations about 'fiction' at the same time they reveal to us—or remind us—how corrosive, distorting and true can be the mirror fiction is supposed to hold up to life. Here is part of Bruce's famous 'Religions, Inc.' routine (from *The Essential Lenny Bruce*, 1967, edited by John Cohen): a character named 'Oral Roberts' is speaking long-distance to a character named 'The Pope':

> Billi wants to know if yew can get him a deal on one o those Dago spawts cahs. . . . Ferali or some dumb thing . . . . . yeah . . . . . yeah . . . . . Willie Mays threw up on the Alcazar? Ha ha That syrup! Really freaked awf!

And here is a speech from Reed's latest novel, *Flight to Canada*. The slaveholder Swile is speaking to Abraham Lincoln, who has just claimed to be able to give the South its 'death-knell blow':

> There you go again with that corn-pone speech, Lincoln. 'Death-knell blow'. Why don't you shave off that beard and stop putting your fingers in your lapels like that. You ought to at least try to polish yourself, man. Go to the theatre. Get some culture.

The two pasages are not interchangeable. But it is obvious that the Reed passage is family-related to the Bruce. It is *dialect* humour, assuming a role, improvising on the possibilities of the role, and finally reducing the role to absurdity (the grim humour of the one-liner about Lincoln going to the theatre to get some culture is what would have been called, during the first years of Bruce's celebrity, a 'sick joke'). This is the humour, and the genius, of that headlong and frantic verbal invention that Jewish comics call the *spritz* and that is known in urban black culture as 'the dozens'. And one way of tracing Reed's development is to note his increasing control over the direction and pacing of his ultiple voices, from the wild but random comic violence of *The ree-Lance Pallbearers* through the inspired fantasia of *Mumbo umbo* and into the austere, pointed bitterness of *Flight to Canada*.

But there is another analogue to the speed and dazzle of his arrative voice, and perhaps a closer one. John A. Williams, a ontemporary writer Reed admires, has said (in John O'Brien's 973 *Interviews With Black Writers*):

> There's an inclination to do to the novel what Charlie Parker did to jazz. I don't know whether you remember this period in jazz music that is called 'Bop', where the method was to take. . . . well, you could take any tune that was standard, say 'Stardust', for example. They would go through it once and then would come through again with all their improvisations, so that it was only recognizable in part. . . . . That's the way it works. And I think that's what's happening to the novel . . . Ishmael Reed's books.

Reed, throughout *Mumbo Jumbo* and in many of the essays in *Shrovetide in Old New Orleans*, argues that VooDoo, an old-world, solemn and slow ritual, becomes speeded up, like everything lse, in America—and emerges as HooDoo, one of the prime manifestations of which is Bop. Of Charlie Parker, 'Bird', the astonishing genius of Bop, he writes (in *Shrovetide*): 'Perhaps you an only relate to a monster in terms of awe, especially the Monter Bird, whose talents were so immense he could invent classics standing on his feet and whose appetites for life were as enormous. . . .' In bop the improvisational art of jazz becomes self-conscious—more highly self-conscious than it had been previously —becomes the *deliberate* 'invention' of classics while standing on your feet. And more importantly, as Williams points out, it becomes aware of the popcult triviality of the material upon which its most towering masterpieces are constructed. What could be cornier, more worn-out than 'Stardust'? Or than that swing-era warhorse, 'Cherokee'? And yet it is upon the chord changes for 'Cherokee' that Parker constructs one of his most stunning improvisations, 'KoKo'.

The boppers—Parker, Dizzy Gillespie, Bud Powell, Thelonious Monk—were not only self-conscious about the value of their music, they were quite self-conscious about it as black music. At least, among the impulses behind the founding of bop was a strongly felt need to play a music so complex and so passionate so distinctively the product of a single voice, that it could not be imitated, trivialized, or mass-produced by commercial white musicians. And while this may have begun as a separatist sentiment, it eventuated in a new and major American art form. Few serious people today would deny that, at their best, Parker, Monk, and Gillespie represent the best and most universal art Americans have produced since the end of the Second World War.

All these elements of bop (and post-bop) are crucial to reading Reed. 'HooDoo', after all, is a contemptuous white name for a native Afro–American religion: literally, with a punning irony Reed would like, a *denigrating* term for a system of belief and ritual. But what is this system? For one thing, it involves possession by the gods or loas rather than, as in the Christian tradition, approximation to the perfection of a single godman: the inspired, shamanistic, but also totally self-conscious moment at which you give yourself to the god who wants to take over your personality And at that moment you use whatever everyday props are available to you to help the god manifest him/herself: it is the improviser's moment of vision, in other words, and the shabbier, the more familiar the props the more impressive the incarnation of the deity within them (this is not, really, very far from the most primitive ideas of the 'scandal' of Christianity—though far indeed as Reed insists, from its most massively institutionalized manifestations). Remember that, for Reed, the business of writing fiction occupies the same kind of psychic space, midway between the lyrical exaltation of poetry and the everyday drudgery of a world of facts.

But VooDoo, or 'HooDoo', is also a religion of the oppressed that turns into a religion of triumph over the oppressor. The saints of the slaveholders' Christianity become new loas in the pantheon of VooDoo—not simply parodied, in other words, but really converted, in this most syncretic of religions, into precisely what they should not (from the orthodox viewpoint) become. At its most creative, VooDoo is a kind of exorcism, the exorcism of the stultifying mythology of the oppressor from the figures of that mythology itself. It is, if you will, *Heart of Darkness* told from the side of the people Mr. Kurtz tries to 'raise', and as such it is

142

liberating, wildly funny, and immensely good-humoured. Parker playing 'Cherokee' or Monk playing 'I Surrender, Dear', or Sonny Rollins playing 'Softly As in a Morning Sunrise' can be taken as the same sort of exorcism.

Reed has said that his most experimental writing to date is the short story, 'Cab Calloway Stands In for the Moon', published in *Nineteen Necromancers From Now*. In *Shrovetide in Old New Orleans*, he writes, 'I wanted to make a crude, primitive fetish and that would put a "writing" on an individual considered an enemy to the tribe.' The sub-title of 'Cab Calloway' is 'D HEXORCISM OF NOXON D AWFUL (D MAN WHO WAS SPELLED BACK-WARDS)' and the story is a grotesque, surreal, obscene narrative of a day in the life of 'President Noxon' as he slips further and further into madness and cretinism. Of course, spelling an enemy's name backwards is one traditional way of gaining power over him. And the whole story, which could easily be mistaken for a dis-organized, though very funny, attack upon the President, really is an exorcism. All the terrible things that happen to Noxon are 'worked' on him by the HooDoo detective and hero, Papa LaBas ('Cab Calloway' was originally intended as part of *Mumbo Jumbo*, where Papa LaBas makes his first full-scale appearance in Reed's fiction).

If we think in terms of VooDoo as a form of creative parody and purification-through-possession, and of bop as an especially fast, especially improvisational form of VooDoo, it is easy to see both how consistent and how deeply serious has been Reed's development as a comic novelist. *The Free-Lance Pallbearers*, his first novel, is a headlong, William Burroughs-influenced satire with more energy than point. Its non-hero, a Black named Bukka Doopeyduk, narrates how he rises from the rank of mere hospital attendant in the mythic kingdom of HARRY SAM to that of media personality, star token Black revolutionary, and almost the new leader of HARRY SAM itself—though at the end he fails in this bid for ultimate power, and is subjected to a grisly public crucifixion. Bukka Doopeyduk is an earnest, well-meaning lad, a careful student of the Nazarene scriptures, a believer in the rightness of HARRY SAM's government, and an altogether assimilated Black man—a fucking dopey dupe, as his name implies—who is almost a working model of everything not to be in Reed's world. In the first chapter of the novel, as the title has it, 'Da HooDoo is Put on Bukka Doopeyduk': the hero finds himself wasting away because of a strange curse that has been worked on him. He finds a man to cure him of the curse, and that of course is his worst mistake, since the rest of his career will be his increasingly frantic attempt to assimilate himself to the grotesque and evil world of HARRY SAM, the white idea of 'normalcy' from which the HooDoo might have saved him.

Nevertheless, the idea of 'HooDoo', and therefore of parody, quotation, possession, and improvisation plays little part in *The Free-Lance Pallbearers*. It appears only as a negative possibility —something bad that can happen to you—but not in its more positive, creative aspects. This may be part of the reason why *Pallbearers*, in retrospect, seems Reed's weakest book. In *Yellow Back Radio Broke-Down*, at any rate, the myth and the image of HooDoo is much more important and mature—and the book is correspondingly vastly more perceptive and entertaining.

If VooDoo is the conversion of Christian saints into pagan loas, *Yellow Back Radio Broke-Down* is the conversion of that most cherished of white middle class psychic shibboleths, the Western, into—literally—Black humour. Here is the first paragraph of the novel:

> Folks. This here is the story of the Loop Garoo Kid. A cowboy so bad he made a working posse of spells phone in sick. A bull-whacker so unfeeling he left the print of winged mice on hides of crawling women. A desperado so onery he made the Pope cry and the most powerful of cattlemen shed his head to the Executioner's swine.

It is, in the purest sense of the phrase, an epic invocation, summarizing the entire action, in sequence, of the book that will follow—but to what Muse? To the Muse of the 'Folks', surely: those folks who were raised on Western radio shows and the entire, white-centred myth of the American West. But the Loop Garoo Kid, the hero of this Western, is not only black, he is Satan himself, the Dark One rejected by the self-confident, daylight religions of Europe and America, returning as an outlaw, sorcerer, and cosmic gunslinger to reclaim his heritage. He is, in other words, a HooDoo hero, a self-conscious and witty parodist and gris-gris-man whose magic is not so much a matter of spells and rituals as it is of the corrosive, mythically alert consciousness itself. Loop's battle against the evil Drag Gibson, trail-boss of the town of Yellow Back Radio, doubles the struggle of Bukka Doopey-duk to enter the presence of the terrible HARRY SAM, leader of the nation HARRY SAM. But here the struggle is even, and Loop knows how phony is the magic Drag Gibson employs to keep his own people down. 'HooDoo', in other words, simply a negative factor in Reed's first novel, has now become a principle of narra-tive and satire. *Yellow Back Radio*, like *The Free-Lance Pallbearers*, ends with the public execution of its hero—with a lynching, that most powerful and most grim detail of the black American experi-ence. But in the second novel, the lynching turns against the lynchers: Loop's tormentor and enemy Drag Gibson is eaten alive by his cannibal swine, and the Loop Garoo Kid escapes. In the baldest terms, it is the symbolic turning of the oppressor's tools against himself, as has been, in fact, the whole course of this inverted Western.

Between *Yellow Back Radio Broke-Down* and *Mumbo Jumbo*, Reed seems to have developed the idea of 'neo HooDoo-ism' into something like a deliberate aesthetic. It is an aesthetic he has recently (in *Shrovetide*) disclaimed and one he has (in *Flight to Canada*) surpassed, but nevertheless it is a central part of his fiction. *Mumbo Jumbo*, which may be his best novel, is in some ways less a novel than it is an exploration of the *idea* of HooDoo, and of its possibilities for the writer. Set in the twenties, *Mumbo Jumbo* tells how Papa LaBas, head of the Mumbo Jumbo Cathe-dral and metaphysical Private Eye, tracks down the 'text' of the jazz craze sweeping the nation (remember: 'Neo-HooDoo is a litany seeking its text') and foils the plans of the 'Wallflower Order', a Teutonic Christian sect of those who can't dance, to stifle the jazz phenomenon by converting it into another pseudo-classical and self-consciously secondary 'Negro movement'.

As in a Charlie Parker solo, the shifts of tone and motif in *Mumbo Jumbo* are too swift and too complicated to transcribe here. But they are all organized around the same central theme, the same hackneyed, standard set of thematic assumptions that the book itself expands, inverts, and remakes. *Mumbo Jumbo* is a detective story, but a detective story with no crime and with no criminals—except for the white members of the Wallflower Order who try to suppress the phenomenon of jazz by turning it into a denatured version of Western modes of imagination. The Wallflower plan is at least partially successful, with the result that the real flowering of HooDoo—or 'Jes Grew', as it is called in this book—will have to wait another thirty or so years; until, in other words, the flowering of the genius of Charlie Parker (who, the book is careful to point out, was born in 1920—the beginning of the book's action) or until the writing of *Mumbo Jumbo* itself.

To find the essential text of Jes Grew, the written liturgy that will make the emotional experience of HooDoo truly religious, truly institutionalized, men will and do kill in *Mumbo Jumbo*. But, the story insists, such killing is not only wrong, it is a betrayal of the text itself. *Mumbo Jumbo* ends in a brilliant parody of the end of the classic detective story. LaBas makes his arrest, and in making it explains the nature of the crime he has been investigating: but that crime turns out to be, not at all the limited, specific act of violence we are used to in the convention, but rather the aboriginal crime through which Set usurped the music and the godhead of Osiris, turning it from cosmic bop into a kind of metaphysical Laurence Welk tune, and through which latter-day magicians like Moses and Christ imitated and transmitted this boring, foxtrot version of a radiant and shattering original vision.

The novel, in other words, moves from pop-parody to cosmogony, from cliché to mythography, and all without missing a beat. It is, in many ways, precisely the 'text' that Jes Grew (or HooDoo) is seeking throughout the narrative, the *right* story that will allow us to understand our whole cultural heritage as, not occlusion or limit to the imagination, but the backdrop for new levels of possession, new reaches of generosity and vision.

The Last Days of Louisiana Red continues the movement of *Mumbo Jumbo,* though in a somewhat muted and more tentative way. It is set in the present, more or less, with the now-aged Papa LaBas in New Orleans, investigating the collapse of the HooDoo business, the 'Solid Gumbo Works', ('Solid Gumbo' is a kind of universal medicine and nourishment). LaBas traces the problem to the usurpation of the business of a cartel of white liberals and black revolutionaries—aided by a passionate and misguided Women's Liberationist—none of whom understand the profound cosmological implications of 'The Business', and all of whom try to warp it in the direction of their own petty interests. *Louisiana Red* has been taken as Reed's unsympathetic, grumpy reaction to the Women's Movement; and, indeed, there is a kind of accidental but distracting *parti pris* to the novel. But it is most interesting—and quite brilliant—as an exercise in HooDoo without apologies and without deflections, an exorcist's division of the world into those who understand the vital powers of the work and those—regardless of race, background, or political affiliation —who do not.

This division continues in his most recent novel, *Flight to Canada*. After two exercises in HooDoo parody at its most extreme, Reed has most lately written a book that is a parody of that most black, as opposed to white, form of popular literature, the slave narrative. *Flight* is the story of Raven Quickskill, an escaped slave who tries to reach Canada but ends up back in the plantation he escaped from, though now as a free man and a liberator of others. *Flight* merges and confuses historical periods, real and imagined characters, and factual and fantastic situations with a grace and a mad subtlety that reminds one of Thomas Pynchon. But the point of the book remains sure and clear from the beginning: this is the narrative of a slave who, through comedy and parody, has ceased to think of himself as a slave and is, therefore, no longer a slave. It is a fiction that completes that archetypal American fiction (which Reed himself has admitted to loving) the *Autobiography* of Frederick Douglass, in which the narrator insists that he became really free at the moment he learned to read and write—the moment, that is, when he took over the tools of his oppressors and learned how to turn them to the uses and needs of his own soul.

Reed, in other words, has passed beyond the idea of HooDoo in his latest book—or, rather, has assimilated that creative idea into a larger and more capacious aesthetics and politics of national liberation and rebirth. Unlike Toni Morrison in *Song of Solomon*, he insists that the mythologies of black people in America are themselves worthy of respect and repetition, without artificial neo-classical embellishments. And unlike James Alan McPherson in

Hue and Cry or *Elbow Room*, he insists that the black experience in America is, of itself, both richly comic and richly humanizing, without the filter of a conventionally 'novelistic' narrative style. But like both these other brilliant contemporary black writers, he is concerned with making the black experience not a revolutionary programme, a marching-song for violence in the streets, but rather the basis for a new polity, a community of charity and good humour—including ribald good humour—that can transform violence into the dance. Like all great comedians, he is a trick-ster whose tricks glimpse not only the abyss but the way out of that pit. And to the reader wondering whatever happened to the black movement in American literature, one cannot do better than requote Pynchon: check out Ishmael Reed.

8

Judgement Day is Coming! The Apocalyptic Dream in Recent Afro-American Fiction

by C. W. E. BIGSBY

Inevitably the political developments of the last twenty-five years are reflected in the nature of black writing. The optimism of the early fifties gave way to an apocalypticism in the middle and late sixties which, more recently, has in turn been largely superceded by a less engaged literature, a literature which, in reflecting on the fierce commitments of that decade, has come to examine more closely its own function and its own betrayals. In the sixties the writer was called upon to subordinate art to life, to acknowledge the functional nature of literature, and to provide the myths of cultural identity and racial dominance required by a community simultaneously threatened and exultant in its new power. The mood was revolutionary, the tone apocalyptic, the imagery eschatological. And yet apocalypse, as Goethe asserted of death, constitutes the abolition of choice, and the revolutionary, no less than the liberal, takes the existence and reality of alternative possibilities as an axiom. Hence, there is a contradiction at the heart of many works in the sixties, a contradiction which emerges sometimes as sheer confusion and sometimes as a powerful and informing ambiguity. So that beneath the imagery of a longed-for racial battle, which will be the culmination of history and the revelatory moment of justice and retribution, is a counter-conviction that the last moment may now be deferred, that a glimpse of the fire may be enough to convert the sinner and give heart to the faithful.

149

Judgement Day is always coming, but its arrival must be per-
petually deferred. Where it does occur, as in LeRoi Jones's *The
Slave*, it is recognized as being destructive not only of injustice
but of all human qualities. That play is thus a warning and a
prophecy rather than a model. With the seventies, when the black
writer felt in some degree released from the immediate task of
serving the cause, novelists like Ishmael Reed and Alice Walker
contemplated the cost in human and literary terms of an apocalyptic mentality. And though Alice Walker was contemptuous of
those who traded in their revolutionary credentials for an insipid
literary solipsism, she has also been dismissive of those who mis-
took image for reality and offered an Old Testament vengeance
where the need was for a New Testament compassion. As her
short stories reveal she is not immune to a conviction that the
self is under immense pressure but what she offers, finally, is
what Ellison offers—the need to rediscover principles buried by
racist and revolutionary alike, principles which recognize the
significance of the individual and which assert the responsibility
of that self not merely to create itself but to acknowledge a duty
towards others. And, paradoxically, that same commitment is to
be found at the heart of the most apocalyptic novels of the sixties, for the central tradition of the black novel since Wright has
indeed been a liberal one, even though that liberalism has had
to wrestle with a potential for mutual annihilation which, in 1967
and 1968, seemed to be enacted on the streets of America's
cities.

In 1963 the novelist John A. Williams undertook a tour of the
United States for *Holiday Magazine*. The resulting articles were to
constitute a personal assessment of the state of the Union. Despite
evidence of discrimination and prejudice, and despite the assassination of President Kennedy, he was able to say, 'I searched and
I came away with hope.'[1] But when the articles were collected a
year later and published under the title, *This is My Country,
Too*, Williams added an afterword which changed the whole mood
of his observations. He had come to believe, he explained, that
Dallas was the symptom of a more widespread malaise which in
its turn was evidence of a steady move towards dissolution. 'I

150

feel that the murder of Kennedy and several other key, though lesser-known people, and the upsurging civil-rights movement, the plunging deterioration of both the Republican and Democratic parties are but the coincidental aspects of a future toward which we have been stumbling all the time. The result is that grim anarchy is but one crisis away, perhaps too, from overwhelming the land.'[2] This apocalyptic tone came to typify the work of several black novelists in the sixties and had done since Baldwin's *The Fire Next Time* had warned of the possibility that Blacks might feel constrained to precipitate chaos and ring down the curtain on the American dream. Seven years later having had a taste of that fire, Baldwin commented that 'what has happened, it seems to me, and putting it far too simply, is that a whole new generation of people have assessed and absorbed their history, and, in that tremendous action have freed themselves of it and will never be victims again'.[3] And it is true that writers like John Oliver Killens, William Melvin Kelley and John A. Williams had become, and indeed remain, fascinated with recreating the history of the Blacks in America and with establishing a link between the plight of the individual and the state of the nation.

This latter concern is of course by no means restricted to black writers. John Updike's *Couples* is structured on precisely this basis; he tries desperately to establish the historical dimension of his characters—the connection between the body and the body politic, the pubic and the public. His failure to establish this nexus stems in part from a failure of craft but in part, also, from the fact that these individuals no longer hold the front line of history. It is simply not convincing now to assert that the destiny of America is enacted in the small New England town nor even, one suspects, in the clash of a Kennedy and a Kruschev. It seems to lie, rather, in the implications of the encounter of black and white. Despite Bellow's attempts to breed a strain of heroes who can match the neurotic frenzy of urban existence with a neutralizing neurosis, it was increasingly the black man who was presented as sliding through the psychic sickness of American society, seeing all, speaking the mystic language of the streets and taking the quickening pulse of a civilization moving towards cataclysm.

As Richard Wright had said in 1957, 'Negro life is [all] life lifted to the heights of pain and pathos, drama and tragedy. The

151

history of the Negro in America is the history of America written in vivid and bloody terms; it is the history of Western man . . . .'[4] Ellison's hero, testing the moral reflexes in South and North, exposed far more than racial intolerance. He revealed an ethical chaos which, Ellison's optimism notwithstanding, threatened the very possibility of order and purpose. History has treated the black American with contempt. He was pushed outside of time and conferred with a social and historical innocence. His return to time, his emergence from slavery and his gradual assertion of rights and cultural identity, precipitated a crisis for black and white alike. And since that crisis had to do with the reality of American democratic principles and the degree to which the individual could break free of history, it was, in reality, a test of liberal ideals, a debate about the authority of the self and the reality of Lockean notions of a social contract.

The eye which surveys the modern world is no longer an innocent one. Armed with the insight which had been the major gift of 'invisibility' the writer moved swiftly from optimistic declarations of natural justice to tracing out the eschatology of the American dream. The romantic confidence drained away; John Oliver Killens' *Youngblood*, (1954), which seems to endorse the work of the NAACP and look forward to inter-racial cooperation, gave way to his book of racial conflict, *And Then We Heard the Thunder* (1968), and the cold threat of *Slaves* (1969); William Melvin Kelley's endorsement of liberal principles, in *A Different Drummer*, is followed ten years later by the surrealistic assertions of *dem* (1967); John A. Williams' *Journey Out of Anger* (1963) is displaced by the destructive insights of *The Man Who Cried I Am* (1967) and the apocalyptic prophecy of *Sons of Darkness, Sons of Light* (1969) and *Captain Blackman* (1972). Williams has said that for many years the Negro believed more fully in the American system than the Whites, and that even during the early sixties 'amelioration had set in . . . enough to push back the boiling point'[5]. But, by the time of *The Man Who Cried I Am*, we are moving in a time in which 'everybody knows everything',[6] and extinction is a real and immediate possibility.

John Oliver Killens was born in Georgia in 1916. His formative years were dominated by the economics and politics of the thirties. He has always played a leading role in cultural and racial affairs and this has seemingly left him with a legacy of competing commitments which have created a central ambiguity in his work. His novels have certainly moved from documents of liberal asser- tion to prophecies of racial cataclysm but he is constantly haunted by the ghosts of old ideologies as well as present convictions. Killens finds himself trapped in a paradox familiar enough to the American Communist Party. On the one hand the Party dedicated itself to forging an alliance between black Americans and poor whites (in essence the old populists' dream), while on the other it seriously advocated the establishment of a separate black state. The Black was seen as both an exploited worker and a victim of colonialism. The result was a curious schizophrenia, with the Party simultaneously committed to minimizing racial differences in order to facilitate working class unity, and stressing racial dif- ferences in order to justify a policy of 'national' independence. Killens is touched with the same double vision.

In *Youngblood* he outlines the historic injustices suffered by Blacks and draws what seem to be inevitable conclusions from a catalogue of violence, injustice and liberal temporising—the need for racial solidarity and ultimately even racial conflict, 'That's the trouble with us Negroes . . . We always fighting each other in- stead of the white man.'[7] But the novel appeared in 1954, the year of the Supreme Court decision on desegregation and a time of some optimism in the area of race relations. Despite the friction between the two racial communities, therefore, Killens commits himself to the possibility of inter-racialism. Slowly, individual poor whites are forced to respect the courage and integrity of the Blacks who are, incidentally, heroic and dignified almost to a man. Brave efforts are made to establish local branches of a union and the NAACP. A tentative but real alliance cutting across colour lines seems possible. Yet while Killens seems intellectually committed to the idea, emotionally he seems to distrust it. There is little in the book to justify the confidence which is voiced by his characters. Belief in the possibility of an alliance between 'the hundreds and the thousands' of Southern Blacks 'and the decent thinking white people'[8] seems to owe more to left-wing optimism than to reality as depicted in the novel itself.

His 1967 book, *'Sippi*, takes the racial battle a step closer to apocalypse. A crudely-drawn account of black/white relations in

Mississippi in the period between 1954 and the voter registration drives of the late sixties, it takes as its subject the slow awakening of black consciousness and a growing militancy. The process whereby the book's black protagonist, and the young daughter of a southern white landowner, move towards sexual and political maturity is offered as a parallel to the new self-perception and manhood of the black southerner, and an emerging, if bewildered, white moralism. But, despite references to white victims, and despite acknowledgements of good will on the part of anonymous whites, the southerners whom he describes are either overt racists or hypocrites. The narrative, indeed, is punctuated with black martyrs, so that the announcement, by an indignant Black appalled at the killing of a civil rights worker, that 'It's time for us to shed some white blood now . . . an eye for an eye, a tooth for a tooth!'[9] establishes the tone for the book's finale.

A black leader is assassinated as he leaves a Mississippi church, in a manner which prefigures Martin Luther King's death the year following the book's publication. The result is a systematic killing of whites and an invocation, by the protagonist, addressed initially to himself, but by extension to all other blacks, to join the Elders—a militant self defence group closely modelled on the Black Panthers. The basis for a cathartic clash between black and white is established.

But, once again, Killens, like Baldwin, seems to be drawn in two opposing directions. On the one hand, he feels obliged to identify some amelioration in the black political situation, to grant some integrity to young white civil rights workers; while on the other, he wishes to indict white America for its historic guilt, to celebrate an impending apocalypse which will tear the veils from the eyes of the innocent and punish the guilty. The result is a pressure on character and action which constantly threatens to reduce the book to crude melodrama. The dialectic is not contained within the individual sensibility; it is crudely assigned according to racial character. Hence, the whites are not merely vicious, they are unbelievably explicit in their hypocrisies and in their racist convictions, the self-deceiving bourbon landowner suddenly lapsing into an uncharacteristic forthrightness when it serves the purpose of the plot. The book's chief virtue lies, perhaps, in its engagement with the contemporary but, by the

154

same token, its crude analysis is equally a product of the moment. It is a potboiler and bears all the marks of one. Hence, sexuality, potentially a powerful subtext of southern life, and used as such by Alice Walker in her excellent novels, degenerates into mere titillation, while the complex pressures which underpin southern racism are rendered in the simplest manner.

But the persistence of Killens's double vision, his continued wish simultaneously to invoke and deny apocalypse, is itself evidence of those subtle pressures which he is himself unable to present with any conviction but which recur in the work of so many black writers as to become almost a distinguishing feature.

Killens's next novel, *And Then We Heard the Thunder*, shows much the same ambivalence, as he assembles the evidence which would seem to justify a cataclysmic inter-racial battle, and then retreats from the logic of his own stance. The book is concerned with the slow and painful initiation of Solly Saunders, a middle-class Black determined, if possible, to 'make it' in the white world. When he is drafted into the army he pursues the same aim, convincing himself that the battle against fascism provides a real opportunity to win the respect of white America. The realities of life in a Jim Crow army offer him repeated chances to appreciate his real position and by degrees he comes to feel that he is living in a genuinely desperate position, and that his only recourse is revolt. The book has as its climax an inter-racial battle whose apocalyptic implications are immediately subverted by a resulting brotherhood which has no justification in terms of the book's central theme and seems little more than a gesture towards the Killens of 1954.

Solly moves towards his new perception with a bewildering slowness. Insulted and beaten by white policemen and soldiers he finds himself in hospital and undergoes a rebirth which is reminiscent of the similar scene in *Invisible Man*. He comes to realise that 'he hated the Great White Democratic Army of the United States of America. They had taken one of their mighty cannons and placed it against his forehead and blown away forever the brains of his grand illusion about the Army and the war.'[10] Together with his fellow black soldiers he now signs a letter of protest sent to the Northern newspapers. The final sentence anticipates the cataclysm towards which the book inexorably moves:

'God only knows why we haven't taken matters in our own hands or when we might . . . .'[11]

Yet, for all this, he still equivocates, wavering between his new militancy and the expedient conservatism which had characterised his life hitherto. Placed in charge of propaganda for his section he finds himself delivering lectures on 'Americanism versus Racial hatred' while being excluded from the significantly-named Booker T. Washington Post Exchange. Finally, confronted with an ineluctable choice, he has to commit himself: 'And now he knew what he hoped he never would forget again. All his escape hatches from being Negro were more illusion than reality and did not give him dignity. All of his individual solutions and his personal assets Looks, Personality, Education, Success, Acceptance, Security, the whole damn shooting match, was one great grand illusion, without dignity'[2]. Only now does he ask the questions implicit in his initial strategy: 'If he signed a separate peace treaty with Cap'n Charlie, would it guarantee him safe-conduct through the great white civilized jungle where the war was raging, always raging? Would his son also get safe-passage? Anywhere anytime any place?' Only now does he realise that he has 'searched in all the wrong places'.[13] Yet, as if to deny the essence of this insight, Killens cannot accept the reality of his own vision. The book ends as Southern white soldiers apologise for their racist brutality. The prophecy of cataclysm is muted into a plea for an eleventh-hour tolerance. 'If I get back home, my brothers, I'll tell the world about your battle here in Bainbridge. Maybe it's not too late yet, if I tell it to the whole wide world, tell them if they don't solve this question, the whole damn world will be like Bainbridge is this morning.'[14] The tone is entirely familiar to anyone raised on the fervent optimism of protest literature, as, curiously, is that seemingly ineradicable schizophrenia. The final page of the novel is a supreme example of Killens' ambivalence, as he looks for a possible solution not only to racial antipathies but also to national divisiveness, while still making compulsive obeisance in the direction of black messianism:

> He wanted to believe whatever was left of the world would come to its senses and build something new and different . . .
> He wanted to believe that East and West could meet somewhere sometime and sometime soon, before it was too late to meet . . .

He wanted to believe that Kipling's lie was obsolete. He wanted fiercely to believe—that all this dying was for something, beat some sense into their heads. If they don't love you they'll respect you . . . Perhaps the New World would come raging out of Africa or Asia, with a new and different dialogue which was people oriented . . . This is the place, where the New World is. The world is waking up again.[15]

Killens returns yet again to the notion of apocalypse in *Slaves*. As its title suggests this poorly written book is set in slavery times (partly inspired, one imagines, by the success of Styron's *The Confessions of Nat Turner*). Plunging further into history, Killens moves, ahistorically, closer to the cataclysm which seems to hound his imagination. As Jericho, a bitter and determined slave, makes his escape with the help of a frustrated white woman, he issues the warning which by now has become a commonplace of Killens' novels, 'Somebody got to pay somewhere, sometime in that great gittin' up goddamn mornin'. It might not come in my time but it's comin' one of these day's it's comin', Luke! Judgement Day is coming. Luke! Judgement Day is coming!'[16] Escape and cataclysm vie with one another; a longed for apocalypse wrestling with a persistent liberalism. It is a paradox which he fails to examine and which, in *The Cotillion* (1971), he simply abandons in favour of a satire on the black bourgeoisie.

William Melvin Kelley obviously writes out of a profoundly different context. Born in New York, he went to Harvard University and studied under John Hawkes and Archibald MacLeish. Like Williams, he has led a peripatetic and decidedly cosmopolitan life, living in Paris, Rome, New York and, more recently and perhaps significantly, Jamaica. His first work, *A Different Drummer*, which won him the Richard and Hinda Rosenthal Foundation Award of the National Institute of Arts and Letters, was a distinguished first novel which owed a great deal to Faulkner in style and mode of approach, and to the nineteenth-century liberal tradition in theme.

The plot itself is extremely simple but, as in *The Sound and the Fury*, is recounted by a number of different characters. Tucker Caliban, after years of service to the State's most important family, the Willsons, suddenly salts his land, shoots his livestock, chops down a tree which for generations had been a landmark for the Willson family, and burns his house and possessions to the ground. When he leaves he is followed by all the Blacks in the state. This crisis serves not only to reveal the confused position of the whites, committed to regarding the Black as expendable but frightened at such a direct attack on the pattern of their existence, but also a potential for action which time and convenvention seemed to have eroded. Tucker's achievement is not that he pursues a line of militant protest but that he rediscovers principles of individual moral responsibility which seem to have died, for the Negro, with slavery, and for the whites with the nineteenth century—killed by the shock of urbanization, the destructive impact of ideology and a nerveless acquiescence in historical momentum. Just as Ralph Ellison's protagonist discovers a basement 'shut off and forgotten during the nineteenth century' at the end of *Invisible Man*, so Kelley's hero acts to reclaim an inheritance of moral self-sufficiency and integrity which historical process and human greed seem to have rendered irrelevant.

The African slave, from whom he was descended, had asserted his integrity the moment he had set foot in America. His 'No! in thunder' had shaken assertions which even then were hardening into assumptions. His descendants, however, had all operated within the terms of those assumptions, excluded from moral responsibility, and thus history, by the whites. But now, with Tucker Caliban's decision to cut all links with the past, the romantic rebellion of his ancestor gains a new vitality. At the end of *Invisible Man* Ellison's protagonist decides to move into history, to end the centuries-long 'hibernation' provoked by white hostility and sustained by black acquiescence. Kelley's hero likewise reclaims his right to shape his own reality and by doing so reveals the potential for action which arises from the courageous exercise of conscience. For Tucker Caliban, belated transcendentalist, it is an instinctual action—the virus dormant through generations becoming active; for those around him it is a lesson to be learned by his example. As David Willson, a descendant of the man who had tried to enslave Tucker's African ancestor, comes to understand, 'he HAS freed himself; this had been very important to him. But somehow, he has freed me too. . . . Who would have thought such a humble, primitive act could teach something to a so-called educated man like myself? Anyone, anyone can break loose from his chains.'[17]

The protagonist of the book is a black Bartleby, resolutely rejecting the social and personal compromises offered to him and gaining dignity precisely through his act of renunciation. But where Melville regarded this gesture as inherently ambiguous—social isolation and wilful nihilism provoking moral problems of their own—Kelley sees Tucker Caliban's action as an attempt to assert pride and identity in the face of a history which has systematically denied both to the Black. In this novel Kelley sets out, with the determination of a John Barth, to re-write history. It is an avowedly fictive world which he creates, in the same way that Hardy's or Faulkner's characters inhabit a country contiguous with, but imaginatively separate from, the world of reality. Yoknapatawpha is recognizably Mississippi but it is simultaneously a fictive projection of Mississippi. Kelley's state has a moral rather than a geographical reality and the changes which are wrought in its confines are achieved within the boundaries of individual conscience rather that political structure.

The book, in other words, is firmly in the liberal tradition. The possibility of action, of moral responsibility, of self-realisation, is available to all, black and white. In the spirit of Kelley's introduction to a volume of his short stories, *Dancers on the Shore*, it is not finally a novel about race, but about the need to reclaim a heritage which had seemed lost but which is within the reach of anyone with the courage to grasp it. By the time he came to write *dem*, ten years later, this possibility seems to have vanished. This America is a nightmare world of unreality in which myth has been superceded by illusion.

dem lacks the control of his first novel, yet in a sense this itself is an expression of a world which is falling apart. It is a world in which fantasy has the authority of reality and reality itself seems no more than a version of absurdity. The white protagonist finds it more interesting and emotionally rewarding to follow the tribulations of a character in a television soap opera than to establish contact with those who surround him. Even when he accidentally encounters this idol he is incapable of seeing her outside of her fictional role. In this surreal world a man murders his wife and

159

children and then entertains his friends in the room below. Yet of course this kind of fantasy is too close to today's bizarre reality to be easily dismissed. And when the protagonist's wife gives birth to twins, one white, one black, we are offered a precise scientific explanation even as the husband sets out for Harlem to track down the black man with whom he shares paternity. The gulf between the races—the hero simply cannot understand the language of the black world and tries to get rid of the unwanted child—is merely one more proof of a fragmenting society. And if this satire does not end, like Nathanael West's *The Day of the Locust*, with a cataclysmic riot, it does picture a society which is slowly destroying itself by believing its own lies and discreetly disposing of realities which become too insistent.

John A Williams's early novels provide a naturalistic insight into black life. Yet while the hypocrisy and nerveless ineffectualness of the white community, liberal and conservative, is exposed, inter-racial relationships can function and black individuals retain at least a tenuous hold on their fate. Thus, despite the bitterness of his early novel, *Night Song*, his characters are not without a sullen determination. Richie Stokes, the jazz playing protagonist, becomes the embodiment of a spirit which has little to do with legal campaigns for justice or direct action for political rights. Stokes is, 'fire and brain; he's stubborn and shabby; proud and without pride; kind and evil. His music is our record: blues . . . Eagle is our aggressiveness, our sickness, our self-hate, but also our will to live in spite of everything. He symbolizes the rebel in us.'[18] His death at the end of the novel does not signify the extinction of this spirit but the vulnerability of one who responds to hatred and suspicion with friendship and love. It is an indictment of racism but it is also an attack on a society which can find no place for humanity in its frantic desire for security and success.

In his succeeding novels anger over individual suffering broadens into a growing awareness of historical process. In *Journey Out of Anger* a character observes that 'a whole process brings a human being to anger. Multiply that eighteen million times over and you don't have a process anymore. You have history.'[19] It is this conviction which leads in his recent work to individuals who dedi-

ate themselves to destroying this system; to interrupting and re-
directing historical process.

Williams is suspicious that his generation would follow those
who had gone before, plunging from innocence to wilful ignorance, and stamped, 'Cause of death: resisting reality.'[20] The
expatriates of *The Man Who Cried I Am* are merely visible evidence of this retreat from truth. The task, as one character
remarks, is to 'tell those people to stop lying, not only to us but
to themselves'.[21] The protagonists of his more recent books have
found themselves living at the moment of historical balance. Like
Ellison's hero they feel the need to emerge from their hibernation. But, unlike Ellison, they do not bring a message of love
and existential awareness; nor do they pledge themselves to renew-
ing democratic principles or realizing the potential of brotherhood.
They are agents become principals. They refuse to conspire in
their own extinction. The conspiracy is exposed and the long-
delayed but logical battle is joined. The cancer eating away at
Max Reddick, the protagonist of *The Man Who Cried I Am*, is
an entirely appropriate image of the dissolution which characterizes the whole system. Nor is this simply a racial observation.
The sickness goes far beyond colour, which, as Reddick reminds
himself, is 'no match for Hiroshima and history'.[22]

The Man Who Cried I Am traces the career of a black writer,
Max Reddick, as his brand of bitter invective attracts the attention of the white world. After an unrewarding first novel, he has
slowly established his reputation and made those contacts with
whites necessary to success in literature and reputation in society.
As a journalist he becomes the tolerated black conscience of a
liberal news magazine and, eventually, speechwriter to President
Kennedy on civil rights; as a writer he delves deeper into his own
psyche and into the reality which threatens not merely his own
developing sense of identity but the very structure of his political
and social world.

He insists throughout on the integrity of his identity, repeating
with a cabalistic intensity, '*I Am, I told you, damn it, I Am*'. But
the very urgency of his statement reveals its falsity. In the
thirty-odd years which the book covers he is led by the logic of
events and by the ironical voice of his own conscience to realise
that he is as much a construction of the whites as the inter-

F
161

national society through which he had worked himself with such avidity. Finally, he discovers the existence of an international conspiracy of whites—the *Alliance Blanc*. This had been established to combat the growing power of blacks in Africa and elsewhere. It operates through agents who organize coups and inspire intertribal hostility. It had contrived Lumumba's assassination and been responsible for much of the instability on the African continent. Observing the success of the *Alliance* abroad, the Americans prepare contingency plans to deal with their own rebellious blacks. At first this is to involve repatriation to Africa but when this is opposed by the Europeans a scheme involving detention followed by genocide is adopted. Another black novelist, Harry Ames, had died because of his knowledge of the plan and now Max has to decide what to do. But as Ames had warned him in a letter, '*Everybody knows everything, now, past and present*'.[23] The truth which his whole life should have conveyed to him now confronts him in a concrete form. He no longer has scope for inaction and passes the information on before he in turn is killed by black agents of the *Alliance*.

Each recurring and ironical affirmation of selfhood marks a stage in his initiation into the reality of history. He is led little by little to the point where he is poised between a deceptive personal fulfilment and full commitment. If these had ever been reconcilable aims they are no longer so. To challenge the white hegemony of history is to sacrifice not merely identity but life itself. And this is where Williams leaves us; on the verge of apocalypse. Reddick makes his decision. He issues the challenge and although he dies for his temerity, the course of history may be deflected. It was after all only by his death that he could hope to reconcile what he belatedly recognizes as the twin goals of his life.

If he had ever imagined that his caustic prose could achieve anything beyond personal fame he is disabused by the white world's ability to pre-empt his anger. Personal and racial abuse is transmuted into literature; fury becomes craft and as such is neutralized. This has always been the dilemma of the committed writer and in many ways *The Man Who Cried I Am* is clearly Williams' appreciation of his own ambiguous position, and, indeed, the all-but-impossible plight of the black American writer.

Richard Wright, James Baldwin, Richard Yates and other novelists and essayists appear in the book precisely because Williams recognizes the failure of any of them to resolve this paradox. Wright, the existentialist, and Baldwin, obsessed with the nature of personal identity, clearly face the same problems as confront Max Reddick, and even polemic and racial exhortation are presented as a substitute for stringent analysis and a massive assault on the status quo. It is arguable, indeed that the novelist's attempts to reshape reality or to cast it in an apocalyptic mould are simply confessions of social impotence. Fiction obviously provides a convenient and secure battlefield for psychic conflicts to those unable to influence their environment or even, in the last resort, to provoke an authentic cataclysm: Williams is fully alive to this, for the novel itself constitutes a coherent critique of his own position. He recognizes with refreshing clarity the paradox which lies in describing entropy in measured prose, in berating white injustice for white publishers at $4.95 a volume, and in criticizing the self-absorption and contemplative inaction of the creative mind at times of crisis. The book is indeed a kind of *mea culpa* disguised as militant prophecy and this gives it a shifting perspective which seems to confer a genuine integrity on his moral postures. The inconclusive ending is perhaps the most honest aspect of the whole book. The truth has been told. Everything is known, not only about the complex contrivances of white society but also, and perhaps more importantly, about the wilful self-deceit of the black victims. Yet the logic of the book leaves Blacks curiously impotent. The Whites control events so effectively that even a revelation of their power can hardly effect their position. There is nothing here then of the messianic role and power of the writer. There are no black heroes here striding manfully through a country nine-tenths white and inspiring fear and cringing admiration. Williams knows all too clearly the limitations of art and the restrictions on action and it is his examination of these realities which gives the novel its force and honesty.

The Man Who Cried I Am is a curious mixture of documentary and fiction; the factual and the fantastic. Many of the characters are clearly identifiable, the fictional names scarcely concealing known details of their lives. Williams seems to create pasteboard masks precisely so that he can strike through them to the intan-

gible but real source of anger and frustration which is his inheritance and the unacknowledged birthright of his protagonist. The
drama itself is enacted against a clearly delineated historical
framework; the 1954 desegregation decision, Gagarin's first flight,
the political assassinations of the sixties. Williams deliberately
intertwines these events with his own fictions until the arbitrary
distinction between the real and the surreal is eroded. The sug-
gestion that Harry Ames (Richard Wright) died at the hands
of a C.I.A. assassin is, in a way, no more absurd than the black
comedy of the events which followed President Kennedy's assassination. Those suspicious of the existence of a vast political and
even cosmic conspiracy no longer seem so paranoid as once they
did. To Williams, the conspiracy which the novel proposes as
being responsible not only for Lumumba's death but also for the
disproportionately high level of black casualties in Viet Nam, is
at least as plausible as the public fictions advanced as explan-
ations of those events. The plot has a truth of its own which protects him as an author from what might otherwise have been
Jamesian ethical problems.

But one is left feeling that there is something a little too casual
about the book and the analysis which lies at its core. If we accept
with him the need to confront reality, to strike through the mask,
the radical simplification of that reality, the deliberate distortion
of the mask, tends to undermine the direct purity of the response.
The rest of the novel goes a considerable way towards validating
his conclusions but it slides away from conviction because of Williams' determination to see history as so completely the contrivance of malicious agencies. As a metaphysical observation this
might be persuasive, as it is when Thomas Pynchon implies the
existence of such a conspiracy and the human need to believe in
such a conspiracy; as a serious comment on social and political
reality it requires something more than the personal experience of
a Max Reddick or the revelations of such convenient plans as
those set out in the contingency arrangements of the *Alliance
Blanc*.

In many ways *Sons of Darkness, Sons of Light*, takes over where
The Man Who Cried I Am left off. Eugene Browning, a black
(Brown?) middle class liberal, incensed by the police murder of
a sixteen-year-old Negro boy, suddenly attains to the clarity of

vision which Max Reddick had only reached at the end of his life. 'How could he not have known the truth about America and Americans, teaching political science as he had? My God, you started lying with the Pilgrims and you kept right on lying. . . . He had been a victim of both accident and design, and he helped the system to function because he, a victim of the lie, abetted it by his presence in that place.'[26] He hires the mafia to murder the policeman. The killing is a catalyst. The mafia agent, himself a Jew experienced in applying the techniques of terrorism as an antidote to persecution, decides to take the revenge a stage further, planning to kill a white southerner who has boasted of killing black children. He is prevented from doing so by a Black who has his own reasons for revenge. These swift, direct actions serve to precipitate a more general violence as long-prepared plans for racial confrontation are put into effect. The police raid the ghettos; the black rebels sabotage New York's bridges.

Sons of Darkness, Sons of Light is Williams' version of *Revelations*. As a black revolutionary recognises, 'Remembering all the years, the false hopes, all the waiting, all the killing . . . now it was 1973 and game-time was over.'[25] Described by Williams as 'a novel of some probability' the book traces out what its author clearly sees as an immediate consequence of years of betrayal and distrust. As the central character discovers, 'working from within instead of outside the system. Can't be done, just can't be done.'[27] Yet, when the simple act of violence with which he had hoped to redress the balance gets out of hand he retreats into an ineffectual liberalism. The Institution for Racial Justice, the organization for which he works, significantly collapses, and it is clearly too late for his decision to return to teaching to have any validity. In Browning's mind the year 1973 joins 1935 (Ethiopia and China) and 1936 (Spain) as a pivotal moment in history, and while Williams refuses, finally, to commit himself on the consequences of the ensuing violence he obviously feels that revelation and restriction are not far distant. The image of regeneration with which the book ends is a fine touch of irony.

Yet in many ways this book marks a step backwards for Williams. Browning's tentative liberalism is sketched in too perfunctorily to carry any real conviction. The genuine dilemmas of his preceeding novel, which grew in part out of the problems of committed writing, are absent from a work which presents a scenario without characters. The caricatures which act out their prescribed roles owe more to the vignettes of a Chester Himes than the kind of compassionate insight which had marked his own earlier books. The novelist cannot afford to demonstrate the kind of callousness, even towards his most ineffectual characters, which he condemns in society. The truth is that with this novel, as he himself has admitted, he capitulated to the pressures exerted on the black writer in the sixties. It was his revolutionary novel and it lacks equally conviction and skill, as it does the imaginative grasp of his next novel.

With *Captain Blackman* Williams probes into the past and projects a mythical future. The novel presents a catalogue of racial abuse and inter-racial conflict, the central thread being provided by the black experience of military life. The protagonist, Captain Blackman is wounded in Viet Nam, and as he lies injured so we are taken in his mind through the black experience of America's wars, from the Revolutionary War, through the Civil War, the Spanish–American War, the First and Second World Wars, to Korea. The conventional ironies of fighting for democracy abroad while denied it at home, defending an American commerce which could find no space for black endeavour, are deepened by the historic panorama. This is history as genocidal conspiracy. The implied conflict, represented in a muted way by the uneasy relationship between Blackman and his equally significantly named white rival, Whittman, eventually reaches its apogee in a battle between white soldiers and black deserters in Tombolo, Italy, during the Second World War. Yet, once again, significantly, the apocalypse is post-dated; it was, by definition, a false apocalypse. And Blackman is fully aware that such a direct battle can never serve the interests of the Blacks. It is, indeed, only in his imagination that he can plot a future in which, operating out of Africa, Blacks can take over the military capability of the United States and turn it against the white oppressor. In fact the novel ends with Blackman lying injured in a Saigon hospital, having been awarded the Congressional Medal of Honour.

Once again the apocalypse is aborted, but now his unease at a retreat which is perhaps no more than an expression of a commitment to the real, is resolved by projecting a fictive apocalypse which need not defend itself against reality or the moral questions which the book has itself invoked. It is an uneasy compromise, revealing in its attempt to transcend its own assumptions.

The crucial point about these novels is that determinism is consistently deflected into hope, that the apocalypse which is a logical extension of social injustice and the collapse of values—an image of the persistent clash of black and white—repeatedly defers to a belief in transcendence, in personal and social change, which is an equally powerful and necessary tenet of faith. The battle between Old and New Testament which characterizes Bladwin's work is equally a factor in most black writing. The need to indict, to lock the white world, and hence, in some degree, the black, into an ineluctable guilt born of the past, does battle with the need to project a future in which the individual is freed of such necessities. But the black man can only be freed by an act of grace towards the whites, in that victim and hangman are yoked together by time and event. For, of course, apocalypse is a moment of simultaneous victory and defeat. As LeRoi Jones suggests, in *Dutchman*, vengeance and suicide are fused together. The moment of truth is potentially the moment of destruction. Hence, if the apocalypse stands as one constant pole of the black imagination, as a present possibility, the other pole is an unfashionable conviction that change is possible—that the ghosts of the past can be laid if only they are freely engaged and honestly confessed.

Wright's early stories were truly apocalyptic but by the time of *Native Son* he was concerned with seeing the self as something other than a victim or agent of history. The momentum carrying Bigger Thomas towards a stance in which personal meaning is to be found only in violence, is deflected into an image of unity and transcendence. In *Invisible Man* the apocalyptic alternative is relegated to a fantasy of emasculation and a reality of self-destructive riot. The imagery of Revelations is finally muted and transformed. For Baldwin, too, the fire is always coming next time, and between the self and destruction there is always a redeeming love, a sense of personal commitment to art, or to other wounded beings, which prevents the apocalypse.

It may be that this resisted apocalypse is an expression of the black writer's conviction that he lives in a period of transition, that his is too much an age of change to make the concept of a end either relevant or tenable. He is still too much in process releasing himself, culturally, politically, and personally, to allow a line to be drawn with too great a finitude. For a white write to assume stasis, and hence to see apocalypse as an appropriat end, may be an expression of a social and metaphysical sense completion—albeit ironic. For the black writer, incompletion is fact of private and public life and the basis for social and cultura hope. The revolutionary flirts with apocalypse, uses its imagery invokes its energy, but rarely embraces its absoluteness. If it true, as Jaspers suggests, that crisis is a defining quality of life how much more so is this true for those whose lives are drama tized by society and hence who become self-dramatizing as means to meet that presumptive arrogation. A certain person apocalypticism is inevitable; it is based on a knowledge of un avoidable fate. Socially, such a presumption deals with possibili ties, not certainties. When John Williams speaks of 'the America twilight' and says that 'we can now calculate the end of our time it turns out that the prophecy of apocalypse is ultimately con nected with an urge to liberal reform, for he goes on to say tha 'we are required to extend our line by doing away with th cancers which have shown us quite clearly where the end of tim is'.[28] History is not to be allowed its own logic. Apocalypse is t be invoked as a reason for the urgency of faith.

The retreat from apocalypse is perhaps an expression of th moral role which the black writer feels called upon to play. Th open ending, the refusal to carry apocalypticism to its logical con clusion is less a product of character or event than it is of privat conviction and public role. The novelist accepts the obligation no necessarily to detail the nature of social possibilities but to endors the existence of those possibilities. That is to say, the blac writer's fictions are like those of the British agent described i Frank Kermode's The Sense of an Ending, whose stories are to b tested by a wholly critical audience—namely, the Gestapo—an which thus become quite literally enmeshed with the business o personal, and, by natural extension, public survival. Thus, th unresolved ending becomes a social as well as a moral duty. A liberal retreat from the brink, whether or not substantiated by th thrust of the narrative, becomes a necessity. As John Williams ha said, 'I think there is a difference in approach to "consciousness" between black and white writers. I don't think white writers have ever had to consciously or subconsciously concern themselves about real problems of life and survival.'[29]

In the case of John Oliver Killens, the retreat from apocalypse is the product of political confusion; in that of John Williams, of ambiguity. For Alice Walker, it is a conscious rejection of apocalypse—a refusal to be contained by definitions of personal and public necessity which allow change to be only a product of violence and which endorse a mythology which identifies epiphany with apocalypse. In *The Third Life of Grange Copeland* (1970), what seems to be a deadly determinism which justifies an apocalyptic violence gives way eventually to a renewed faith in change and the power of love. Grange, overwhelmed by what seems to be his inability to control his own life, abandons his wife and child to a lonely suicide, and convinces himself, like Bigger Thomas, that his life gains meaning only with the murder of a white woman. But in the end that conviction gives way to the notion that violence is only redemptive when it serves a purpose beyond the self—if the individual, that is, is willing to offer himself as sacrifice.

So, too, with her second novel, *Meridian* (1976). This is clearly a post-sixties novel, not only in the date of its publication but in its assumptions about racial relationships and in its concern with the connection between craft and conscience. It begins with it's heroine's refusal to embrace murder as a personally legitimized strategy for social advance, and attempts to untangle the complex interplay of sexual, racial and psychological tensions which the sixties had sought to short-circuit with the bullet. The immediate lesson of assassination did indeed seem to be the need to neutralize sophisticated prevarications and justifications with a purifying violence; the conclusion which her tortured characters work their way towards is the culpability of each individual who chooses to endorse the chaos which surrounds him by enacting its brutal premise. It is true that the sentimentalities of the early sixties could not survive the simplicities of public violence, that the heroine's uncomplicated compassion is broken by the assaults of a reality which will not respond to spontaneous kindness. But there remains a tenacious will which survives its own disillusionment—a courage which is the residue of idealism and a reminder of an innocence which, if no longer fully functional, can outlive a cynicism which, by definition, will destroy itself, and a callous exercise of power which contains no transcendence. As her name implies, it is Meridian, and not the racist or the revolutionary, who is at the heart of human experience, who feels most directly the individual needs which prompt compassionate action. Refusing to succumb to the pressure to capitulate to either extreme, she assumes the responsibility of mediating between them. It is a responsibility which, though threatening her peace of mind, is the source of her personal identity.

The tangled motives which drive black and white together and which pull them apart—motives composed partly of guilt, partly sadism, partly desperation—are both the product of history and an explanation of it. Meridian is an expression of the need to break free of this. Conceding the fact that the future may belong to the revolutionary, she sees herself as endorsing older values. 'Perhaps', she suggests, 'it will be my part to walk behind the real revolutionaries—those who know they must spill blood in order to help the poor and the black and therefore go right ahead —and when they stop to wash off the blood and find their throats too choked with the smell of murdered flesh to sing, I will come forward and sing from memory songs they will need once more to hear'.[30] What she offers is neither a purifying violence nor a redemptive innocence; it is compassion. As she herself writes, in a poem:

> there is water in the world for us
> brought by our friends
> though the rock of mother and god
> vanishes into sand
> and we, cast out alone
> to heal
> and re-create
> ourselves.[31]

As a result she raises up both herself and those she serves, becoming both an agent and a model of change.

For Toni Morrison, in *Song of Solomon* (1977), apocalypse is a natural enough product of recent history. And when a group of

Blacks forms an assassination squad, called the Seven Days (one assassin being assigned to each day of the week), it is a logical response to the violence inflicted on blacks. As one of the characters laments, 'Everybody wants the life of a black man. Everybody. White men want us dead or quiet—which is the same thing as dead. White women, same thing. They want us, you know, "universal," human, no "race consciousness". Tame, except in bed . . . But outside the bed they want us to be individuals. You tell them, "But they lynched my papa," and they say, "Yeah, but you're better than the lynchers are, so forget it".'[32] But when this logic leads them to propose the murder of four white children, in revenge for the death of four black girls killed in a Sunday school bombing, the response is clearly too implacable. And the murder of whites, with its own necessary injustices, inevitably leads to the murder of Blacks, until it becomes clear that the real offence is against human life and individuality, and the real responsibility to a version of truth which exists to one side of a murderous nature which is drawn too easily to the brink of annihilation.

Ishmael Reed, in *The Last Days of Louisiana Red*, denies apocalypse through parody and irony, Alice Walker and Ralph Ellison, (and Ronald Fair, whose *Hog Butcher* moves from threatened apocalyptic revolt to individual transformation), through the invocation of a moral responsibility apparently out of tune with the times. For Alice Walker the revolution is over. What it has left behind is not a conviction as to the efficacy of violence, but a conviction that the private and public world can be transformed: 'I believe in change: change personal, and change in society.'[33] The agency of that transformation is a self which can first imagine the world which it then creates. Nor is it without relevance that so many of the characters in *Meridian* should be writers. For their achievement is ultimately to break free of a myth which requires the resistance of the oppressor in order to sustain an identity. The world which she pictures is, as she has admitted, almost wholly menacing. Apocalypse is indeed a logical extension of its social and metaphysical cruelties. Yet, at its heart is the resistant individual, slowly constructing a self, a society and a culture from the detritus of human passions and neglect. And this is the heart of the liberal enterprise which, largely, is the black American novel of the Second Renaissance.

171

NOTES

1   John A. Williams, *This is My Country, Too* (New York, 1966), p. 153.
2   *Ibid.*, p. 156.
3   James Baldwin, *The Guardian*, 12 December, 1970, p. 9.
4   Quoted in *Images of the Negro in American Literature*, ed. Seymour Gross and John Hardy, (Chicago, 1966), p. 25.
5   John A. Williams, *Sons of Darkness, Sons of Light* (London, 1970), p. 194.
6   John A. Williams, *The Man Who Cried I Am* (London, 1968), p. 370.
7   John O. Killens, *Youngblood*, (London, 1956), p. 137.
8   *Ibid.*, p. 560.
9   John Killens, *'Sippi* (New York, 1967), p. 295.
10 John O. Killens, *And Then We Heard the Thunder* (New York, 1963) p. 132.
11 *Ibid.*, p. 174.
12 *Ibid.*, p. 482.
13 *Ibid.*
14 *Ibid.*, p. 483.
15 *Ibid.*, p. 485.
16 John O. Killens, *Slaves*, (New York, 1969), p. 142.
17 William Melvin Kelley, *A Different Drummer*, (New York, 1965), pp. 136–37.
18 John A. Williams, *Night Song* (London, 1962), p. 110.
19 John A. Williams, *Journey Out of Anger* (London, 1965), p. 18.
20 Williams, *Night Song*, p. 84.
21 Williams, *The Man Who Cried I Am*, p. 50.
22 *Ibid.*, p. 68.
23 *Ibid.*, p. 188.
24 *Ibid.*, 370.
25 Williams, *Sons of Darkness, Sons of Light*, p. 6.
26 *Ibid.*, p. 181.
27 *Ibid.*, p. 258.
28 John Williams, ed., *Beyond the Angry Black* (New York, 1971), p. xvii.
29 John O'Brien, ed., *Interviews With Black Writers* (New York, 1973), p. 229.
30 Alice Walker, *Meridian* (New York, 1976), p. 201.
31 *Ibid.*, p. 213.
32 Toni Morrison, *The Song of Solomon* (New York, 1977), p. 222.
33 *Interviews With Black Writers*, p. 194.

9

Landscapes of Reality: The Fiction of Contemporary Afro-American Women

by FAITH PULLIN

This essay is dedicated to Pat Earnshaw in Mbabane, Swaziland, and Pearl Marsh in Berkeley, California

> The wound is the wound made upon the recognition that one is regarded as a worthless human being.
>
> —James Baldwin: Foreword to
> *Daddy was a Number Runner*
> by Louise Meriwether

Much of contemporary writing by black women in America takes as its starting point the revolutionary cultural nationalism and feminism of Zora Neale Hurston.[1] Her life was proof that personal autonomy and writing devoid of self-pity were possible. Given the circumstances of her time (she died in 1960), Hurston was forced at times to accommodate and manipulate the white power structure in order to be published at all, but, as her recent biographer Robert Hemenway has pointed out,[2] she always spoke directly and honestly to black audiences. Hurston's work as a folklorist and anthropologist convinced her that black America had produced an authentic subculture with its own richness and vitality, owing nothing to white middle-class norms and values. However much this view derived from her specialised experience of her all-black home town of Eatonville, Florida, and however much it was influenced by the romanticism of the Harlem Renaissance, it served an invaluable purpose in emphasizing the uniqueness and self-sufficiency of the black world view. Hurston consistently presents Blacks as innovators and creators, and denies that black culture is merely a defensive strategy of pathological origin, arising out of poverty, powerlessness and cultural deprivation. Hurston confirms that Blacks have made a major contribution to American life in cultural terms and she resists accommodation to the white world; a world unable to perceive Blacks, and particularly black women, in any but stereotyped forms.

It has been said that much of American literature is concerned with establishing a sense of identity; this is particularly so in the case of black American women who have always had to struggle against the definitions imposed on them by others, not least by black men. In an interview of 1973, Alice Walker was asked:

> Why do you think that the black woman writer has been so ignored in America? Does she have even more difficulty than the black male writer, who perhaps has just begun to gain recognition?

Her reply was as follows:

> There are two reasons why the black woman writer is not taken as seriously as the black male writer. One is that she's a woman. Critics seem unusually ill-equipped to intelligently discuss and analyse the works of black women. Generally, they do not even make the attempt; they prefer, rather, to talk about the lives of black women writers, not about what they write. And, since black women are not—it would seem—very likable—until recently they were the least willing worshippers of male supremacy—comments about them tend to be cruel.[8]

She goes on to remark that Nathan Huggins, in his *Harlem Renaissance* (1971), never quotes from Zora Neale Hurston herself, 'but rather the opinions of others about her character. He does say that she was "a master of dialect," but adds that "Her greatest weakness was carelessness or indifference to her art" '. Having read, and taught, Hurston's work, Ms Walker feels that her writing, 'far from being done carelessly, is done (especially in *Their Eyes Were Watching God*) almost too perfectly. She took the trouble to capture the beauty of rural black expression. She saw poetry where other writers merely saw failure to cope with English.'

This persistent refusal to acknowledge the achievement of a

174

writer of the calibre of Zora Neale Hurston is the result of class
and racial inhibitions on the part of critics. It has been difficult for
all those who are not black women to understand and evaluate the
black female experience because of the prevalence of the myths surrounding it—myths such as those enumerated by Michele Wallace
in her 'Black Macho and the Myth of the Superwoman' (1979):

> Sapphire. Mammy. Tragic mulatto wench. Workhorse, can swing
> an ax, lift a load, pick cotton with any man. A wonderful house-
> keeper. Excellent with children. Very clean. Very religious. A ter-
> rific mother. A great little singer and dancer and a devoted
> teacher and social worker. She's always had more opportunities
> than the black man because she was no threat to the white man
> so he made it easy for her. Curiously enough, she frequently ends
> up on welfare. Not beautiful, rather hard-looking unless she has
> white blood, but then *very* beautiful. The black ones are exotic
> though, great in bed, tigers. And very fertile. If she is middle-class,
> she tends to be uptight about sex, prudish. She is unsupportive
> of black men, domineering, castrating. Very strong. Sorrow rolls
> right off her brow like so much rain. Tough, unfeminine. Opposed
> to womens' rights movements, considers herself already liber-
> ated.[5]

One has only to read a pre-Civil Rights Movement work like
Gwendolyn Brooks' *Maud Martha* (1953) to see the falsity of these
stereotypes, imposed by both the black and the white worlds. The
integrity of Ms Brooks' writing reveals her heroine's insight into
and understanding of the effect of colour symbolism on her husband's perception of her. Maud Martha realises that her husband
has no affection for another girl who is 'white as a white':

> 'Not,' thought Maud Martha, 'that they love each other. It oughta
> be that simple. Then I could lick it. It oughta be that easy. But it's
> my color that makes him mad. I try to shut my eyes to that, but
> it's no good. What I am inside, what is really me, he likes okay.
> But he keeps looking at my color, which is like a wall. He has to
> jump over it in order to meet and touch what I've got for him. He
> has to jump away up high in order to see it. He gets awful tired
> of all that jumping.'[6]

Maud Martha's insight here is translated into her own dealings
with the white world when lack of money forces her to take work in

175

a white woman's kitchen. What is being described is a power situation, based on colour-caste:

> It was while Maud Martha was peeling potatoes for dinner that Mrs Burns–Cooper laid herself out to prove that she was not a snob. Then it was that Mrs Burns–Cooper came out to the kitchen and, sitting, talked and talked at Maud Martha. . . . She went on listening, in silence, to the confidences until the arrival of the lady's mother-in-law (large-eyed, strong, with hair of a mighty white, and with an eloquent, angry bosom). Then the junior Burns–Cooper was very much the mistress, was stiff, cool, authoritative.
>
> There was no introduction, but the elder Burns–Cooper boomed, 'Those potato parings are entirely too thick! . . . . for the first time, she understood what Paul endured daily. For so—she could gather from a Paul-word here, a Paul-curse there—his Boss! when, squared, upright, terribly upright, superior to the President, commander of the world, he wished to underline Paul's lacks, to indicate soft shock, controlled incredulity. As his boss looked at Paul, so these people looked at her. As though she were a child, a ridiculous one, and one that ought to be given a little shaking.'[7]

When Maud Martha leaves work that night, she has already decided never to return. Explanation would be impossible—'I couldn't explain *my* explanation'. But the explanation comes in the concluding lines of *At the Burns–Coopers*': '*One was a human being*' (my italics). It is this fact and the failure of the white world to realise it that makes communication impossible:

> What difference did it make whether the firing squad understood or did not understand the manner of one's retaliation or why one had to retaliate?

The necessity for articulating the complex of emotions experienced by Maud Martha in this and other passages is expressed in Langston Hughes' 'If anybody's gonna write about me, I reckon it'll be /Me myself!' Ms Brooks' success in writing about her character Maud Martha lies in the fact that she has a total perception of the situation in all its ambiguities and is able to balance subtle social satire against the real horror of the Burns–Coopers' pathological inability to perceive the highly intelligent, resourceful and aware Maud Martha as anything but a foolish child:

> Shall I mention, considered Maud Martha, my own social triumphs, my own education, my travels to Gary and Milwaukee and Columbus, Ohio? Shall I mention my collection of fancy pink satin bras?

Although destructive enough, Maud Martha's experience of the white world is at least not confusing. Unlike that of the heroine of Nella Larsen's earlier novel, *Quicksand* (1928). However much this character is the product of the romantic tradition of the tragic mulatto, the material of the novel obviously derives from Larsen's own painful history. Unlike Claude Mackay's optimistic but facile treatment of a similar theme in *Banana Bottom* (1933) Larsen's protagonist does not enjoy an ecstatic reunion with the folk, but rather 'discovers her ironic destiny in spiritual oblivion amidst a sect of fundamentalist Alabama sharecroppers.'[8] Helga's confused identity is revealed by her constant attraction and repulsion to both the black and white worlds. She is part of both, but belongs to neither. Alternately, she feels an 'uncontrollable desire to mingle with the . . . multicolored crowd' and that 'she had come home' if she were shut up, boxed up, with hundreds of her race, closed up (64–5) and yet is soon overcome with a terrible claustrophobia 'as with that something in the racial character which had always been, to her, inexplicable, alien.' (101). She is drawn to Harlem emotionally but repelled intellectually:

> For the hundredth time she marveled at the gradations within this oppressed race of hers. A dozen shades slid by. There was sooty black, shiny black, taupe, mahogany, bronze, copper, gold, orange, yellow, peach, ivory, pinky white, pastry white. There was yellow hair, brown hair, black hair; straight hair, straightened hair, curly hair, crinkly hair, wooly hair. She saw black eyes in white faces, brown eyes in yellow faces, gray eyes in brown faces, blue eyes in tan faces. Africa, Europe, perhaps with a pinch of Asia, in a fantastic motley of ugliness and beauty, semibarbaric, sophisticated, exotic, were here. But she was blind to its charm, purposely aloof and a little contemptuous, and soon her interest in the moving mosaic waned. (108)

Here, Larsen is clearly using terms related to ideas of exoticism in Harlem Renaissance thinking, and, many times, her control of language is insecure; yet the psychological truth of her narrative is always convincing. Particularly in the sickening sense of loss and insecurity and, above all, dissatisfaction with every area of life

177

that Helga experiences. The dichotomy resolves itself neatly into the two geographical areas of her inheritance; a European/African schizophrenia:

> This knowledge, this certainty of the division of her life into two parts in two lands, into physical freedom in Europe and spiritual freedom in America, was unfortunate, inconvenient, expensive. It was, too, as she was uncomfortably aware, even a trifle ridiculous, and mentally she caricatured herself moving shuttlelike from continent to continent. From the prejudiced restrictions of the New World to the easy formality of the Old, from the pale calm of Copenhagen to the colourful lure of Harlem. (p. 163)

There is no resolution of Helga's dilemma. In an unconscious attempt to end the unbearable ambivalences of her life, she enters a kind of living death, drugged by sex and religion. When the initial effect of these wear off, as the result of a difficult childbirth, she realizes that she has trapped and entombed herself in a loveless marriage in a deprived section of the rural south. 'She couldn't, she thought ironically, even blame God for it, now that she knew that He didn't exist' (p. 214). Helga can never escape since she would find it impossible to abandon her own children, as she had been abandoned herself as a child.

Quicksand expresses in the most overt, often melodramatic, manner the black woman's painful condition of double jeopardy; the double strain of being a woman in a sexist society and black in a racist one. In *Quicksand*, Larsen also confronts the dilemma of passing. It is possible for Helga to exist and to marry in both societies. The problem comes from the fact that she is satisfied by neither. Helga can survive as a solitary Black in Copenhagen, suffering reverse discrimination treated as 'some new and strange species of pet dog being profoundly exhibited' and at the price of loneliness and isolation. And yet, the practical difficulties of life in America are crudely appalling, even if she can be with her own people:

> Go back to America, where they hated Negroes! To America where Negroes were not people. To America, where Negroes were allowed to be beggars only, of life, of happiness, of security. To America, where everything had been taken from those dark ones, liberty, respect, even the labor of their hands. To America, where

if one had Negro blood, one mustn't expect money, education, or, sometimes, even work whereby one might earn bread . . . Never could she recall the shames and often the absolute horrors of the black man's existence in America without the quickening of her heart's beating and a sensation of disturbing nausea. (p. 141)

Larsen's achievement in this novel is to express the mental and emotional stresses to which her very existence exposes her heroine. She takes over too easily the racist identification of blacks with emotional and instinctive life and whites with destructive rationality, but she conveys to the reader a disturbing sense of the nervous tension Helga is constantly forced to live under, in whatever situation or society she finds herself. In her role of outsider, forced to live in a series of alien value systems, she is a forerunner of the contemporary black heroine. However, the events of the sixties and the influence of the Women's Movement have meant that the protagonists of the novels of Gayl Jones and Toni Morrison do not retreat into mindless masochism, but strive to establish themselves as autonomous and active figures in their worlds. They may also be destroyed, but they fight. They do not share the self-destructive anger and despair of Helga Crane:

> She had resolved never to return to the existence of ignominy which the New World of opportunity and promise forced upon Negroes. How stupid she had been ever to have thought that she could marry and perhaps have children in a land where every dark child was handicapped at the start by the shroud of color! She saw, suddenly, the giving birth to little, helpless, unprotesting Negro children as a sin, an unforgivable outrage. More black folk to suffer indignities. More dark bodies for mobs to lynch. No, Helga Crane didn't think often of America. (p. 131)

Contemporary black women writers are effectively expressing their own, often conflicting, experience, the two sides of which are articulated in two well-known poems by Nikki Giovanni. The first is the autobiographical *Nikki-Rosa*:

> and I really hope no white person ever has cause
> to write about me
> because they never understand
> Black love is Black wealth and they'll
> probably talk about my hard childhood

and never understand that
all the while I was quite happy

Woman poem, in contrast, generalizes rather than personalizes the issues:

joy is finding a pregnant roach
and squashing it
not finding someone to hold
let go get off get back don't turn
me on you black dog
how dare you care
about me
you ain't got no good sense
cause i ain't shit you must be lower
than that to care

in this circular poem, the end is the beginning:

my whole life is tied
up to unhappiness
cause it's the only
for real thing
i
know[9]

What emerges from the juxtaposition of these poems is, first, an affirmation of the emotional strength of the black family, and the misinterpretation of this by the white world and, secondly, the realism implicit in the expression of a fundamental sense of worthlessness inculcated by living in a minority group not esteemed by the majority society. The task of the contemporary black female writer is to resist imposed definitions; her fiction must provide new material by means of which more accurate assessments of the black female experience can be made. The first section of *Woman Poem* contains the lines

i wish i knew how it would feel
to be free

It's psychological freedom that's being discussed here; the freedom to reject 'the recognition that one is regarded as a worthless human being', always at the base of the white man/blackman/white woman/black woman power structure.

One major way in which black women have set out to deny the stereotypes imposed by others is in their account of their own sexuality. Writers like Gayl Jones have broken new ground in their treatment of black lesbianism; and, in very many respects, the whole spectrum of black women's experience, sexual, economic, religious, has been delineated for the first time by major new talents like Alice Walker, Toni Cade Bambara, Toni Morrison and Gayl Jones. Alice Walker's recent collection of stories, *In Love and Trouble* (1973), consisting of work written between 1967 and 1973, is particularly valuable in its range of subject and technique and in its obvious relationship with the work of African women writers, such as Bessie Head in Botswana and Ama Ata Aidoo in Ghana. Alice Walker's use of an epigraph from Rilke indicates her awareness of the problems she has set herself:

> it is clear that we must hold to what is difficult; everything in Nature grows and defends itself in its own way and is characteristically and spontaneously itself, seeks at all costs to be so against all opposition.
>
> (Letters to a Young Poet)

The first story, 'Roselily', uses the simple device of phrases from the marriage service interspersed with the protagonist's thoughts to reveal a complex situation, and does so with elegance and economy. Roselily is to be removed from Mississippi to Chicago; although going through the motions of a Christian marriage, her new husband is a Muslim and will expect her to live a sober life 'of black and white. Of veils. Covered head.' The husband, with missionary zeal, is taking her away from the delusions of Mississippi and her hard life as the single mother of three children:

> She knows he blames Mississippi for the respectful way the men turn their heads up in the yard, the women stand waiting and knowledgeable, their children held from mischief by teachings from the wrong God.[10]

Roselily's whole past history and probable future is contained in these few pages. Incidentally, we learn that one of her sons lives with his white Civil-Rights-worker father in New England: 'Was a good man but weak because good language meant so much to him he could not live with Roselily. Could not abide TV in the living room, five beds in three rooms, no Bach except from four to six on

Sunday afternoons. No chess at all.' From a practical point of view, Roselily's move to the North can be seen as nothing but good and yet her extreme ambivalence is shown in her sense of belonging to her past:

> She feels old. Yoked. An arm seems to reach out from behind her and snatch her backward. She thinks of cemeteries and the long sleep of grandparents mingling in the dirt. (6)

and in her fear of the future with its welcomed respectability but unnerving restraints. Her life has been unsatisfying till now but there is no sense of freedom in her apparent escape—'She thinks she loves the effort he will make to redo her into what he truly wants'. Roselily's problem is that 'she wants to live for once' but she is trapped, by the conditions of her life as a poor black woman in Mississippi and now as the manipulated wife of a husband who literally stands in front of her and 'in the crush of well-wishing people, does not look back'.

In 'Roselily', Ms Walker, using an extremely simple vocabulary, manages to convey a strong sense of the conflicts within black society and the virtually inescapable exploitation of a poor black woman. In 'Really, Doesn't Crime Pay?' a more sophisticated persona is used, that of Myrna, a middle-class aspiring writer who is used and cheated by both husband and lover. Myrna's husband wants to make her into a mere accessory—an object that will sit neatly in his new house. Myrna fits into her new surroundings perfectly, 'like a jar of cold cream melting on a mirrored vanity shelf'. The broken time scheme functions effectively here to emphasize the fragmented nature of Myrna's experience and the frustration of her creativity. Ruel, the husband, sees writing, like having a baby or shopping, as an equivalent way of passing the time—since her role is not to be a separate agent, but merely a means of reflecting credit on himself, 'No wife of mine is going to embarrass me with a lot of foolish, vulgar stuff.' Ms Walker realistically avoids the sentimentality of Myrna's lover awakening her to sexual pleasure and helping to get her stories published. On the contrary, he steals her work and publishes it as his own. Her response is to try to murder her husband with one of his own chain saws. Society's attempts to adjust Myrna cause her to transform herself into the archetypal consumer housewife:

> I go to the new shopping mall twice a day now; once in the morning and once in the afternoon, or at night. I buy hats I would not dream of wearing, or even owning. Dresses that are already on their way to Goodwill. Shoes that will go to mold and mildew in the cellar. And I keep the bottles of perfume, the skin softeners, the pots of gloss and eye shadow. I amuse myself painting my own face. (23)

Her passive revenge for the exploitation she has suffered takes the form of 'religiously' using the Pill. 'It is the only spot of humour in my entire day.' Her strategy is to exhaust her husband with her submissiveness and finally leave him. Against the present of loss and humiliation, she sets a vision of possibility:

> A famous authoress, miles away from Ruel, miles away from anybody. I am dressed in dungarees, my hands are a mess. I smell of sweat. I glow with happiness. (18)

Many elements in this description combine to constitute a rejection of the role set out for women by society. Dungarees, instead of dresses; sweat instead of perfume; nail-bitten hands; in other words, a person making her own individual contribution to life. This is the vision that contemporary writers are presenting as valid and necessary for the mental health and indeed the survival of black women in America.

In an important article in *Ms.*, May 1974, Alice Walker made a claim that black women in America have been, perforce, suppressed artists whose creativity has been expressed in devious ways. In the present intellectual and emotional climate, creative black women can emerge. Certainly, the work of black men has received recognition previously denied to women, but one of the purposes of an essay such as the present one, is to attempt to change this situation. What is hopeful is that black women writers do not feel the reassuring need to produce idealistic stereotypes to offset the destructive characterisations often found in the writing of other authors. Black women writers are beginning to provide their audience with the truth about themselves. These are the stories, poems, novels and biographies that Mary Helen Washington, in her perceptive introduction to her collection, *Black-Eyed Susans* (1975) asserts are needed. She asks for writing about black women who have nervous breakdowns, not just the ones who endure courageously; stories about women who are overwhelmed by sex; wives who are not faithful; women experiencing the pain and humiliation of divorce; single women over thirty or forty, trying to make sense out of life and perhaps not being able to; and what about black women who abuse and neglect their children, or those women whose apparently promiscuous behaviour has caused them to be labelled "easy," or those black women in interracial relationships?[11]

One of the many strengths of Alice Walker's 'Really, Doesn't Crime Pay?' is that the heroine does not leave home but puts off her rejection of all that it means to some unspecified point in the future. In this way, the story acquires psychological credibility and depth and avoids mere propaganda. In a similar way, 'Her Sweet Jerome' has a heroine who deludes herself into rabid jealousy over an imaginary rival for the love of her younger goodlooking husband. She is an ugly woman who has, in effect, bought a younger lover. Ironically, the rival turns out to be the revolution itself. Her apocalyptic revenge—the burning of his books—involves her own physical destruction. In spite of the limpid style of these stories, the subject-matter is often violent, even melodramtic. The pressures and tensions of the black woman's life often resolve themselves on a physical level. This is true of the story, 'The Child Who Favored Daughter', whose subject is incestuous jealousy complicated by interracial sex. Here, the child is actually mutilated by her father, who cuts off her breasts and flings them to his dogs. Horrific though this is, it is a clear representation of the bitter and tortured emotions involved. Nor is the daughter presented merely as a victim. There is no blame in this story but a full understanding of the father's needs and traumas as well as those of the daughter:

> In a world where innocence and guilt became further complicated by questions of color and race, he felt hesitant and weary of living as though all the world were out to trick him. (40)

The story, 'Everyday Use', deals with a problem in all societies, the conflict between generations; but in black society this conflict is made more intense by questions of culture and nationality. The protagonist here has two daughters, one of whom, Dee, has escaped from her rural background and is caught up in a spurious African identity. All the objects associated with her past, previously treated with contempt, are now sought after as proofs of a rich folk heritage. The mother is intimidated by her aggressive, successful daughter. 'She was determined to stare down any disaster in her efforts.' The mother belongs to an older, conformist generation who accepts her background and is unnerved by her daughter's new insistence on it. There is another sister, Maggie, who has been permanently injured in a house fire in their childhood. Dee rejoiced in the burning of all that she despised and resisted. Now, the urge to recover her culture makes her demand the quilts made by her grandmother. But the mother refuses; her cultural imperative states that the quilts must be inherited by Maggie when she marries. They are to be used, not to be looked at. Ironically, the mother is functioning as a true African here, since the concept of art for art's sake is foreign to Africa—all objects are for use. Dee has involuntarily taken over a very western attitude towards art and its material value. She has come back to her family parading a phony African personality, which is as unreal as her former rejection of the quilts at any earlier stage of her development.

> 'The truth is,' I said, 'I promised to give them quilts to Maggie, for when she marries John Thomas.'
> She gasped like a bee had stung her. 'Maggie can't appreciate these quilts!' she said. 'She'd probably be backward enough to put them to everyday use.' 'I reckon she would,' I said. 'God knows I been saving 'em for long enough with nobody using 'em. I hope she will!' I didn't want to bring up how I had offered Dee (Wangero) a quilt when she went away to college. Then she had told me they were old-fashioned, out of style.
> 'But they're *priceless*!' she was saying now, furiously; for she has a temper. 'Maggie would put them on the bed and in five years they'd be in rags. Less than that!'
> 'She can always make some more.' I said. 'Maggie knows how to quilt.' (57–8)

In spite of the superficial comedy created by these misunderstandings, the basic mood of the story is tragic. None of the characters has a strong sense of identity. Even Maggie is too subdued and deprived to use and enjoy her society, limited though it is. All the characters are grappling with the fact that they exist parallel with the dominant white society, but not as part of it. They know that they have something of their own, but they don't know what it is or who they are.

All the women portrayed in the stories of this collection are seeking to find or retain some dignity in their lives through the assertion of their own personalities and needs. Sometimes, this assertion takes the form of straightforward revenge, as in the story, 'The Revenge of Hannah Kemhuff' where the heroine loses everything as a direct result of the lack of compassion of a 'little white moppet'. Again, Ms Walker allows the situation its full ironic complexity. The Kemhuff family appeared not to be starving because they were wearing castoff clothes, as a way of retaining self-respect, so that on one level, the young white woman is right to refuse them food, prosperous as they appear to be. With this story, Alice Walker pays open homage to Zora Neale Hurston whose anthropological research lead her to the belief that voodoo was an authentic religion. In 'The Revenge of Hannah Kemhuff', the narrator recites the curse-prayer 'straight from Zora Neale Hurston's book, *Mules and Men* . . . I was moved by the fervor with which Mrs. Kemhuff prayed. Often she would clench her fists before her closed eyes and bite the insides of her wrists as the women do in Greece.' (72)

The voodoo death spell works, after Hannah herself has died. The superior intelligence and manipulative skills of the narrator and her instructress cause the white woman's death, by playing on her fear.

Alice Walker interprets religion in a broad sense. Much of her fiction constitutes an attack on Christianity because of its racism and anti-feminism. In the interview previously quoted, she admits to being intrigued by the religion of the black Muslims.

> By what conversion means to black women, specifically, and what the religion itself means in terms of the black American past; our history, our 'race memories' our absorption of Christianity, our *changing* of Christianity to fit our needs. What will the new rituals mean? How will this new religion imprint itself on the collective consciousness of the converts? Can women be free in such a religion? Is such a religion. in fact, an anachronism? . . . In other stories, I am interested in Christianity as an

imperialist tool used against Africa ('Diary of an African Nun') and in Voodoo used as a weapon against oppression ('The Revenge of Hannah Kemhuff'). I see all of these as religious questions.[12]

Certainly the two stories in *In Love and Trouble* dealing with Christianity are hostile to it. In 'The Welcome Table' an old black woman is forcibly ejected from a white church and dies later on the road. The old woman meets Jesus and walks with him to her death. The old woman's entry into the white church is seen as an intrusion on a tribal ritual and the whites close ranks against her; religion has nothing to do with it, but self-preservation and the maintaining of privilege do:

> Some of them there at the church saw the age, the dotage, the missing buttons down the front of her mildewed black dress. Others saw cooks, chauffeurs, maids, mistresses, children denied or smothered in the deferential way she held her cheek to the side, toward the ground. Many of them saw jungle orgies in an evil place, while others were reminded of riotous anarchists looting and raping in the streets. Those who knew the hesitant creeping up on them of the law, saw the beginning of the end of the sanctuary of Christian worship, saw the desecration of Holy Church, and saw an invasion of privacy, which they struggled to believe they still kept. (82)

This kind of satirical comment is more in keeping with the thrust of the story as a whole than the somewhat heavy and facile symbolism of the ending:

> Some of them wondered aloud where the old woman had been going so stoutly that it had worn her heart out. They guessed maybe she had relatives across the river, some miles away, but none of them really knew. (87)

Nevertheless, there is a stark and effective contrast between the sentimentality of the vision that inspires the old woman—it is a white Jesus, taken from a white lady's Bible, while she was working for her—and the brutality of the white view of the event. 'Most of them heard sometime later that an old colored woman fell dead along the highway.' Ms Walker is operating out of a double vision here; on the one hand, there is the sense that Christianity is an oppressive device used by whites to keep blacks quiet (and at the same time a means of preserving their own class/ caste position); and, on the other, the sense that the old woman is nearer to a God than anyone else. A simpler, and less effective, use of ambivalence is made in 'The Diary of an African Nun'. In this story, Ms Walker is dealing, in her own words, with 'Christianity as an imperialist tool used against Africa.' Ms Walker's gifts of acute observation and sense of the complexity in human relationships could have been better deployed if this story had taken a different form. What comes over very successfully is the sense of the imposition of an alien culture; one which distorts the personality of the young African girl and does not fulfil her needs. What is not convincing, however, is the alternative, symbolized in an erotic, midnight dance. The language is at fault here—Ms Walker descends into an uneasy poetic prose which is surprising in a writer with such a fine control of tone:

> Silence, as the dance continues—now they will be breaking out the wine, cutting the goat's meat in sinewy strips. Teeth will clutch it, wring it. Cruel, greedy, greasy lips will curl over it in an ecstasy which has never ceased wherever there were goats and men. The wine will be hot from the fire; it will cut through the obscene clutter on those lips and turn them from their goat's meat to that other. (116)

This seems typical of the worst kind of nineteenth-century European romanticism about savage Africa, rather than the writing of an aware modern black woman. The problem perhaps comes from Ms Walker's personal unclearness about the subject: 'Like many, I waver in my convictions about God, from time to time . . . I seem to have spent all of my life rebelling against the church and other peoples' interpretations of what religion is—the truth is probably that I don't believe there is a God, although I would like to believe it.' There is a falsity in this story which is compounded by the language itself. Ms Walker, like other black women writers, is engaged in a search for a new medium to express what she, uniquely, has to say. A new language has to be created for these new experiences. Ms Walker has the courage to make this exploration and it's inevitable that there will be some failures along the way. What she is interested in is 'the plastic, shaping, almost painting quality of words . . . a new dimension to the language . . . I am trying to arrive at that place where black music already is; to arrive at that unselfconscious sense of collective oneness; that naturalness, that (even when anguished) grace.[13] All the stories in *In Love and Trouble* have important things to say, vital information to give us; whether concerning the love between the young and the old, in 'To Hell With Dying', the perverse sacrifice of himself to a 'savage idol' of the boy John in 'Entertaining God', or the dignity of a deprived black girl who asks for the white doctor for her dying son, and is refused in 'Strong Horse Tea', or the affection of a middle-aged Polish refugee for a young black student in 'We Drink The Wine in France'; the reader can know these things only from Ms Walker, who has an original talent. Finding the means of expression for this new material is a constant and vital endeavour. In Ms Walker's own words:

> The writer—like the musician or painter—must be free to explore, otherwise she or he will never discover what is needed (by everyone) to be known. This means, very often, finding oneself considered 'unacceptable' by masses of people who think that the writer's obligation is not to explore or to challenge, but to second the masses' motions, whatever they are.[14]

One of the major problems with which the black woman has to grapple in her own life is the intimidation of colour. Many writers have borne witness to their education by their community into the desirability of being light-skinned, with 'good hair'. This is a trauma suffered only by black women, and the evidence of their writing is that it is a particularly vicious and destructive one. As Mary Helen Washington has pointed out, black male writers do not seem to feel affected by their shade of skin or type of hair, nor is the reaction of other people a factor. In *The Bluest Eye*, (1970) Toni Morrison has documented the horrific dimensions of this problem. The cute, white, baby-doll image of beauty in America destroys the self-esteem of black girls when they are children. It focusses the fact of their rejection and makes them unacceptable even to themselves, sowing seeds of self-hatred that will distort the rest of their lives. The character of Pecola sums up, in an extreme form, the facts of rejection and lack of self-esteem with which black women have to come to

189

terms. The narrator maps out at the beginning of the novel the community in which Pecola has to live and suffer:

> Being a minority in both caste and class, we moved about any-way on the hem of life, struggling to consolidate our weaknesses and hang on, or to creep singly up into the major folds of the garment.[15]

Pecola enters the narrative at the beginning, having to be taken in as she has nowhere else to go after the disaster of her rape by her own father. Ms Morrison's method is to present the initial situation and then trace back the reasons for it, giving full weight to the human pains and difficulties of each character. The baby-doll image is an immediate cause of dissension in its current manifestation in the blue-and-white Shirley Temple cup:

> She was a long time with the milk, and gazed fondly at the sil-houette of Shirley Temple's dimpled face. Frieda and she had a loving conversation about how cu-ute Shirley Temple was. I couldn't join them in their adoration because I hated Shirley. (19)

The blue-eyed, yellow-haired, pink-skinned baby-doll represen-ted the standard of beauty to the black community. It means that the white shop-keeper cannot even see Pecola because she is a total deviation from this norm. 'He does not see her, because for him there is nothing to see.' What Pecola sees in his eyes is dis-taste for her blackness. Sensing this fear and repulsion, Pecola learns a sense of inexplicable shame. The relevance of the colour/shade problem for them is brought home to the narrator and her sister by the treatment accorded to Maureen Peale, 'a high-yellow dream child' who enchanted the black and white worlds. Maureen's accusation, 'I *am* cute! And you ugly! Black and ugly . . .' is, in terms of societal values, nothing less than the simple truth. The two black children are forced to confront the assumptions that will influence their lives and inevitably restrict their personal free-dom:

> We were sinking under the wisdom, accuracy, and relevance of Maureen's last words. If she was cute—and if anything could be believed, she *was*—then we were not. And what did that mean? We were lesser. Nicer, brighter, but still lesser. Dolls we could destroy, but we could not destroy the honey voices of parents

and aunts, the obedience in the eyes of our peers, the slippery light in the eyes of our teachers when they encountered the Maureen Peals of the world. What was the secret? What did we lack? Why was it important? . . . And all the time we knew that Maureen Peal was not the Enemy and not worthy of such intense hatred. The *Thing* to fear was the *Thing* that made *her* beautiful, and not us. (61–2)

Similarly, Pecola's mother, Pauline Breedlove, had had her sense of herself, and value in her world, destroyed by the ideal of female beauty portrayed in films, her only escape from reality. Loneliness in the city, the result of her inability to adapt from her country life-style, made her take refuge in the cinema. But there she is introduced to the ideas of romantic love and physical beauty. 'Probably the most destructive ideas in the history of human thought'—this is the narrator's gloss on Pauline's initiation. Pauline was never able, 'after her education in the movies, to look at a face and not assign it some category in the scale of absolute beauty'. The sinister element is in the equating of physical beauty with virtue so that Pauline 'collected self-contempt by the heap'. She begins to punish her husband for her lack of material possessions and her self-righteousness is one of the many indirect causes of his maltreatment of their daughter. Pauline's experience of reification, or rather, the reduction to the status of animal, extends to the hospital where she is literally treated as a brood mare by the white male doctors:

When he got to me he said now these here women you don't have any trouble with. They deliver right away and with no pain. Just like horses. (99)

Pauline is forced to assert her status as a woman, like any other:

The pains wasn't as bad as I let on, but I had to let them people know having a baby was more than a bowel movement. I hurt just like them white women. (99)

The child born is Pecola and, because she is black, Pauline 'knowed she was ugly. Head full of pretty hair, but Lord she was ugly'.

Pecola's father, Cholly, had himself been dumped by his mother on a junk-heap and was rescued by his Great Aunt Jimmy. When

191

Cholly was a young boy, this aunt died and the occasion of her death gives the narrator the opportunity for a definitive apologia of the life of black women. In spite of its occasional Faulknerian undertones, this is an impressive summation and worth quoting in full:

> But they had been young once. The odor of their armpits and haunches had mingled into a lovely musk; their eyes had been furtive, their lips relaxed, and the delicate turn of their heads on those slim black necks had been like nothing other than a doe's. Their laughter had been more touch than sound.
>
> Then they had grown. Edging into life from the back door. Becoming. Everybody in the world was in a position to give them orders. White women said, 'Do this.' White children said, 'Give me that.' White men said, 'Come here.' Black men said, 'Lay down.' The only people they need not take orders from were black children and each other. But they took all of that and re-created it in their own image. They ran the houses of white people, and knew it. When white men beat their men, they cleaned up the blood and went home to receive abuse from the victim. They beat their children with one hand and stole for them with the other. The hands that felled trees also cut umbilical cords; the hands that wrung the necks of chickens and butchered hogs also nudged African violets into bloom; the arms that loaded sheaves, bales, and sacks rocked babies into sleep. They patted biscuits into flaky ovals of innocence—and shrouded the dead. They plowed all day and came home to nestle like plums under the limbs of their men. The legs that straddled a mule's back were the same ones that straddled their men's hips. And the difference was all the difference there was.
>
> Then they were old. Their bodies honed, their odor sour. Squatting in a cane field, stooping in a cotton field, kneeling by a river bank, they had carried a world on their heads. They had given over the lives of their own children and tendered their grandchildren. With relief they wrapped their heads in rags, and their breasts in flannel; eased their feet into felt. They were through with lust and lactation, beyond tears and terror. They alone could walk the roads of Mississippi, the lanes of Georgia, the fields of Alabama unmolested. They were old enough to be irritable when and where they chose, tired enough to look forward to death, disinterested enough to accept the idea of pain while ignoring the presence of pain. They were, in fact and at last, free. And the lives of these old black women were synthe-

192

sized in their eyes—a purée of tragedy and humor, wickedness and serenity, truth and fantasy. (109–10)

The emphasis here is on creativity and on life, in spite of its restraints, lived richly and fully. It is not merely a matter of endurance, but of celebration. The concept of 'de nigger woman as de mule uh de world'[16] is here deftly manipulated to bring out all its positive aspects. But the negative aspects are dominant in the case of a frustrated personality like Pauline Breedlove's. In the kitchen of her white woman, Pauline is happy because here she can touch and arrange beautiful things: the instinct for design that she had shown as a young child is given free reign as it cannot be in her own environment: 'Mrs. Breedlove's skin glowed like taffeta in the reflection of white porcelain, white woodwork, polished cabinets, and brilliant copperware.'[17] Pecola's fear and hunger in this white kitchen cause her to spill a pie. Mrs. Breedlove's savage anger is in ironic contrast to her honeyed words, 'soothing the tears of the little pink-and-yellow girl'. Again, Toni Morrison achieves a total view of the pain of this incident for all concerned. Pauline is afraid for her job and ashamed of her own child and the poverty of her home. Her violence to Pecola and her desire to remain in the ordered and beautiful kitchen are in themselves indications of her frustrated love and hopeless aspirations. She has bought a kind of security at the price of real self-respect ('Her calling Mrs. Breedlove Polly, when even Pecola called her mother Mrs. Breedlove, seemed reason enough to scratch her').

The dénouement of this densely written and wonderfully inclusive novel transcends its own pathos and horror. Pecola seeks help from a magician, an interpreter of dreams, to save herself from the terror of her own blackness. She goes to him to ask to be granted the gift of blue eyes. It is characteristic of Toni Morrison's intricate fictional strategy that even this request, in all its devastating simplicity, is caught up with the interpreter's sexual preference for little girls and his killing of his landlady's dog. This is accomplished with a gratuitous horror, reminiscent of Southern Gothic, which precipitates Pecola into genuine madness.

Take this food and give it to the creature sleeping on the porch. Make sure he eats it. And mark well how he behaves. If nothing happens, you will know that God has refused you. If the animal behaves strangely, your wish will be granted on the day following this one. (138)

The poisoned dog jerks horribly; Pecola takes this as a sign and runs from the yard. Her insane conversations with herself that end the novel focus on her desire to have not only blue eyes but the bluest eyes in the whole world. The narrator's final view of Pecola if of a scapegoat on whom her community directed all that they felt, or were made to feel, was repellent about themselves:

> All of us—all who knew her—felt so wholesome after we cleaned ourselves on her. We were so beautiful when we stood astride her ugliness. (159)

The humanity and compassion of *The Bluest Eye* are striking. It is a profound book in that it dares to face and understand the deepest psychic fears of black women; its images work to express and develop the most subtle shades of meaning and emotion. In itself it is a triumphant refutation of the prevailing assumption mentioned by Alice Walker when she claimed that black writing has suffered,

> because even black critics have assumed that a book that deals with the relationships between members of a black family—or between a man and a woman—is less important than one that has white people as a primary antagonist. The consequence of this is that many of our books by 'major' writers (always male) tell us little about the culture, history, or future, imagination fantasies, etc. of black people, and a lot about isolated (often improbable) or limited encounters with a nonspecific white world.

I suggest that writers such as those I have been discussing here *are* already producing the work for which Ms Walker calls, comparable to that of African writers—work that 'exposes the *subconscious* of a people, because the people's dreams, imaginings, rituals, legends etc. are known to be important, are known to contain the accumulated collective reality of the people themselves'.[18]

Certainly, Toni Morrison's next novel, *Sula* (1973) fulfils these requirements, concentrating on the ambivalent relationship between an autonomous black woman and her uncomprehending

194

community. Sula is another of the frustrated artist figures with whom many black women writing today are concerned:

> Had she paints, or clay, or knew the discipline of the dance, or strings; had she anything to engage her tremendous curiosity and her gift for metaphor, she might have exchanged the restlessness and preoccupation with whim for an activity that provided her with all she yearned for. And like any artist with no art form, she became dangerous.[19]

The danger that Sula constitutes is in her implicit questioning of the predetermined role of a black woman in the society of the Bottom. Sula refuses to marry, nor does she have children, nor will she undertake the servile work expected of her. She is therefore a divisive influence and there is relief at her early death. When Sula becomes disillusioned with the one experience of love she has had ('I didn't even know his name. And if I didn't know his name, then there is nothing I did know and I have known nothing ever at all'), she literally lies down and begins to die. When she returned to the town after a long absence, she was unable to talk to any of the other women since the lifestyle they had chosen was so different from her own. They were already old, used up and narrow in their views and lives:

> Those with husbands had folded themselves into starched coffins, their sides bursting with other people's skinned dreams and bony regrets. Those without men were like sour-tipped needles featuring one constant empty eye. (105)

She attacks societal norms by refusing relationships with men, but merely using them for sex. The one relationship to which she consents, with Ajax, works (until he leaves, fearing commitment) because he sees her as an equal:

> He did not speak down to her or at her, not content himself with puerile questions about her life or monologues of his own activities. (110)

When Ajax leaves, Sula feels she has no more to experience, or rather she has used up all the limited opportunities available to her ('I have sung all the songs there are'). All that Sula represented in her idiosyncratic life in terms of (unfulfilled) potential is contained in the anguished cry of her alienated friend Nel after Sula's burial:

> the loss pressed down on her chest and came up into her throat. 'We was girls together,' she said as though explaining something. 'O Lord, Sula,' she cried, 'girl, girl, girlgirlgirl.' (149)

At this late point, Nel has discovered what Sula knew before her: 'she had been looking all along for a friend, and it took her awhile to discover that a lover was not a comrade and could never be—for a woman'. This is the deepest truth for Sula and Nel and all the women in the novel. Sula's mother, Hannah, and grandmother, Eva discount the idea of love verbally, but their actions prove otherwise—their whole lives are directed towards securing the survival of their daughters. The first questioning of the conventional idea of love is by Hannah herself when she asks Eva, 'Mamma, did you ever love us?' to which the short answer is ' "No, I don't reckon I did. Not the way you thinkin' " '. Her explanation is that times were so hard that the best she could do for her children was simply to stay alive for them and care for them, rather than abandon them or neglect them. This caring *is* an active kind of love. Eva expresses it in crude terms to hide the strength of the protective emotion:

> You settin' here with your healthy-ass self and ax me did I love you? Them big old eyes in your head would a been two holes full of maggots if I hadn't. (59)

It's Eva, a one-legged woman, who precipitates herself through a window to try to save Hannah from the fire. And it's Eva who burns her only son because she can't bear to watch him destroy himself and return to an unnatural state of childlike dependence. Earlier, Hannah herself, in a realistic conversation with two of her friends, tells the truth about maternal love:

> "Can't help loving your own child. No matter what they do.'
> 'Well, Hester grown now and I can't say love is exactly what I feel."
> "Sure you do. You love her, like I love Sula. I just don't like her. That's the difference."
> "Guess so. Likin' them is another thing."
> "Sure. They different people, you know. . . ." (48–9)

196

The naked honesty of these remarks involves the re-examination of the relationship between black parents and children. In all they write, black women are querying false concepts thrust on them by outsiders. One of the most valuable aspects of *Sula* is that it forces a reassessment of what 'love' between parents and children —men and women—really means and *is*.

Sula herself is considered a witch by many people in the Bottom, because of her non-conformity and apparent lack of responsibility. They fear what she reveals in themselves: 'Sula never competed; she simply helped others define themselves.' This doesn't mean that she isn't critical, or ironically aware of the myths by which others protect themselves. When Nel's husband, Jude, indulges in self-pity and rehearses a current wrong done to him—'a Negro man had a hard row to hoe in this world', she responds with a different explanation:

> Sula was smiling. 'I mean, I don't know what the fuss is about. I mean, everything in the world loves you. White men love you. They spend so much time worrying about your penis they forget their own. The only thing they want to do is cut off a nigger's privates. And if that ain't love and respect I don't know what is. And white women? They chase you all to every corner of the earth, feel for you under every bed. I knew a white woman wouldn't leave the house after 6 o'clock for fear one of you would snatch her. Now ain't that love? They think rape soon's they see you, and if they don't get the rape they looking for, they scream it anyway just so the search won't be in vain.
>
> 'Colored woman worry themselves into bad health just trying to hang on to your cuffs. Even little children—white and black, boys and girls—spend all their childhood eating their hearts out 'cause they think you don't love them. And if that ain't enough, you love yourselves. Nothing in this world loves a black man more than another black man. You hear of solitary white men, but niggers? Can't stay away from one another a whole day. So. It looks to me like you the envy of the world.' (89)

The problem that Sula represents to her community is that she thinks original thoughts and lives an experiential life. This makes her a disturbing presence since she refuses to submit or to come to terms with the apparent conditions of her life. She is a brave experimenter, exploring her own thoughts and emotions. This is hard for a people circumscribed by poverty and ignorance to admit. She is a threat to the existing order of things because she points to new approaches to reality. Her role is the same as that of Alice Walker's Meridian, in the novel of the same name. Both *Sula* and *Meridian* (1976) explore the question Alice Walker presents in her interview: 'Why women are always condemned for doing what men do as an expression of their masculinity. Why are women so easily "tramps" and "traitors" when men are heroes for engaging in the same activity? Why do women stand for this?' (O'Brien, p. 197).

Meridian, too, rejects a conventional life style, though she is early caught up in an unwanted schoolgirl pregnancy and marriage. She breaks free from the confines of her life as a young mother through her contact with Civil Rights' workers and the Movement. In refusing to play her preordained role according to the womens' magazines—in which 'Woman was a mindless body, a sex creature, something to hang false hair and nails on'—she is really carrying on the rejection that her schoolteacher mother felt, but was not strong enough to act out. Her mother

> could never forgive her community, her family, his family, the whole world, for not warning her against children . . . her frail independence gave way to the pressures of motherhood and she learned—much to her horror and amazement—that she was not even allowed to be resentful that she was 'caught'. That her personal life was over. There was no one she could cry out to and say 'It's not fair!' And in understanding this, she understood a look she saw in the other womens' eyes. The mysterious inner life that she had imagined gave them a secret joy was simply a full knowledge of the fact that they were dead, living just enough for their children.[20]

Meridian, through her work in voter registration, starts out on a spiritual quest; as though she has to purify herself to make the Movement succeed. In the course of this spiritual development, she becomes a leader and a kind of saint, not only to the people in small towns among whom she goes to live, but to other Movement workers. Particularly to Lynne and Truman, an inter-racial couple whose lives seem inextricably bound up with her own. Finally, Meridian gathers strength to return to the world and passes on her role and work to Truman. The three of them have worked through sexual relationships with one another and have come to a more caring and less self-seeking kind of affection. *Meridian* is basically documentary, rather in the manner of Doris Lessing's *Four-Gated City*, with a mystical element superimposed. It is informational in the truest sense since it reveals what the experience of a black girl, not especially brave or strong, actually was in the South in the sixties. But to explain Meridian, Ms Walker has to explain her whole background and family, the forces and people that have made her. Ms Walker manipulates this varied material with great finesse; she is an accurate and skilful storyteller and she is dealing with what was a truly heroic historical episode. This novel does not quite fulfil her proposal that it would be

> about several women who came of age during the sixties and were active (or not active) in the Movement in the South. I am exploring their backgrounds, familial and sibling connections, their marriages, affairs, and political persuasions, as they grow toward a fuller realization (and recognition) of themselves.[21]

Meridian's friend at college, presented initially as a foil to the more complex and diffident character, is Anne-Marion, a more confident revolutionary but one who is lost sight of in later years, apart from the angry letters she still feels impelled to send. Meanwhile, she is apparently pursuing the upper-middle class life-style for which Saxon college prepared her. One of Meridian's main successes in her example to others is the fact that she educates Truman out of vanity and affectation into a less shallow view of life, so that he becomes, in effect her disciple. Both Lynne and Meridian change their attitudes towards each other, getting beyond white and black female stereotyping. Ms Walker's fictional method excels when she has the opportunity to present a set-piece, which sums up a series of themes—as in the scene of the burial of Wile Chile or the episode in the black church with its new, unresigned, ritual. The nature of its subject-matter means that *Meridian* must use a naturalistic method, and this at times assorts oddly with the assumed mystical level of meaning. Meridian's vision on the Indian land of her father's farm is presented, not as the spirit's escape from the body, but rather as a way to a greater intensity of physical life. Nevertheless, this visionary quality is stated rather than worked for in the novel as a whole. More obviously effective are the vignettes of voter registration, which are done with a reporter's eye for the significant, often grotesque, detail. All in all, *Meridian*, as was intended, works well as social history. It lacks the timeless poetry of *Sula* and *The Bluest Eye*.

A third major writer to have emerged during the seventies is Gayl Jones. The sensational nature of her subject-matter in *Corregidora* (1975) and *Eva's Man* (1976), with its emphasis on the power of sex in human lives is less apparent in her collection of stories, *White Rat* (1977). One of the key stories deals with a daughter's initiation into the fact of her mother's homosexuality and the pressures on her to enter on her own sexual life before she is ready for it. Much of Gayl Jones' writing deals with the sexual abuse of black women, often when they are small children. These early experiences create a situation where they are always frightened and/or frigid. When they do begin to have the confidence to trust a relationship, they are often rejected by their men: often, as in *Eva's Man* they are confused by many destructive experiences and can't focus on one individual. Eva is kept virtually a prisoner in Davis' room (a foretaste of the actual prison she will go to when she has killed him); all her sexual knowledge up till then, whether her own or that learned from observing other people, is bound up with violence and exploitation. Eva kills Davis because she is beginning to love him and knows that he will leave her. The emotional dependence and physical pleasure are too threatening. Associated with her ambivalent responses are her accumulated rage and hatred—the result of episodes of brutality practised on her since the age of five. Ms Jones' technique is to present Eva's consciousness as a theatre in which many scenes are taking place at the same time and they are all meaningless. Eva can be said to be out of touch with reality and yet she is in touch with the psychic reality of her brutalized life. Gayl Jones' earlier novel, *Corregidora* is a less specialized story of revenge, but deals equally with sexual abuse and the response to it of a woman who refuses to remain passive and submit. The narrative ranges back and forth in time because Ursa's female ancestors were determined not to let the knowledge of their oppression by their Portuguese slavemaster die; the events are mercilessly passed down from generation to generation but the sexual suffering continues when Ursa is beaten up by her husband and made barren. The pain of her heritage of incest and her present maltreatment by her husband are turned to creative effect in her compelling singing of the blues. The compensation for Ursa's wounds, physical and emotional is that she is a successful artist.

> I wanted a song that would touch me, touch my life *and* theirs. A Portuguese song, but not a Portuguese song. A new world song. A song branded with the new world.[22]

Having a talent means that she escapes having to work for someone else, in a kitchen, or on a factory line. Most of the women Ursa comes into contact with are also on their own, supporting themselves in some entrepreneurial way—like the hairdresser, Cat, who is in love with Ursa. As such they are examples of the women admired by Meridian, who couldn't see that white women were good for anything:

> On the other hand, black women were always imitating Harriet Tubman—escaping to become something unheard of. Outrageous. . . . They commanded attention. They deserved admiration. Only the rejects—not of men, but of experience, adventure —fell into the domestic morass that even the most intelligent white girls appeared to be destined for.[23]

Corregidora has a happy ending: Ursa and her husband come together again, after many years of separation. Ursa has come to terms with her past and the devastating question as to how much love was involved in it as well as how much hate. She manages to establish her own identity and to stop reliving the past, a past that has meant that for much of her life she has not been able to disentangle her mother's/grandmother's/great-grandmother's lives from her own. Apart from its compelling psychological insights, *Corregidora* succeeds on a simpler level as a documentary of the life of a small-town singer and her relationships with a variety of friends and clients. It is also a convincing analysis of the punitive relationships between black men and black women and proof of the validity of Lynne's statement in *Meridian*, 'black men and women *are* scared to death of each other'. Gayl Jones' stories show a wider range of technique and feeling than either of her novels. Several of them deal with subjects like sexual love between women;

the unrequited love of an older woman for a homosexual man; tenderness between men and women; a lynching; the fate of a retarded teenage boy, the problems of a schizophrenic student obsessed with religions. The title story concerns a man whose colour means that he is constantly mistaken for white. In some of these stories, the control of tone can be shaky, but overall they represent, in technique and content, an important achievement for so young a writer.

The confident experimentation, technical accomplishment and original content of writing by black women in America today leads to great hope for the future. Already, Toni Morrison's *Song of Solomon* has received international acclaim. It is impossible to analyse so rich and intricate a novel in the space of this brief survey, but there is no doubt that *Song of Solomon* represents the culmination of recent developments in black literature and is the result of the new determination by black women to express themselves in their own terms. The lively and ingenious stories of Toni Cade Bambara, the autobiographical writing of Maya Angelou and Louise Meriwether, all the complex and varied work that has been produced in recent years, depends on the heritage that has gone before; on Paule Marshall, Gwendolyn Brooks and on the pioneering writing of Zora Neale Hurston and Nella Larsen. Contemporary women writers have seen the necessity for speaking for themselves and developing innovatory techniques with which to do so; their work is not merely informative but is extending the bounds of literary possibility in many new directions. The assurance and energy of contemporary black writers proves that, like Fannie Lou Hamer, 'they're sick and tired of being sick and tired'.

NOTES

All references are to paperback editions, unless otherwise stated: *Black feeling Black talk Black judgement* (1970); *In Love and Trouble* (1973); *Black-Eyed Susans* (1975); *The Bluest Eye* (1972); *Sula* (1975); *Meridian* (1977); *Corregidora* (1976); *Eva's Man* (1st edn. 1976; paperback 1978).

1 On 15 August, 1973 Alice Walker placed a gravestone in the Garden of Heavenly Rest in Fort Pierce, Florida. The inscription reads, Zora

Neale Hurston 'A Genius of the South' 1901–60 Novelist, Folklorist, Anthropologist.

2 In his *Zora Neale Hurston: A Literary Biography*, 1977.
3 *Interviews With Black Writers* edited by John O'Brien, 1973, p. 201.
4 *Ibid.*, p. 201–2.
5 *Ms*, January 1979, p. 45.
6 *The World of Gwendolyn Brooks*, 1971, p. 213–14.
7 *Ibid.*, p. 287–88.
8 Dust-jacket blurb to the Collier–Macmillan edition, 1971.
9 *Black feeling Black talk Black judgement*, 1970, p. 59, 79–80.
10 *In Love and Trouble: Stories of Black Women*, 1973, p. 3.
11 *Black-Eyed Susans*, 1975, p. xxxi–xxxii.
12 *Interviews With Black Writers*, p. 205–6.
13 *Ibid.*, p. 204.
14 *Ibid.*
15 *The Bluest Eye*, 1970, p. 18.
16 Zora Neale Hurston, *Their Eyes Were Watching God*, 1978 reprint, p. 29.
17 *The Bluest Eye*, p. 86.
18 *Interviews*, p. 202.
19 *Sula*, 1973, p. 105.
20 *Meridian*, 1976, p. 50–1.
21 *Interviews*, p. 197.
22 *Corregidora*, 1975, p. 65.
23 *Meridian*, p. 108–9.

10

Beyond Realism: Recent Black Fiction and the Language of 'The Real Thing'

by GRAHAM CLARKE

> It was as though a veil had been rent. I saw on that ivory face the expression of sombre pride, of ruthless power, of craven terror—of an intense and hopeless despair. Did he live his life again in every detail of desire, temptation, and surrender during that supreme moment of complete knowledge? He cried in a whisper at some image, at some vision—he cried out twice, a cry that was no more than a breath—'The horror! The horror!'
>
> —Joseph Conrad: *Heart of Darkness*

> A Negro Literature, to be a legitimate product of the Negro experience in America, must get at that experience in exactly the terms America has proposed for it, in its most ruthless identity.
>
> —LeRoi Jones: 'Myth of a Negro Literature' in
> *Home: Social Essays*[1]

1

The novels I am concerned with, Julian Mayfield's *The Hit* (1957), *The Long Night* (1958), and *The Grand Parade* (1961), Ronald Fair's *Many Thousands Gone* (1965) and *Hog Butcher* (1966), Cyrus Colter's *The Rivers of Eros* (1972) and *The Hippodrome* (1973), Robert Deane Pharr's *The Book of Numbers* (1969), *S.R.O.* (1971) and *The Soul Murder Case* (1975) and Hal Bennett's *The Black Vine* (1968) and *Lord of Dark Places* (1970), do not immediately come to mind in a period dominated by the work of James Baldwin, Ralph Ellison, and LeRoi Jones (Imamu Baraka). Yet such writing not only confirms the depth of the contemporary black achievement, it marks the development of a fiction, and a style, which aspires to the 'ruthless identity' which LeRoi Jones demands. While essentially realist writers, they go beyond realism to what I want to call 'the real thing'.

The distinction is crucial. When, for example, Robert Bone argued in *The Negro Novel in America* (1958) that 'to deal successfully with racial conflict a new style will be required, for the naturalism of the Wright school has lost its power'[2] he implied that 'realism', in the way it had developed in black writing since *Native Son* (1940), had reduced itself to a set of tired and worn racial prescriptions from which the writer intent on social protest and commentary was powerless to escape. Clearly, that 'new style' is most obvious in a consciously black modernist voice or even in the 'universalism' which Bone so admired about Ralph Ellison's *Invisible Man* (1952). And yet my contention is that we can equally see its development in precisely that tradition of Afro–American realist writing which Bone saw as so worn and frenzied.

Part of Wright's achievement in *Native Son* was the assertion, and the realization, of a black literary voice which placed black experience at the centre of American realism. As he declared in the autobiographical *Black Boy* (1945), it was as if his own life had 'shaped' him for 'the realism, the naturalism of the modern novel'.[3] The brutality of the world he depicts, like the fate of Bigger, is urged upon the reader in a style which, as he declared in 'How "Bigger" Was Born', is consciously 'hard and deep'. Yet one of the weaknesses of *Native Son*, as with Ann Petry's *The Street* (1946) and of some of the early Chester Himes, is the extent to which the authorial voice, as spokesman, impinges on the interaction between character and society and pulls the energy of its vision, the often ferocious violence of its language, into a thesis constrained by the limits of social determinism. This sociological mechanism cuts into the achieved detail and 'life' as much as it does in Frank Norris's *The Octopus* (1901) or Theodore Dreiser's *Sister Carrie* (1900). 'Protest' locks the fiction into a viewpoint intent on making the message 'stick' and hit home. It is surely this aspect of Wright and the others that led Lloyd Brown to accuse them of producing a literature which depended on a 'narrow range of frenzy, shock brutality, and frustration'.[4]

It might be argued that LeRoi Jones's call for the laying bare of a 'ruthless identity' seeks little more than an extreme form of Wrightian realism, but this is to ignore the particular nature of its effect as it emerges in the writing of Colter, Pharr, and Bennett. In their work we receive a distinctive and challenging style which moves beyond 'protest', beyond Wright and realism towards the 'legitimate Negro Literature' which LeRoi Jones demands. It is an art which consciously opposes the world it is forced to confront. The 'exactness' it seeks urges the writer to a vision of America as brutal and unflinching as the history of black Americans, but its achievement is something more than realism. The force behind that 'ruthless identity' works to unmask the very nature of white America's language, its limitations and lies. As Jones declares in *Home: Social Essays* (1968), the 'Black Artist's role in America is to aid in the destruction of America as he knows it'.[5] Whitey's words declare and control a world antagonistic to the creative basis of that role, a role committed to the realization of a language and style intent on forging an absolute aesthetic of race, of blackness. The implications of such a development are as portentous as that blackness 'ten times black' that Melville found in Hawthorne; its presence on the page as daunting as Babo's gaze at the close of 'Benito Cereno'.

I want to argue that there has emerged a language and style intent on determining a particular *kind* of sensibility and consciousness, at war with—and openly undercutting—the world in which it moves. If it is to fulfil its destiny it must both make and unmake meaning, effect a simultaneous creative surge and destructive will as its energy, its life, proclaim the force of its independent being. Unlike Wright's language, this is a language freed from ideological restriction, able to transcend the 'conflicting loyalties of race and art'[6] because the style is the concrete assertion of both: the art *is* the race. And yet this view of style, of language, is characteristically American. As Tony Tanner, in *City of Words* (1971), suggests, American fiction, particularly since the fifties, has consciously concerned itself with the 'possible nightmare of being totally controlled by unseen agencies and powers'. If the white writer is obliged to take on these forces, for the black writer the implications are doubly compelling. He must both encounter and fight a world and a language which is neither of his making or of his choosing. He faces an environment and a language which, inherently, is 'limiting, directing and perhaps controlling his responses and formulations'. If the black writer is to assert 'the real thing' he must demonstrate 'to himself and other people that he does not accept nor wholly conform to the structures built into the common tongue, that he has the power to resist and perhaps disturb the particular "rubicizing" tendency of the language he has inherited'.[7] While Mayfield and Fair offer a language adequate to the 'realistic' picturing of black life, at home in its own environment, Colter, Pharr, and Bennett, I want to suggest, go further into that 'real thing'. In them we see the word set free, forcing it to live on its destructive and existential impulses. In Wright the fiction is determined by the society of which it is a part. In these writers language seeks to cut itself loose from such determinants. The brutality in their art is the self-laceration of a vocabulary which actively purges the world it seeks to control and transcend.

In *Native Son* Bigger's murderous actions create 'a new world' for him. His violence, as with Joe Christmas in *Light in August*, achieves the freedom of identity which he seeks. And yet that freedom, like the visceral language which 'hits' the reader, is firmly rooted in character and story. If, as Baldwin has argued, Bigger is a 'monster',[8] it is because he is seen as the end product of a society and environment which is itself monstrous. The 'real thing' is as murderous (and monstrous) but its energies propel the reader to a different *kind* of language, a freedom of the word rather than character. Like the narrator of *Invisible Man* its impulse is to 'shake off the old skin and come up for breath'[9] and its method, as proclaimed by Eldridge Cleaver in *Soul on Ice* (1968) is to 'employ the tactics of ruthlessness' and 'look at white America through these new eyes'.[10] It is an act of becoming. Yet the language's movement into an absolute ruthlessness does not, finally, push it into the 'black dada nihilismus' of LeRoi Jones. Rather, it seeks (and achieves) what Eugene O'Neill saw as one of the Black's greatest assets, the potential to tap 'an untouched world of deep reality'.

Clearly the novels do not present an equal level of achievement, but to see them as a whole is to recognize this shared development into ruthlessness. To move from Mayfield's *The Hit* and *The Long Night*, both fine but essentially 'traditional' realist works, to Bennett's meteoric *Lord of Dark Places* is to feel the extent to which something quite distinctive *has* happened. One has the sense of a black lexicon painfully discarding its white inheritance, loosening the naturalistic holds and opening up its own energies as protest is distilled into revolt and negation. It is a fiction where the trigger is increasingly at the reader's head. Bennett, in one of his stories from *Insanity Runs in Our Family* (1977), has two images which cunningly evoke the nature of this development, this style, that I am concerned to suggest:

> As always, when he thought a woman was stalling him, Cliff felt the nigger in him rise like an erection. It was a tremendous surge of anger that erupted like a rocket from the hairy black prison where he kept it surrounded and subdued by the paler flesh of pretending to be white.

and again:

> His voice was cool and carefully controlled—a white man's voice—as though he had pulled a jock-strap over the black point of his emotions, bending and dulling the deadly head under strong, white elastic.[11]

The sexual imagery is typical of Bennett, but it seeks more than merely emotional and physical intensity. This is a style, a language, whose energy works against constricting structures and pressures as its creative impulse, that 'tremendous surge of anger', feels its way towards a purity of the word. The art pushes against a prescribed reality and language as its blackness swells and disgorges itself onto the page via its 'deadly' force. This is a process of confrontation, stretching the naturalistic fabric to its breaking point, to the limit of its nerve ends as it cuts its way towards the 'real thing'. It wants the reality of the word itself rather that the depiction of a given world. As Robert Creeley has asserted, in his introduction to *The New Writing in the USA*, the 'usual critical vocabulary will not be of much use in trying to locate the character of writing we have now come to'.[12]

2

Crucially, these novels inhabit an environment which is wholly urban: *l'immonde cité* of New York, Chicago, and Newark; a desolation row of black ghetto life—poverty, squalor, crime, violence, drugs, and the depiction of every kind of sexual activity. One might argue that American realism has always been a fiction of the city intent on revealing its brutality, anonymity and poverty, but these writers go beyond the depiction of decay and social corruption. They do not so much reveal as assert the power of their fictional voice amidst incipient chaos.

Hubert Selby's *Last Exit to Brooklyn* (1964) is an example where the distinction is clear. Its extreme realism is as 'hard and deep' as anything Wright sought, forcing upon us a reading experience that is both painful and disgusting. As its title implies, one can 'go' no further. The style compels a view of city life which, like the scab one of the characters tries to remove, 'hurts'. The veracity of its vision depends for its force on the reader's sensibility being so battered that, in the end, the picking of a nose becomes as nauseous as the horrific and painful description of a sickening gang rape in a Brooklyn waste lot. The human has, quite literally, been squeezed out. The realist perspective exists through a language which is as begrimed and degraded as the life it depicts. The ethos, quite obviously goes beyond Dos Passos's *Manhattan Transfer* or Burroughs's *Junkie* just as it goes beyond *Native Son* and *Invisible Man*. The language can do nothing else than bleed to death so that the final sense one has of the novel is of a recalcitrant puss staining the page. In short, a vocabulary of response and feeling has been cut and pummelled to death.

Pharr and Bennett can be as extreme as Selby, but the impending 'void' is fused into something wholly different. In Selby the verbal energies are laid waste by the environment they encounter. In Pharr and Bennett the language fights this environment, intent not only on survival, but on possession and transcendence. *Last Exit to Brooklyn* is a judgement on a white American culture from within the detritus of its own language. Pharr and Bennett reveal that 'ruthless identity' but do not fall prey to it. In them the imperatives of style and language exist in that contradictory mix which LeRoi Jones found to be so central to Harlem's particular nature: an 'existential joyousness' surrounded by 'every crippling human vice'. It is a language of survival which insists on staying alive, but on its own terms and with its own integrity.

And yet there is a crucial difference between the way this style

209

asserts its status, its self, in the earlier novels of Mayfield and Fair, and the later writing of Colter, Pharr, and Bennett. Mayfield, in *The Hit* and *The Long Night*, celebrates Harlem, creating through an intense verbal alacrity, a sense of life and energy amid poverty and despair. Pharr and Bennett seek the same verve but more ruthlessly and with greater 'cool'. In Fair's *Hog Butcher*, for example, a white cop (in civilian clothes) decides to open himself to black ghetto life and walk through its streets. Against a background of urban corruption and racial tension, his 'journey' elicits one of the central rhythmic impulses of the novel's world. He enters an urban culture which, in its capacity for survival and pride, is celebrated:

> It was Saturday and there were many people on the street. John had always carried the impression of Negroes as being slow-moving creatures, shiftless and lethargic by nature. But today he was seeing differently. It seemed to him that they were moving much more rapidly than he had ever noticed in the past. And there was something else new, too: their grace. God, he thought, its like a . . . like a . . . yeah, like a ballet. They just seemed to glide along.[13]

The reader, like John, has to be careful here, for it would be too easy to fall into a clichéd emotional judgement about the meaning of the scene. Yet Fair works *through* the tourist eye, guiding it towards a surface celebration and discovery. But if John works close to stereotype there is in this clash of cultures a deeper significance behind his eye-level wanderings. The final sense of the passage is of a particular and felt presence: a surity of feeling as the journey into the ghetto evokes a particular kind of sensibility. The crucial terms are 'rapidly', 'grace', and 'style', for these offer a vocabulary appropriate to a specific way of being. The movement here is, finally, a ballet-like precision: a quiet freedom and *élan* set free from its urban surroundings.

This is not simply a question of description. In Pharr's *The Book of Numbers*, for example, Dave, a central character, asks another his name:

> The young image grinned slyly. 'Blip-Blip, but you can call me Blip for short, if you wants,' he said. 'The kid here is Flick, or Flick the kid for short, or even Kid Flick. Nobody knows for sure.'

He turned to introduce the third man. 'But this here is jest plain Randy Jones.' Blip-Blip paused for effect in the approved Blueboy manner, and then said offhandedly, 'This here's Dave Greene, Pigmeat Goin's latest victim.'[14]

The conversation propels itself forward by its own energies. In this extract it is the language rather than a character which speaks to us. The style itself answers the question, emitting a vibrance held within the names themselves. They are informal, imaginative, and slangy, but 'sly' and mannered in the 'approved' way. The names belong to a vocabulary of its own making, its own freedom, and will. This is partly the 'joyous existentialism' which LeRoi Jones celebrates and which, in part, these writers mine. It is one part of an aesthetic bent on its own survival and yet this spirit, in Mayfield and Fair, is almost too one-sided. In them the realist impulse emits a 'passive' blackness locked into social commentary. In Pharr, Bennett, and Colter style and language are fused into the very essence of black ghetto life as they move into that 'heart of darkness' which is the final impetus of their writing.

3

The Afro–American has, from the beginning, confronted an alien American culture and yet one which, paradoxically, determined the nature of his world, ethic, and style. As Edward Margolies has rightly stated, 'the Negro is himself more a product of the American environment than most others'.[15] Black art is centrally American and urban: Blues and jazz, like the street, have shaped the defining rhythms of self and world appropriate to the culture from which they come. My point, however, is that in these writers we can see the development of a black realism which, while dependent upon its heritage, transcends the historical and political, the ideological and social, to refine an aesthetic *of* race. The style *is* the protest as it fights a given reality with its own ruthlessness. Its dialectic hovers between the void and the totality of self. Pharr, Bennett, and Colter evolve a series of verbal incantations whose alchemical intensity denies the vacuum into which their fiction moves. They assault whitey's world and language intent on both challenging and assaulting the reader by the sheer force of their presence.

211

It is much to the point, for example, that so many of these novels are concerned with numbers and the numbers racket (*The Long Night, The Hit, The Book of Numbers, S.R.O., The Grand Parade*). In the most obvious sense they can be seen as metaphors for the black American's life in the ghetto, a life determined by chance, circumstance and the continual hope of escape against overwhelming odds. Yet in the later novels they emerge as an image of the way the language works. The existential randomness posits a style and language which breaks away from any given view or pattern of meaning towards exploration and discovery. The style subverts and destroys assumed codes and values in an effort to achieve its own self, its own individuality. In *S.R.O.* it is the centre of the blackness that Pharr seeks. Sid Bailey, the narrator, is speaking of his progress as a writer:

> Ten days passed and I had completed twelve chapters. Sure they were rough, but they also had something. I was working out of a bog no other writer had used. I often wondered why no other Black writer had gone to the numbers racket for a locale or milieu. For numbers are as Black and American as jazz, the Renny, Small's and sweet potato pie.[16]

Yet numbers are not the 'subject', for, we are told, he is 'not writing a novel about the numbers racket' but 'about some characters who just happen to be in the numbers racket'. On being asked what the difference is his advice is to 'read some of my stuff and find out'. The difference, of course, is in that 'reading', for we are here speaking of a reading experience, and of a style, which is the essence of numbers. Indeed, this is the crucial distinction between Pharr's *The Book of Numbers* and *S.R.O.* for the first (and earlier) novel *uses* the numbers racket for its subject, while the second novel inculcates it into the heart of its aesthetic and being.

The 'S.R.O.' of the title is a single room occupancy hotel, The Logan, in Harlem. The sense of loneliness suggested by the title is compounded by the presence of the ghetto, a 'hell's kitchen' where lines of destructive energy chart the make-up of the novel's milieu. Thus *S.R.O.* is a world of freaks and outsiders: junkies, pushers, alcoholics, gangsters, pimps and prostitutes embroiled in a violent and Dantesque inferno. Into this world comes Sid Bailey, who finds release from his own alcoholism by writing about his experience in The Logan. Yet the realism of the novel is not simply a picture of raw and grotesque lives. The novel, like the voice which speaks to us, lives on its style. When Bailey enters this world, for example, he wonders if he can 'make the rest of the way on nerve alone'. The sense of nerve here exhibits a view of style, and language, committed to 'getting high' and seeking possibilities at the risk of its own extinction. Like the junkies in the novel who 'mainline', the language is 'strung out as far as it can go'. What emerges is a 'prayer from the damned' kept alive by 'nervous prostration' in a 'house of people without god' and full of 'crippled lovers'. The style edges deeper and deeper into its hell-hole:

> Wasn't a realistic writer supposed to descend into the very pits of all that was not quite normal so that he could inform his readers? (p. 454)

Once again, we are not to take this on the level of description. Pharr creates a language which is itself that 'pit', shaping a style the effect of which is to suggest 'a new kind of loneliness'. We experience a 'ruthlessness' whose hardness is apocryphal rather than simply brutal. In one of the third person narrative sections, for example, a pusher (Kingfisher) is being repaid for selling cut heroin. His attacker

> got down aside Kingfish. With one hand he opened the lid of Kingfisher's left eye and with the other plunged the needle all the way in. Then he refilled the hypo and did the same thing to the King's other eye.
> He got up and went to lean backwards against the dresser, panting. After a while his breath came easier; once he started to go to King and pull out the needle. But he changed his mind. Instead he put out the light and left the room. 'Now do it again', he said softly, 'you lemon-selling motherfucker'. (p. 494)

This is appalling, as cold and penetrating as the hypo which hits the reader's eye as much as it does Kingfisher's. And yet its power lies precisely in the way its nerve works through a controlled 'coolness', It is determined to 'tell it as it is' but conscious of its own voice and movement. As with the world it measures, the natural is emptied *into* the eye so that words such as 'Kingfisher', 'panting', and 'softly' exist as vestiges of a human vocabulary which can find no place in which to survive. Indeed they intrude as obscene terms. Like the needle, the style here is committed to go 'all the way in'. It cuts its way through the human. But this is not the camera-eye of Dos Passos or Isherwood, just as it is not the extremism of Selby. Equally its treatment of New York is distinct from Baldwin's achievement in *Another Country* (1961). There we feel the city's 'danger and horror' as it impinges on the lives of the characters. But in Pharr style and language consciously 'fix' themselves towards intensity and self-destruction. The 'real' here is to test and define the limits of a language which no longer has the power to assert the human, the 'truth' in the way we would want it to do. It digs into the underside of the word in order to find an energy that will 'see it through':

> The silent room was filled with a furious kind of savagery. These three men were kinetic. My nerves could not have been more on edge if they had drawn knives on each other. (p. 32)

In many ways this distinguishes the novel's style: the exploration of a 'savage' kinetic, the tapping of a dynamic from which the human has been extinguished:

> For one of the few times in my life I wanted to shout out that I was a decent and a square. But I couldn't. I was so charged that I couldn't give out the words. It was like the Sinman was always saying: sin and sinning were dynamic. Goodness and decency can only be told in the silent tongue of the pussy. (p. 280)

The Sinman is the centre of this 'pit of the purely profane' to which the language is drawn. He is called a 'pure genius', one of the 'originals', recalling that 'original genius' of Melville's *The Confidence Man*. The compelling negation of language in Melville's novel has given way here to its final and violent dénouement. But where Melville's novel ends by moving into darkness, Pharr's begins in it, committed to getting through to the other side.

4

Sinman, surrounded by decay, exists as a dynamic centre which pulls style and language into its death-like vortex. Indeed, as in many of these novels, the impact is like an exorcism of the word and the positing of one style, one language, against another. Certainly this would seem to be the case with Cyrus Colter whose two novels, *The Rivers of Eros* and *The Hippodrome* reveal the development of a 'passive' realism into the dynamic, the kinetic, that the Sinman offers. Indeed, on one level *The Rivers of Eros* offers an internal debate on the warring positions open to the the black writer. It brings together a series of figures in a Chicago ghetto who, in their individual ways, are expressive of different levels of black consciousness. Each is measured against the plight and decline of the major character, Clotilda Pilgrim, whose guilt-ridden past finally overcomes her and she ends in a mental hospital after murdering her grand-daughter. Her anguish achieves a tragic dimension and the texture of the novel elicits a depth of feeling and controlled pathos reminiscent of William Faulkner.

I want to comment briefly on two characters in the novel in which we can see Colter offering two alternative black positions, two *styles* measured against the living presence and fate of Clotilda. The first is Hammer, a postman and amateur historian who is writing a book on 'the negro' in American history. The second is Alexis, a young radical who smokes dope and reads Kierkegaard. Alexis and his friend, Dunreith, laugh at a lecture Hammer gives on the subject of his book. Later, Hammer meets Alexis in his room and their conversation develops into a confrontation of two versions of blackness, two kinds of language by which to view and shape the world. To Alexis, Hammer's preaching and concern for being 'decent, being patient, being patriotic' is 'guff'. For Hammer the black American is on the 'threshold of great things' but for Alexis on 'the threshold of nothing'. Each reveals a shaping vocabulary and viewpoint which determines the way their world is read: Hammer's, historical, traditional, liberal, rational, and humanist; Alexis's, radical, anarchic, nihilistic, and existential:

> O, Mr. Hammer, we must go somewhere—if not physically, then spiritually, emotionally—away, away, away, anywhere to ourselves, and disentwine our frantic arms from around the white man's neck.[17]

This is more than 'political'. Two traditions are being weighed here, two aesthetics impelled against the barbarous fate of Clotilda. By the end of the novel Hammer is reduced to feeling 'desperate, absurd' and has a 'bitter urge to laugh'. *The Rivers of Eros* is an impressive achievement, and I have simplified its effect, but its major force lies in the struggle between styles measured against the reality which the Black is seen to inhabit. When we reach *The Hippodrome* it would seem that Hammer's defeat is final.

The Hippodrome creates a style which consciously seeks a 'spirit of the perverse'. Yaeger, the central character, has killed his wife and her lover, severed her head and carries it around the streets as a macabre trophy. The manic beginning, however, gives way to a fictional energy in a novel where the realist props are only the surface of its impact and force. Yeager ends in a 'bizarre house', a brothel called 'the Hippodrome'. The building, his 'refuge and prison', is a theatre of prostitution where black performers provide sexual entertainment to a willing white audience. But the novel's effect lies in the way that the hero's plight, like the house, becomes a metaphor for the writing process. James's 'house of fiction' undergoes a daunting metamorphosis for it is not so much characters who enter this 'black' theatre as a language committed to a ruthless exploration and analysis of itself as, like Yaeger, it seeks the nature of its identity, its self. Colter forces the language in upon itself with an almost religious ferocity, burning it away from prescribed roles and performance. Its vision of sickness draws the reader, like the audience, into its vacuity, in turn to judge him as voyeur or friend.

The effect of *The Hippodrome* works through a style which is 'cold and murdering'. As a literary structure it exists, like the house, as a 'great cavern of blackness' extolling a 'ringing silence' and 'a musty smell'. It is against this emptiness, this putrifaction of the word, that Yaeger decides to destroy all that the Hippodrome represents. He plans to 'kill' the sickness by plunging a knife into his stomach in a final performance on the stage. The 'death' will be acted out in a dance-like trance. This is to be the 'mounting of an apocalypse' in front of a 'savage' and 'sick' audience in a 'foul, disgusting setting'. If language is to survive it must indulge in a communion with the damned for what we have here is, once again, the stylistic exorcism of the word as it turns from entertainment to a ruthless exposure of its deadness. Yaeger

216

doesn't kill himself, but the ritual achieves a catharsis, a purity which frees him from the imprisoning influence of the theatre. By the end of the novel he, like the language, can 'only be sure of nothing' but it is a *nada* of his own making and will.

5

The Hippodrome is a remarkable stylistic achievement; nervous and edgy it is obsessed with its own compulsive voicing. Along with *The Soul Murder Case* and *Lord of Dark Places* it reveals the fullest effect of a 'ruthless identity'. Its perversity and paranoia, however, are controlled properties—style in the purest sense. Indeed, these three novels achieve the essence of the 'real thing' and I want to look briefly at *The Soul Murder Case* and *Lord of Dark Places* to suggest the final nature (and implications) of such a style for the thrust of these novels is towards an aesthetic and language which gives to realism a new dynamic. It is a fictional energy appropriate to the culture which it both confronts and questions.

The Soul Murder Case offers the confessions of an addict. Bobbie Dee, ex-singer, jailbird, and now literary agent and writer, has become involved with a black singer, Candice, the effect of which is to make him question the whole nature of his own blackness. While the story moves inevitably towards murder the confessions are essentially concerned with the nature of *Soul* as Dee digs deeper and deeper into its meaning. Openly aggressive to 'Whitey', the narrative voice cajoles the reader into a daring confrontation with the nature of its aesthetic for we are to experience the naked exposure of the 'soul' of Soul. Dee relates accounts of sex and violence through a style which taps its rhythms for Soul is 'cool'. Like *S.R.O.* it mainlines on its own destructive energies. What the novel achieves is not so much a concern for character or ideology as the opening up of a particular way of feeling, a sensibility openly assertive and black:

> The next one was called 'Black I came'. And it made you wonder what the hell was poetry anyhow. This was a hymn without music. I mean it was a kind of shout in the dark. It had a beat, a real stomp. It sang of its own accord in your head.[18]

Dee is here reading a poem by Candice which he recognizes as the 'real thing'. As he reads he knows what it is 'to meet a soul that really is SOUL'. The effect here, as it assaults our response, is to lay bare the ruthlessness of its aesthetic and style: desolate, agonized, and unfeeling. Soul here is 'gut, a real ballbreaker'. Thus, 'kids like to think of soul as something nice, but there isn't a damned thing nice about solid soul. It is the ugly part of you that doesn't know how to die.' (p. 8)

The voice of the novel, like the spirit and poetry of Candice, *is* soul, but it is also 'cool', a 'manically cool' and *cold* language. There is no casual sense of a hip vocabulary here, no soft use of the term. In *Junkie* William Burroughs speaks of learning hipster slang (so celebrated in Norman Mailer's 'The White Negro') where 'cool' is 'an all-purpose word indicating anything you like or any situation that is hot with the law'.[19] But the sense of 'cool' in Pharr, as with 'soul', is to imbue its presence and effect as an integral part of the style, totally distinct from 'Whitey's' sense of it. It is part of a specific, controlled, and heartless energy that will not be made safe, will not allow itself to be played with. Its manic force empties the language of moral and social axes as it cuts its way through a culture in which it is determined to survive:

> I was scared because I could not read a single thing in Candice's face. I was lost. It was the kind of awesome fear you get when you look down into the Grand Canyon. The thing itself scares you with its very inhuman bigness until you realize the real thing to fear is the forces that created the vast insanity of that canyon. (p. 153)

To 'dig' this, as Dee says, is to face the compulsive rawness of a language attempting to 'put on paper exactly like it was'.

This seems to me to be the peculiar effect of Bennett's *Lord of Dark Places* for the style here involves us in a reading experience which moves us ever inward to a declared 'heart of darkness'. Beginning in Virginia, the novel moves to Newark, New Jersey (and Vietnam) as we follow the almost picaresque journey of its black hero, Titus, who, from his youth, has been dominated by his imagined status as the saviour of 'The Church of the Holy Disciple'; a sect invented by his trickster father and dedicated to the 'celebration' of the phallus. His life exists through acts of prostitution, buggery, homosexuality, rape, suicide, murder and finally execution in the electric chair. It is a fictional world of orgy and orgasm, of conscious scatology and violent extremism which recalls Burroughs. This is a fiction where the 'human' has been expunged. Titus becomes the exemplary of a monstrous society in which 'goodness' and 'truth', as in *S.R.O.*, are both meaningless and impossible. Once again, however, it does not work through character. Rather, the language and style become the dominant forces of the novel's impetus, of its moral vision. The language, rather than Titus, attempts to lead us to some kind of silent and renewed faith in the possibility of a human world. The style here tests itself, goes all the way out, as the sexual and violent extremities edge towards conscious caricature and satire. The perspectives of the word overcome the impending void of the world we are given, undercutting the pornographic imperatives as they force the language to a final and self-conscious ejaculation. The novel's extremism pushes the style towards a stasis, a moment of death as, after frenzied word play, it, like the hero, is executed and burnt away. As in *The Hippodrome* there is the sense of an overriding sickness as language relinquishes layer upon layer of meaning seeking to re-emerge as a pure presence. Like Joe Christmas, Titus finds release in death and, like Wright's Bigger, freedom in murder as he overcomes the label of 'nigger stud'. Crucially, however, this is essentially a freeing of the language, for it is style here that has achieved its own death, its own blackness:

> A terrible, flaming spirit entered his being, almost stifling his breath with the onslaught of its coming.
>   *I am the Holy Ghost, I have come to redeem the world.* He heard the divine words plainly inside the captivity of his mind, and he knew how he would die.
>   Strapped in that devil chair like Mr. Cobb, insanity denied, all appeals exhausted, prayed over by that nigger chaplain in the death room.
>   *Does the condemned man have any last words?*
>   Yes. The condemned man does have last words.
> The very fact of being human panics us into the most grotesque play-acting imaginable; and we deal in absurdities to keep life from being a total waste, like one constant jacking-off party.

Now please suck my dick. All you slimy motherfuckers, black and white alike.[20]

This is an awful release of the word. We have come a long way from that 'faint, wry, bitter smile' of Bigger's as he heard the steel door shut at the end of *Native Son*, for this is not simply the symbolic death of a black character, it is the ritual catharsis of a language and style which seeks a purity and freedom beyond the world it mirrors. Yet it is not simply a language of despair or brutal realism. Bennett's stylistic destructiveness and extremism looks towards a cleansing of the word, to a *human* language precisely because the realist impulse has reached the limits of its veracity. Its achievement is a fiction that negates itself in order to stay alive. Eliot's 'The Hollow Men', like Melville's *The Confidence Man*, plunges towards a darkness where the word 'locks in upon itself'. But in these writers, as they seek that 'real thing', the effect is towards the eye-searching presence of Babo's unflinching gaze into the distance at the end of 'Benito Cereno'. As Baldwin has said, this 'world is white no longer, and it will never be white again'.[21]

'Mistah Kurtz—he dead'

NOTES

1 *Home: Social Essays* (London, 1968), p. 113. The essay is central to the thesis of this chapter. Significantly, in his introduction, Jones speaks of becoming 'even blacker' as the essays develop.

2 Robert A. Bone, *The Negro Novel in America* (Yale, 1958). Sixth edition, 1969, p. 251.

3 *Black Boy—A Record of Childhood and Youth* (Stockholm, 1946). Wright tells us that he 'couldn't read enough' of the naturalists.

4 Quoted by Bone, p. 245.

5 *Home: Social Essays*, p. 251.

6 *The Negro Novel in America*, p. 243.

7 *City of Words* (London, 1971), p. 16. All quotations are from this page although the whole of Chapter One is relevant to the discussion.

8 See Baldwin's essay 'Many Thousands Gone' in *Notes of a Native Son* (London, 1964). It is also in this essay that he speaks of murder, for Bigger, as an 'act of creation'.

9 *Invisible Man*, Penguin edition (Harmondsworth, 1965), p. 468.

10 Eldridge Cleaver, *Soul on Ice* (London, 1969), p. 23.

11 Hal Bennett, *Insanity Runs in Our Family* (New York, 1977). From 'Where Are the White People?', pp. 52–3.

12 *The New Writing in the USA* ed. Donald Allen and Robert Creeley (Harmondsworth, 1967), p. 19.

13 Ronald L. Fair, *Hog Butcher* (New York, 1966), p. 103. For its full effect the whole sequence in the ghetto should be quoted. The sense of city life is consciously related to the 'Hog Butcher' of Sandburg's poem 'Chicago' and Wright's view of Chicago in 'How "Bigger" Was Born'.

14 Robert Deane Pharr, *The Book of Numbers* (London, 1970), p. 28.

15 Edward Margolies, *Native Sons: A Critical Study of Twentieth Century Negro American Authors* (New York, 1968), p. 14.

16 Robert Deane Pharr, *S.R.O.* (New York, 1971), p. 383. All subsequent page numbers quoted in the text refer to this edition.

17 Cyrus Colter, *The Rivers of Eros* (Chicago, 1972), p. 145.

18 Robert Deane Pharr, *The Soul Murder Case* (New York, 1975), p. 12. All subsequent page numbers quoted in the text refer to this edition.

19 William Burroughs, *Junkie* (New English Library edition, London, 1966), p. 145.

20 Hal Bennett, *Lord of Dark Places* (Bantam edition, New York, 1971), p. 309.

21 *Notes of a Native Son*, p. 148.

11

Making New: Styles of Innovation in the Contemporary Black American Novel

by A. ROBERT LEE

> No-one says the novel has to be one thing. It can be anything it
> wants to be, a vaudeville show, the six o'clock news, the mumb-
> lings of wild men saddled by demons.
>
> > Ishmael Reed: *Yellow Back Radio Broke-Down* (1969)

> The American black is a new race of man; the only new race of
> man to come into being in modern time.
>
> > Chester Himes: *The Quality of Hurt* (1972)

1

Since the appearance within a year of each other of Ralph Ellison's
Invisible Man (1952) and James Baldwin's *Go Tell It On The
Mountain* (1953), there can be little doubt of the health, the
sheer imaginative energy, of recent black fiction in America. An
extraordinary range of talent and interests has been evident. The
novelists whose work this essay considers—William Demby, John
Wideman, Charles Wright, Carlene Hatcher Polite and Leon Forrest—thus represent but one group from a far busier landscape. I
don't, however, want to offer these five as some kind of coterie, an
avant-garde writing from shared assumptions to a shared audience, nor indeed as writers with equal claims. But I do suggest
that their novels, in common with others I call attention to (which
include Chester Himes's *Série Noire* detective fiction), reflect the
spirit of Himes's remark about a 'new race' and assuredly the

refusal of the recent black novel to be any 'one thing'. Theirs is a fiction which is rightly to be thought innovatory, new in vision and in modes of making narrative. In this sense I believe they represent serious new directions and take Afro–American fiction on not only from Richard Wright, in whose *Native Son* (1940) the modern black novel has its starting-point, but on from Ellison and Baldwin. In their separate and distinct ways, they display a freedom from past models and assumptions about black writing in America, a confidence in their own sense of direction.

Ellison and Baldwin, nevertheless, made (and continue to make) an essential contribution to the process, and in this respect they deserve pause. For not only did their two novels carry obvious imaginative weight, they inaugurated a succession to Richard Wright. The novels themselves, and the hypnotic essays which accompanied them and which were later gathered in collections like *Note Of A Native Son* (1955) and *Shadow And Act* (1964), engaged with almost all the ancestral issues of race and blackness and the shaping imagination, but with a wholly new resonance, a fresh departure of accent. The peculiarly black powers of the imagination as Afro–America has evolved them in Jazz and Blues, and in the spoken languages of bible Christianity and the inner-city street and in the rich tissue of folklore, found a new incarnation in their prose. Both writers offered a distinctive idiom, an inner articulacy, infinitely too subtle to be dealt with as 'protest', dissent on the same assumed Wrightian basis as before.

The media were quick to respond to both writers, though less for their fiction than as 'spokesmen'—a role Ellison had honourable reasons for declining, but which Baldwin, a ready sermonist, seized upon and then used for ends which were always shrewder and more generous than any supposed self-publicity. For just as, in the same decade, Saul Bellow and Bernard Malamud had been wooed in their recent literary triumphs to 'speak' for Jewish America, and less certainly a pair as inherently dissimilar as Flannery O'Connor and William Styron for the New South, a South at any rate subsequent to Faulkner, so Baldwin especially was designated the high custodial voice of black America, a lettered 'inside' interpreter to the nation of the ghetto and the pulse behind the urban riots of the sixties. Baldwin, however, like Norman Mailer (an affinity diagnosed in Baldwin's 'The Black Boy Looks At The

White Boy'[1]) danced his own odd dance for the media, an infec-tious monologuist who performed stunningly before the cameras and the press in the very act of decrying racism, and each terrible assassination, and his country's Asian and Third World adventures. Who ultimately will be judged to have made better use of the other isn't yet clear.

What isn't odd, or unclear, is the urgent intelligence Baldwin has consistently brought to his literary activity, an intelligence which, like Ellison's, finds form in one of the marvels of modern prose style, in the essays perhaps above all, and which has con-tinued to win honour for the vitality of the truths carried upon its cadences. Both Ellison and Baldwin occupy a crucial place in the modern American canon at large, but they also, as black writers, fundamentally renewed, and re-made, Afro–American literary tradition. They established a sense of what was imagina-tively possible in fiction and in the essay after Wright, demonstrat-ing that the black writer need not be locked for ever inside inflexible prescriptions about 'realism' and 'protest'. Their impact as powers to free and enlarge black literary performance compares in this with earlier moments in the tradition, Alain Locke's pio-neer anthology and the manifesto of the Harlem Renaissance, *The New Negro* (1925), for instance, or Richard Wright's *Native Son* (1940), both crucial points of departure for later writers.

None of which is to suggest there haven't been lapses, a rather spectacular one in the case of Baldwin's *Another Country*, but that the fierce nervous eloquence of early essay collections like *Notes Of A Native Son* (1955), *Nobody Knows My Name* (1961) and *The Fire Next Time* (1963), and of *Go Tell It On The Mountain* and of no small part of the fiction Baldwin has since written right through to *Just Above My Head* (1979), testifies to prodi-gious talent, as equally does the novel which issued from Ellison's quite different kind of imagination, *Invisible Man*. If Ellison and Baldwin rank as precursors, they do so as black literary moderns, essential antecedent presences against whom the new fiction I discuss here takes its place. There have, of course, been dissenters, none more so than Eldridge Cleaver in his attack on Baldwin as a castratus, a sexually confused and self-hating fawner upon white people.[2] Even *Invisible Man* came under fire in some black nationalist quarters as too white and 'European' a work, a novel insufficiently abrasive in its indictments of racism and the indignity of the ghetto (a charge Ellison deals with in 'The World And The Jug'). And yet, against these and other odds—the attack upon Baldwin's unviolent brand of liberalism and upon his several flights from an America he has felt moved to indict for its murders and racial and sexual phobias and the jibes at Ellison's low public profile and seeming unwillingness (one hopes it isn't his inability) to bring out his long promised second novel—theirs has been a deserved eminence, an honour earned above all in the effort of their writing.

2

While both men, however, have attained the high ground in critical estimation, to an extent also by their individual kinds of presence as well as the feats of their fiction and essays, there has been emerging in its turn a body of fiction quite subsequent to them, easily as various as that of the Harlem Renaissance, and unwilling to be bound by past stereotypes. And ironically, as for Ellison and Baldwin, Richard Wright was a legacy to be negotiated (at least for Baldwin as he demonstrated in 'Alas, Poor Richard'—Ellison in 'The World And The Jug' says he 'simply stepped round him'[3]), so for their successors they have become influences to be fought against and assimilated, even while being admired. The newer spirits have been many, and have pursued a variety of new paths.

Perhaps, and deservedly, the best-known reputations belong to LeRoi Jones (Imamu Amiri Baraka), an established poet and activist whose place in the politics of black liberation has been vital and whose fiction, *The System of Dante's Hell* (1965) and *Tales* (1967) notably, underlines the breadth of his experimental flair; to William Melvin Kelley, from among whose novels and stories, his subtle black comedy, *dem* (1967), should assure him of a continuing attention; and to the California-based Ishmael Reed, whose fiction has been almost startling in its 'tall tale' effects of voice and adaptations of American social and historical myth and whose *Yardbird Readers* have provided an essential outlet for different ethnic literary talent (Volume 3 is given over, for instance, to Asian–American writing). Another gathering of talent has remained close to the vein of Richard Wright, John A. Williams outstandingly, especially in *The Man Who Cried I Am* (1967), a novel loosely based on Wright's own expatriate years in Europe, and also John O. Killens. A slightly newer fiction, mainly published first in the sixties, by Hal Bennett, Cyrus Colter and Robert Deane Pharr, among others, shows the continuing power of the black realist aesthetic, and indeed establishes the case for thinking the tradition of realism to have moved into, and beyond, a new apotheosis. Such, at least, is Graham Clarke's contention in this volume.

Other lines of departure have been equally evident. In *Train Whistle Guitar* (1974), the talented essayist Albert Murray composed one of the best 'Blues' novels yet to appear, a novel whose nuances echo the rich ballad life it draws upon and which Murray has studied in several of his lectures and non-fictional books.[4] James Baldwin might equally be thought to have written Blues in *If Beale Street Could Talk* (1974), his urban lyric story of a young couple's love set in New York and Puerto Rico which explores the meanings of the enduring black family bond. At another reach, there has been the phenomenon of Alex Haley's *Roots* (1976). When television, with lavish publicity and a budget to match, as well as an impeccable commercial sense of its audience, made *Roots* into an international media sensation, it gave America, and the world, an up-dated *Gone With The Wind*, though from a supposedly black perspective. America, especially, marvelled at the boldness of its truths, however much, on reflection, the whole enterprise smacked of a confection, de-fused and neutered costume history. It also somewhat eclipsed other important works about black family and community origins, Margaret Walker's slave-epic, *Jubilee* (1966), for example, and more importantly, Ernest Gaines's *The Autobiography Of Miss Jane Pittman* (1977), an intimate story of kinship and continuity also adapted for the screen but in more subdued manner. Gaines's triumphs across a body of fiction, beginning from *Catherine Carmier* (1964) and *Love and Dust* (1967) and moving on to *Bloodline* (1968) and most recently, *In My Father's House* (1978), which probes the lost connection between a black small-town preacher and his radicalized son, have still to receive due recognition. Al Young, similarly, an associate editor of *Yardbird Reader*, has written novels (and poetry) of serious strengths, *Snakes* (1970), *Who is Angelina?* (1973), and most recently, *Sitting Pretty* (1976), a wry piece of narrative which offers in Sidney J. Prettymon a possible successor to Langston Hughes's Jesse Simple. Another contemporary who belongs in the company of Murray, Gaines and Young is Robert Boles, the author of two novels, *The People One Knows* (1965), a delicate portrait of emotional breakdown and an expatriate European love-affair set in an army context, and of *Curling* (1968), the story of a murder in Boston with implications which verge increasingly on the absurd.

There has been emerging, further, as Faith Pullin's contribution to this collection underlines, a gallery of important black literary women, heiresses to Zora Neale Hurston, Ann Petry and Gwendolyn Brooks, writers of the diversity of Paule Marshall, Alice Walker, Gayl Jones, Toni Morrison, Kristin Hunter, Toni Cade Bambara, Louise Meriwether, Ruby Guy, Sarah Wright and Nikki Giovanni. To them, I would add Octavia E. Butler, whose unusual Science Fiction allegories, *Patternmaster* (1976) and *Mind Of My Mind* (1977), yield unexpected perspectives on the racial connundrum. Unlike her, however, her distinguished black fellow creator of SF, Samuel R. Delaney, hasn't given his novels a discernible racial dimension. The last decade has also seen the powerful Chicago city fiction of Ronald Fair, particularly *World of Nothing* (1970) and *We Can't Breathe* (1972); Barry Beckham's novels, *My Main Mother* (1969), a tale told as a fictionally 'literal' diary of self-discovery, and *Runner Mack* (1972), which re-works baseball as a source of different 'life' myths and a novel to compare with Robert Coover's *The Universal Baseball Association Inc* and Bernard Malamud's earlier *The Natural*; Clarence Major's two resolutely experimental novels, *No* (1973) and *Reflex And Bone Structure* (1975), both rich in the play of memory upon the present and in the uses of fictional voice; and a first novel as assured in its resort to black folklore as Charles Johnson's *Faith And The Good Thing* (1974).[5] In an account of the short story, an essential place would have to be given to James Alan McPherson's two sculpted collections, *Hue and Cry* (1969) and *Elbow Room* (1977). The energy of modern black fiction has clearly been a matter of bulk as well as imaginative quality.

3

The writers who concern me here have also written as part of, and within, a period of accelerated racial and political change, a period not perhaps immediately to be thought conducive to the writing of novels and stories. This nerve of cultural change can be dated from Kennedy's New Frontier and the new liberal promise of serious desegregation, and taken through the Civil Rights crusade and the busing and voting marches that followed. The change took an explosive turn as expectations, and increasingly they became demands, outran results. Riot, assassination, media images of police and army brutality and of America's burning cities, became almost commonplace. The commanding voices belonged, irresistibly, to Malcolm X, Stokeley Carmichael and Rap Brown and the Panthers, to Eldridge Cleaver and to the 'Soledad Brother' George Jackson, and the martyrs were many, from Medgar Evers and Martin Luther King to the front-line black troops in Vietnam. In time, the fuse dampened, energies had run their course, until reaching the apparently quieter waters of the Carter Presidency. Already, Selma, the Nixon years, and the Asian wars begin to seem somewhere behind. An important part of the fiction alluded to here, then, was written through a time, or soon after, when the public declaration of written or spoken witness—in autobiographies, prison letters and diaries, broadsheets and speeches—seemed more to the point than the deliberated creation of the novel or short story. Yet it was an extraordinary and productive time for fiction. These different politics and upheavals actually strengthened, and made increasingly self-aware, the making of black fiction.

Then, too, for the black writer, it was a time when Negro gave place to Black (and Black became not only Beautiful but marketable), an alteration in racial and minority consciousness which spread dramatically through almost all strata of American life— Black, but also Indian, Hispanic, Gay and Feminist. In Afro–American academic and literary circles, one aspect of this emergent new consciousness issued in the debate about the Black Aesthetic, which demanded a revolution in the assumptions by which black art and literature were to be evaluated,[6] and which at different times directly embroiled writers like LeRoi Jones and Clarence

Major and eventually brought riposts from Ishmael Reed and Ralph Ellison. It came to a point of acrimonious focus in black literary reactions to William Styron's 'meditation upon history', *The Confessions of Nat Turner* (1967).[7] An aesthetic formed out of black criteria was arguably a necessary act of cultural reclamation, a timely piece of recovery and self-assertion, but its arguments have by no means been unambiguous (Ellison was moved to warn against a 'stance of cultural self-segregation').[8]

For many black contemporaries no single requirement about 'criteria', either about subject-matter or form, has been thought to suffice. Some have clearly kept faith with the Wrightian heritage. Others have sought their form in Blues, or in surrealism, or black comedy, or thrillers, styles which, with typical brio, Ishmael Reed once listed as 'Fantasy, Nationalism, the supernatural, HooDooism, Realism, Science Fiction, Autobiography, Satire, Scat, Erotica, Rock, K. C. Blues, International Intrigue, Jazz . . .'.[9] Nor can it be doubted that the American end of the debate about postmodernism has played a part. The search for untapped resources of form among black writers of the novel has been as active as it has been throughout almost all post-war American fiction (witness Reed's own purposive Hoo-Doo interests, or Clarence Major's experiments with syntax and plot-sequence in a novel like *Reflex And Bone Structure*, or Leon Forrest's uses of dream). If, in aggregate, these new voices can be said to come together in any one respect, it might well lie in the observation Ralph Ellison made in 'Change The Joke And Slip The Yoke', an essay written in 1958:

> For the novelist of any cultural or racial identity, his form is his greatest freedom and his insights are where he finds them.

In this, a contentious view given the controversies about what black American writers should and should not be doing in their fiction, Ellison is echoed two decades later by Ishmael Reed. Certainly, the novels Reed himself has written so dazzlingly, as much as any by his innovation minded contemporaries, have refused to be the 'one thing'. 'Freedom in form', in fact, might easily be taken for the hallmark of this entire new black fiction, but especially that written by Demby, Wideman, Wright, Polite and Forrest. In this respect they can stand as instances of a wider urge to 'make new', and to take the novel towards a fresh realm of possibilities.

229

4

As a preface to the names on my list, I want to acknowledge briefly the achievement of Chester Himes, whose roots lie deep in an earlier generation, but whose recognition as a force for innovation (and as the creator of an important body of fiction and an autobiographer of note) has come only belatedly, and not without reservation. In part, and little to his personal satisfaction, this has been because critics proved too ready to label him, usually in company with Ann Petry and Willard Motley, a member of Wright's 'school', a tough but predictable naturalist voice from the Depression and Roosevelt years. Wright's exact contemporary (they were born within a year of each other) and his friend and long-time fellow Paris and European expatriate, Himes began publishing as early as 1932 with a run of prison and crime short stories. By the time *The Primitive* (1955) appeared, his fifth full-length novel in a decade, it should have been clear that he wrote with far subtler powers than those of a formula 'protest' writer. His ability to blend into an ostensibly realist plot-line his powerful satiric wit, and his different dream and fantasy materials, now can be seen to confirm a writer of unusual inventive flair. At least, so he has been judged by Ishmael Reed and other younger writers on whom he has exerted an influence.

The interest in experimentation showed stronger still in his two next novels, *Pinktoes* (1961), a *jeu d'esprit* and his mock-scatalogical look at inter-racial and sexual behaviour on New York's liberal social circuit (and first published by Olympia Press which established it as something of an underground classic), and *Une Affaire De Viol/A Case of Rape* (1963), the story of a white woman's death in the company of four expatriate black Americans in a Paris hotel and of their subsequent experiences of white, European law in a French court. Issued in what Himes says is an abbreviated version, it looks at the inter-secting paths of European, American and African colonial history in terms of a search for the roots of racial mythology. It remains, still, available only in obscure French translation. But it was above all with his detective stories that Himes came decisively into his own. In 1957, largely at his friend Marcel Duhamel's urging, he wrote *For Love Of Imabelle* (later re-titled *A Rage in Harlem* and *La Reine Des Pommes* in France), the first, to date, of nine *romans policiers*, for Gallimard's *Série Noire*, which at last brought him international acclaim and a decent income.[10] Hollywood wasn't slow to spot a good bet and in short order *Cotton Comes To Harlem* (1965), then *Come Back Charleston Blue* (originally *The Heat's On*, 1966), were made into films, with Raymond St. Jacques and Godfrey Cambridge in the detective roles and direction by Ossie Davis. Despite the Harlem sets, and some inventive screenplay by Davis, neither film quite recaptures the antic wit and sheer street pace of the thrillers on which they are based. Nevertheless, with the rise in the sixties of black cultural nationalism, Himes was obviously a name waiting to be re-discovered and the films were part of the tribute.

The Harlem Himes in fact does create in his detective series is an imagined world of rare, almost surreal, proportions. His Harlem functions as a parish of bizarre happenings and is peopled by invented types of every hue and sexual taste, calling not only upon Himes's mastery of black street life, but his well-tuned ear for ghetto and crime argot. For though Himes has often been dismissed as merely a writer of potboilers, 'urban Westerns' in one critic's phrase, his quite unique recreation of the world of Harlem's 125th Street and Amsterdam Avenue, and of the Apollo theatre, the bars and tenements, deserves serious note. His imagination is ample and resourceful: he writes plots of rich invention, the wit is wildly and often improbably funny, he makes his language vivid, close to live speech. And, above all, his two 'Harlem sheriffs', as he calls them, Coffin Ed Johnson and Grave Digger Jones, serve as the perfect custodians of this black mythical kingdom, tough, laconic guardians of America's central black metropolis, Manhattan's exotic, impoverished, city-within-a-city and, as Himes tells it, a hothouse of crime and the daily human hustle to survive at all costs. The effects are beguiling, and likely enough, profound.

Nowhere are those effects more strikingly given form than in the latest of the novels, *Blind Man With A Pistol* (1969) which, when taken with its predecessor, *Cotton Comes to Harlem*, shows Himes to have taken the detective-thriller to its outer limits. The novel offers an almost prophetic vision of racial collapse, a parable up to his usual richly comic level, yet apocalyptic, closer in kind

231

with William Melvin Kelley's *dem*, or Nathanael West's *The Day Of The Locust* (1939), than detective writing by, say, Raymond Chandler or Dashiell Hammett, or his fellow black writer of detective stories, John B. West. Re-titled *Hot Day Hot Night* in American paperback (and *L'Aveugle Au Pistolet* in Gallimard), *Blind Man With A Pistol* weaves a number of apparently disparate plots one into the other: an inter-racial sex scandal; a rejuvenation caper (run by a wonderfully conceived black Mormon who advertizes for 'fertile womens' and has leads into syndicate crime); and a spate of political marches which put Harlem dangerously on edge. Himes also feeds into the novel considerable reference to Black Power and Malcolm X and to the accelerating tempo of street shoot-outs and confrontations with the police. The plot thus reads at times like a seeming fast-moving comedy of errors, a litany of comic blunders each of which underscores the darkening racial picture. The climax is a berserk blind man firing off his pistol, wildly, indiscriminately, on a New York subway. This last sequence, which Himes depicts as wholly gratuitous, is perhaps his purgatorial metaphor of a society his novel suggests is fast going racially insane and for which the formal discontinuities and turnabouts of pace in *Blind Man With A Pistol* act as the perfect expression. The upshot of holding in fealty upwards of a million black Americans in New York's urban box has produced an intolerable, anarchic human pressure. Thus blindness of the violent kind set out in the novel begets only further blindness. Ostensibly sighted 'passengers' see through blinkered, and blinking, eyes. Suspicion, fear, the retreat into safe mythologies of 'law and order', become the standard. Himes glosses the world his novel explores in typically abrupt manner:

> Everybody reacted immediately. Some thought the world was coming to an end; others thought that the Venusians were coming. A number of white passengers thought the niggers were taking over; the majority of soul people thought their time was up.

What keeps *Blind Man With A Pistol* going, apart from the untiring good wit and Himes's ability to give his spirals of plot a larger human vision than might be expected of the thriller, is his handling of the novel's form. Himes isn't merely unravelling a mystery, his novel makes the mystery into the very shape of his narrative. In a series which all along promised to become more, this latest effort transforms an apparently 'pop' genre into visionary fiction, given its limits and an idiom whose authenticity is established in the scabrous 'down-home' extracts which serve as a preface, quite as sure of touch as Ellison's *Invisible Man*.

Himes must rank, from within a long tradition of writing about Harlem, as black Manhattan's most companionable archivist. Each of the nine novels shows his abundant knowledge of his territory's flavours, its brownstone and dives, its soul-food and music, the bars and citizenry. Thriller after thriller puts on view a milling population of con-men and preachers, matriarchs and gaudy prophets, pimps and their chippies, shysters and their victims. Real, or truly a mythic kingdom of Himes's own imagining, his Harlem comes over as a paradox: an enclave of poverty which finds release in all manner of criminal glamour, a people depicted as prone to every imaginable frailty yet as strong on human resilience as the Londoners of Dickens's novels. It is, however, Himes's ability to use the form of the thriller to so unique and diverting an advantage that claims the attention.

For his thrillers exceed their brief. Himes's fashioning of his stories, and his mastery of the Harlem textures which give his plots their human detail, argue for a craftsman with a rare angle of vision, an authentic comic wit. In an interview he gave his friend, John A. Williams, Himes observed:

> American violence is public life, it's a public way of life; it became a form, a detective story form.[11]

Few thriller-writers have better understood, or done as much with, the equation. Only lately, however, in his Spanish retreat at Jávea, has Himes begun to win his due as a serious experimentalist and as one of America's senior literary native sons.

5

Like Himes, William Demby also left America for Europe in the fifties, settling in Rome rather than Paris or Spain shortly after the publication of his first novel, *Beetlecreek* (1950), a close-wrought, existential parable, set in a West Virginia hill-town. A decade later followed *The Catacombs* (1965), a venture altogether more 'modernist' in kind, and an experiment as much in its view of human consciousness and its perception of time as its narrative means. The two novels read very much as a diptych, linking visions of human loss and subsequent recovery. Demby has since been at work on a third novel, a confessional narrative in the mould of Malcolm X's *Autobiography* (1965) or Eldridge Cleaver's *Soul On Ice* (1968), to be called *The Journal Of A Black Revolutionary In Exile*, a work which promises a yet further development in the fiction of fact.

In *Beetlecreek*, Demby's mode is insistently naturalistic, a controlled linear accumulation of images of death made over into a story. The novel depicts a triangle of characters, each in his own way the victim of small-town suffocation. Bill Trapp, a white, ageing ex-carnival man and a recluse is burnt to death in his ramshackle house at the town's outskirts; Johnny, the neophyte black adolescent hero becomes the unresisting agent of Trapp's death, despite being helped and befriended by him; and David Biggs, sign-painter and the unloved husband of a rising church-woman (he is also Johnny's uncle) abandons his hopes of becoming an artist for the fast city charms of a schooltime girlfriend long 'gone north' and returned for her mother's funeral. The novel derives its claustrophobic impact from Demby's dense imagery of entrapment, stasis, closed doors and windows, coffins and beetles, a catalogue of death and ways of suppressing the instinct for life. The final act of arson, particularly, serves the novel as an emetic, a violent terminal act of release from the town's racial paralysis. Demby has acknowledged in interview that *Beetlecreek* signified his own leave-taking from America, a society he then believed impossibly locked inside its racial myths and dead-ends.[12] The deliberateness of Demby's prose and the care with which his novel uses major images of death were sure signs of promise.

The Catacombs more than fulfilled that promise, a novel which bids for, and in my judgement achieves, genuine new ground, especially in exploring human connections which run greatly deeper than race. Demby himself calls his novel an experiment in 'cubistic time', narration which seeks to bind different levels and kinds of consciousness one into the other as if time were a shared, simultaneous present, and by which he confirms his affinity with moderns like James Joyce and Virginia Woolf (he also speaks admiringly of Izak Dinesen's African Gothic fiction). The novel in fact draws upon a range of modernist sources: foremost Demby's interest in the visual arts. His considerable training in art history and collection shows in the novel's pattern of allusions to painterly form. He also borrows from different post- and neo-realist film strategies, having done translation and screen-writing for Italian directors like Antonioni and Rosellini. Given that the novel was being written in the early sixties, and is actually set between Easter 1962 and 1964, it reveals in Demby an alert response to the then new accounts of a post-Gutenberg Galaxy being explored in Marshall McLuhan's writing and to emerging developments in the mathematics of time-theory and probability. The philosophical roots of his novel he readily acknowledges to be Teilhard de Chardin's evolutionary Christianity, the credo of human ascendence and convergence. Hence, his novel's most resonant touchstone, Rome's ancient sites of Christian sanctuary, the catacombs, serve as points of spiritual and temporal meaning in a manner which recalls E. M. Forster's Marabar Caves. Demby's second novel is self-avowedly 'complex', and runs the risk of mystification, but it controls with great sureness the ambition behind the form.

Though in part a self-reflexive composition (Demby intervenes several times to advise his reader of the kind of novel he is reading), *The Catacombs* keeps steadily in view the world external to itself. It is organized as montage of sorts, a careful inter-working of the 'facts' of world news and change with the 'facts' of its imagined author's life. In one sense it is a book about the world, and about historical process; it is also a book about a book, about its own imaginative provenance. The centre is a work-in-progress being written by one 'William Demby' about his muse and lover, Doris, in reality a black show-girl in Rome with a minor part in the film 'Cleopatra', starring Elizabeth Taylor. She sleeps with both the 'author' and the Count he has introduced her to, a minor aristocrat whose lineage no longer protects him from the modern world of advancing technology. Suitably he works for an airline as an executive, a servant of the new media and means of travel. The novel's last picture is of Doris pregnant, unsure which man has impregnated her (and thus unsure whether she has 'white' or 'black' seed in her body), fleeing like the muse she has become to the further edges of the catacombs. She carries within her the author's fugitive vision, his commitment to a greater kind of human consciousness.

Around this triangle, Demby constructs a narrative which reflects the high-speed technological world of transaction and change. His novel uses extracts from newspapers, weeklies, diaries, personal journals and letters, to re-capture the bewildering speed with which history can now be seen to be in process. He alludes thus to the newly fought Algerian war; the neo-Fascist backlash in France and Italy; the quickening space race between America and Russia; the changes in western fashion, dress styles and art tastes; the increasing hold of TV and the instant visual media; and recurrently his belief in a philosophy of time and human redemption which transcends the events of any one immediate now. The novel abounds in these mutual echoes and refractions, mirroring patterns of cross-reference, and holds them to a credible narrative rhythm—not least because there is always to hand a preceptible line of story in process of being discharged.

The climax of these different shifts of energy and contrast takes place when the Count, long habituated to pain and doubt about his own meaning, finally sees through time, both as he himself has known it and as it is reflected in the new media, and grasps that the catacombs, where death has been stored for centuries, is also a means back into life—that Doris, in truth, incarnates the life-principle. His epiphany is also the 'author's', and the reader's, a final point of clarification in a novel which throughout has explored the fatal costs of compartmentalizing human consciousness along simple lines of nationality or race, or to a single measure of time. It makes for a singular moment in a singular novel. *The Catacombs* offers an important endeavour to 'make new', a fiction whose ambitions are matched in the overall achievement.

6

'I had a real interest in experimenting, in expanding the form of the novel'[11]—John Wideman's ambitions for his first novel, *A Glance Away* (1967), the story of the destructive Easter home-coming of an ex-addict to his inner-city roots, holds good both for Wideman's contemporaries in general and for his own two other novels, *Hurry Home* (1970), the narrative of a journey

through ghetto America and on into Europe and an Africa con-
jured up in the hero's mind, and *The Lynchers* (1973), which
depicts the fevered conspiracy of four Philadelphia black men to
lynch a white cop and thereby put to America *the* symbol of its
own historic racial inhumanity. All three novels attempt new ter-
rain, and if Wideman's innovations don't always come exactly into
balance, his imagination is clearly one of enormous gifts which on
occasion soars. He requires mention in any serious estimate of
change in the recent Afro–American novel.

Wideman's interest in experimental narrative took an early academic turn when, as a young Rhodes Scholar at Oxford in the sixties from the University of Pennsylvania, he did research on Laurence Sterne (an influence he emphasises) and on the rise of the
novel as genre. Yet for all his experimental inclinations, and they
take the reader frequently into an interior world of dream and
memory, each of the novels rests solidly upon a strong forward
sense of story, which Cecil Braithswaite, the itinerant protagonist
of *Hurry Home*, likens to a process of 'awakening'. Of his com-
positional habits, Wideman has mentioned a number of debts:
to T. S. Eliot and the polyphonic structure of 'The Waste Land'
(he also has several Prufrock-like characters, the most affecting
being Robert Thurley, a broken-down college professor in *A
Glance Away*); to painters like Bosch and the Spanish baroque
masters whose uses of colour obviously fascinate him and whose
canvases he makes an explicit motif in *Hurry Home*; and in *The
Lynchers*, his most black-centered novel, to the 'open' form of
Jean Toomer's *Cane* (1923) and the fiction of Richard Wright and
Ralph Ellison. Wideman's novel falls somewhere between the
realistic and experimental, a middle-ground he is evidently aware
of and exploits with considerable adroitness.

All three novels, in seeking to understand the determining impact
of the remembered past upon the present, use memory in often
new and engaging fashion, so much so, that I want to approach the
experimental nature of the writing through this play of memory
and remembering. In *A Glance Away*, Eddie Lawson's day-long
descent into the abyss, is told against the background of the larger
Lawson family, kin of a troubled and mutually damaging kind:
Daddy Gene, the wine-happy grandfather recalled in snippets of
song and gesture; Gene, the spectral elder brother killed in Guam;

Martha, Eddie's betrayed and unbending mother; Bette, her cowed daughter; Brother Small, the gargoyle albino sidekick whose mind never quite clears; and Alice, Brother's sister and Eddie's one-time love, a dancer by training but now a whore. This background of people, and the feelings they represent, Wideman evokes through different increments of memory, so that they move in and out of Eddie's day of return like angry, hurt ghosts. Against this background is set another, that of Robert Thurley, would-be aesthete, of white-genteel stock and a homosexual with his family roots in the magnolia South. Their mutual and downward spiral finally is made to converge at Harry's Bar, a last resting station before the novel's ultimate catastrophe. Against these collapsing lives, Wideman sets off the Easter Passion, in the form of a concert Thurley attends and in a body of allusion to Easter music and the pascal liturgy, the expression of a hope of redemption neither can attain. The voices of memory build, throughout the novel, into a gathering whole, a delicate balance of the past impinging on the present and of human connections which have given way to loss. Wideman's hold on his narrative's energies rarely falters and for a debut *A Glance Away* offered a striking accomplishment in making form of Eddie Lawson's life.

In *Hurry Home*, the emphasis is even more upon dream, reverie, the intoxication with landscapes of memory. Cecil Braithswaite, the novel's protagonist, once a law graduate and now working as a janitor, dreams a Joycean book of dreams: of his past at the University supported by the patient Esther, on whom he simply 'walked out', and of their dead son, Simon (named for Daedalus?); of his sojourn through the great galleries and cities of Europe as the adopted ward of a white painter; and of his fascination with a lost Moorish African leader, a figure enclosed in myth as much as the dark continent of his origins. The novel resorts freely, yet purposefully, to different diaries, letters, vivid patches of recollection, past sights and sounds and smells, until the reader begins to recognize that Cecil's 'journey', his dreaming, in fact *is* the narrative, the remembering consciousness as itself a literary form. The result is haunting, the novel in the form of a single sustained dream monologue.

The Lynchers, by contrast, is essentially a novel in four voices, each the outlet for a past full of confusion, angry momentous long-ings for revenge. It reads at great pace drawing the reader into the accelerating 'passage' of its four would-be lynchers who plan a final, implacable ritual gesture of dissent against the racial order they have inherited. Wideman's narrative thus takes up, and enacts, the fever each man feels, moving easily from one run of consciousness to another. But in no traditional sense is the novel a work of 'protest'; like *Hurry Home* it embodies within its own momentum and idiom the rising energies of the act the lynchers plan to perform. That their plan ends in confusion, disarray, is in part the outcome of attempting a supreme anachronistic act, history repeated. They are, in fact, men caught out-of-time, and in a noose as tightly drawn as the one they would place about their intended victim's neck to bring about 'an event so traumatically symbolic that things would never be the same afterwards'. Wideman's language carries in its lively metaphors and imagery a detailed sense of the present's pastness (indicated also in the long series of opening historical extracts about lynching and slave abuse). Like Wideman's other two novels, *The Lynchers* deserves wider acknowledgement for its sweep of vision, its invention.

7

If Charles Wright's novels, *The Messenger* (1963), *The Wig* (1966) and *Absolutely Nothing To Get Alarmed About* (1973), could be said to claim a spiritual forbear, it would be Nathanael West, to whom he explicitly addresses a letter as the conclusion to his third novel. For like West, though in a style always distinctively his own, Wright depicts a city world which borders on phantasmogoria, Baudelaire's *cité fourmillante*. His world is thus as utterly New York as West's is Hollywood in *The Day of the Locust*, but also a world seen as though in hallucination, in the fragments of a continuous, accelerated dream. The narrator of *The Messenger*, Charles Stevenson, puts his feelings of disjuncture in the following terms:

> Here in this semi-dark room, I become frightened. Am I in America? The objects, chairs, tables, sofa are not specifically American. They, in this room, have no recognizable country. I have always liked to believe that I am not too far removed from the heart of America (I have a twenty-five dollar U.S. Savings

Bond) and I am proud of almost everything American. Yet I am drowning in this green cornfield. The acres stretch to infinity. I dare not move. This country has split open my head with a golden eagle's beak. Regardless of how I try, the parts won't come together. And this old midtown brownstone is waiting mutely for the demolition crew, these two-and-a-half rooms which have sheltered me for two years. A room with a view: the magical Manhattan skyline, and all for five dollars a week because I have connections.

It is through, and around, this 'magical' Manhattan that Charles operates as a messenger, the connecting human link between the different messages he delivers, just as Charles Wright, author, acts as messenger for his novel's different 'messages'. *The Messenger* thus moves with great speed between different locales and types, between New York's contrasting zones and regions and between people as different as the Rockefellers, for whom Charles works, and dead winos and abused city children. He finds himself reporting on a whole gallery of ethnic and street life, especially the worlds of drag queens, pick-ups, party-goers and bar-flies—a spoiling, multi-sexual constellation of New Yorkers who pass across, and in and out of, his times like actors on a revolving reel. Wright's novel also includes memories of his Missouri childhood, Korea, different Harlem adventures, and extraordinary moments of tenderness with children like Maxine, his neighbour and fellow creative spirit with a taste for 'the fantastic'. But the novel's tone is set in the references Charles makes to himself as variously 'a sea-lion landlocked', as 'dying the American-money death', and as being 'drunk with dreams of leaving New York, of going to Europe, going any place'. And by the end of the novel, a still moment after so much sound and fury, he imagines himself having reached 'a time of stock-taking'.

The design of *The Messenger* is appropriately episodic throughout, like the life it gets so tangibly and busily upon the page, a novel which sees this life as 'magical' and 'fantastic' as it pours in from and out on to the New York streets. Wright's vision belongs, on its own terms, in the line of Céline and William Burroughs and, as I suggest, of Baudelaire, a New York vision which also finds special analogies in the poetry of Frank O'Hara, Kenneth Koch and John Ashberry. The city's space, its 'unreal' permuta-

240

tions and design, he speaks of as an intimate of all New York's energies and crevices, all the changing connections and power. *The Messenger* reads as an urban book of fragments, a log of the modern Western city, held within a single, intimate gaze.

In *The Wig*, Wright's taste for the fantastic is given explicit free rein (a prefatory Author's Note confides that 'the story itself is set in an America of tomorrow'). It tells the story of a modern ingénu, a black Candide, Lester Jefferson, whose aspirations to Lyndon Johnson's Great Society Wright renders as a grotesque *rite-de-passage*, a journey through a world of fraudulent 'success' and myths of endless American opportunity which ends, as it must if Lester is to understand anything at all, in a scene of castration. Wright decks out his ingenuous hero in a magical wig, 'burnished red-golden hair', and takes him on a Pilgrim's Progress through America's worst consumer landscape. Lester, a fantasist supreme (Wright calls him 'Walter Mitty's target-colored stepson') takes on an array of different identities, all aimed at 'scoring', attaining the supreme American success of being a public celebrity, a media 'event'. He passes through the film and soul music world, the world of advertising and the media, a victim ready to act out its silliest demands. He also encounters a special fairground of all-American grotesques: his hysterical apartment neighbour, Nonnie; Little Jimmy Wishbone, recording star and shaman of the Motown world; the Deb, an all-American girl type; Miss Sandra Honover, transvestite and parody woman. Lester himself is finally incarnated as a living advertisement gimmick, The Chicken Man, a ridiculous, high-paying, commercial nemesis. But, and finally, he is 'unwigged' by the Harlem undertaker, Mr. Fishback, an Ishmael Reed type of Hoo-Doo man. *The Wig* risks a fair degree of plain pop-art silliness but its idioms and Wright's eye for America's fatal attraction to easy panaceas and commercial 'uplift' is never without its shrewdness. In lambasting America's entrepreneurial myths, and their debasement of human life, Wright joins older company, like Melville, Twain and Nathanael West, in decrying a major betrayal in America's promise to its people.

Absolutely Nothing To Get Alarmed About, which Wright originally called *Black Studies: A Journal* (an ironic title he dropped for fear his novel would be wrongly classified in book-

241

stores and libraries), continues much in the vein of *The Messenger*, a highly personal chronicle and progress-report on America under Lyndon Johnson's aegis, the country stalked by riot, war protest and hippiedom. Wright's geography is once more New York: Union Square, Times Square, The Village and East Village, the Bowery (which he describes as 'a cinema in hell where classic films play forever'), the fortress of Wall Street, with occasional forays into Harlem and into the moneyed realms of Upper Manhattan. Wright again charts with a ready fluency his city world of different and competing energies, New York as at once America's exhilerating and first major metropolis and its urban nightmare, a stone prison of violence and poverty and human decay. This novel, also, seeks form for the city's spatial energies and contrasts, the skyscraper opulence, the street pace, and the welfare and tenement blight, in its episodicity, its incremental sequences of action and reporting.

Wright, or his fictional *persona*, speaks as someone consummately street-wise, yet always a fugitive presence, measuring on his own body and psyche the costs of so rapid a life rhythm. He speaks as the city's Defoe-like eye, both compelled yet alienated, for which his different jobs in the city's restaurants and kitchens and in the holiday resorts of the Catskills Mountains give him a special vantage point. Not without self-irony, however, does he observe 'I became frightened and felt like a character out of a Kafka novel.' The novel's detail fills out to embrace memories of Langston Hughes; Union Square hippie life ('the games of affluent space-age children'); an almost Burroughsian 'disgust' and 'suffocating sense of horror' at 'the black and white American majority', yet always an alertness to 'whitey's historical dealing with my people'. Busy, and as fast-paced as *The Messenger*, *Nothing To Get Alarmed About* exudes something of the flavours of a modern *Notes From Underground*, a 'subterranean' chronicle of desperation, rapid surges of change, lives often marred and erased by New York's criminal and drug cultures. And always, for Wright, there exists New York's sexual aura, the city's power to arouse instantaneous sexual heat and needs. Yet for all the copious detail Wright gives his novel, it rarely fails to hold its overall shape. Even the sex romp which rounds out the novel, a coda suitalby grotesque for Wright's actual and phantasied scenes of modern city life, fits into the larger pattern. Wright uses the novel as chronicle, as an expression of individual witness and testimony to a city which is at once literal New York and supremely his 'Unreal City'.

8

The first of Carlene Hatcher Polite's two novels, *The Flagellants* (1967), like Chester Himes *romans policers*, initially saw print in French translation, partly the outcome of her different stays in France after training with the Martha Graham Dance troupe and various stints doing political and civil rights work for the Democrats in Michigan. In a discussion with Hoyt Fuller of *Black World* about a kind of fiction he has long thought of attempting, Himes also unintentionally provided a useful gloss on Polite's first novel:

> I would like to see produced a novel that just drains a person's subconscious of all his attitudes and reactions to everything. Because, obviously, if one person has a number of thoughts concerning everything, there is cohesion. There has to be because they belong to one man. Just let it come out as the words generate in the mind, let it come out in the phrasing of the subconscious and let it become a novel in that form.[18]

The 'thoughts' in *The Flagellants* belong, in fact, to two lovers, Ideal and Jimson, a black Greenwich Village couple, whose love for each other Polite renders as an ornate, obsessive colloquy, the expression of a passion in itself histrionic, draining in all its tilts and demands. In the course of their alternating speeches and soliloquies, we learn of two pasts—Ideal's in the black Southlands amid conjure women, exotic guitar men and a childhood of Halloweens and witches, and Jimson's as the zen-influenced son of a protestant preacher. Their dialogues range over the competing myths of black and white sexuality; the issues of evolutionary Civil Rights as against revolt; the costs of each daily negotiation of a white American world of taboos and subtle social and racial rites. These, and abundant other related concerns, are located within the unremitting confessional war of their love-affair, a battle-ground of words, gestures, eruptions of deepest anger and despair.

243

The Flagellants, rather unexpectedly, is anything but casebook realism, however. It takes the form of a baroque, almost stylized, interplay of two voices, each driven, intense. Polite takes a considerable risk in this. Her novel teeters on the edge of sounding overwrought, simply too strained. But for all its fastidiousness, her idiom delivers. She manages to depict a love full of dissonance, wildness, a narrative in two juxtaposed and urgent registers of need. The wilder, and more accusatory, each outburst, the more formalized Polite makes her fictional language. Ideal and Jimson are thus rightly described as a 'reeling couple', their love 'an irrevocable trauma'. Both pivot, muster force against each other's arguments and expositions, fall into depression, fight, act out, until the novel's ending takes them to a last separation, their mutual passion at last, or momentarily, spent. The ornateness of Polite's language, and the novel's resort to so stylized an idiom, gives *The Flagellants* a unique, or at least highly unusual, temper, as if this particular love could be understood only as ritual, feelings elaboratley 'drained' as Himes puts it. The hermetic pressure of their love is met in the novel's style and organization, a style which at first looks slightly oblique, inappropriate, but which takes on its own rhythm as the novel unfolds. For what stays in the mind, ultimately, is the dexterity with which Polite manipulates her style, the expressiveness of the means she uses to make her reader understand the meaning of her lovers' mutual 'flagellation'. It is as though she had deliberately chosen a style which would work as counterpoint to the volatility of her lovers' passion, a style to play against and contain their erotic fury. *The Flagellants* represents serious experiment.

Polite's subsequent novel, *Sister X And The Victims of Foul Play* (1975), Ishmael Reed has described as 'jazz writing', a free-form narrative very much in the manner of his own *The Free-Lance Pallbearers* (1967), or Charles Wright's *The Wig*. It is set in Paris, amid the dance and review 'boîtes de nuit', and serves as an obituary to Sister X Arista Prolo, an exotic dancer, and to the death of a particular black life-force and skill that died with her as she was overtaken by mere strip-tease and the sex-shows. The two survivors around whom the novel is built are Abyssinia, Sister X's dress-maker, and Black Will, a travelling man and ex-convict, in whose mutual integrity lies a counterweight to the world of

244

dollars and greed all about them. For all its 'camp', its fancy pirouettes in laying out the printed page, this second novel is clearly intended as a tract for the times, a sermon against the cash-nexus and the replacement of the lost arts of serious dance by cheap titillation. Abyssinia puts it as an argument against 'a trap, a trick bag, Brother, a Dead World'. Polite's concern is to map this Dead World, the cost of putting the dollar above human needs and feeling. The story of Sister X's (quite literal) fall and death is offered as a cautionary tale, a warning. Like *The Wig* on occasion it almost gives in to mere show, pop-cartoon gimickry, but the wit is considerable. *Sister X And The Victims Of Foul Play* isn't major fare by any means, but its touch should earn for Carlene Hatcher Polite a continuing ragard.

9

When asked to advise an aspiring black writer about the art of narrative, Leon Forrest, in an interview with *The Massachusetts Review*, gave the following answer:

> He must develop a writer's mind, which is highly associative —and deeply reflective—and constantly see story material possibilities in patterns, in symbolic connections, word transitions in the world about him and within him. He must develop a fury for re-writing, for it is only via re-writing, endlessly, obsessively, that he can ever write into currents of energy, felt-knowledge memories. The writer's mind is possessed by a long and deep memory of the way things fit or are in paradox, but he must train his mind to find his form.[14]

Forrest's observations, those of a working novelist, bear most usefully on his own fiction, two novels of rare 'symbolic connections' and 'felt-knowledge memories', *There Is A Tree More Ancient Than Eden* (1973) and *The Bloodworth Orphans* (1977). As Ralph Ellison observes in his Foreword to *There Is A Tree More Ancient Than Eden*, the reader needs time to establish his bearings in Forrest's world, but the returns are ample, and on occasion, amazing. Few black contemporaries have tried to do more with their language, to make it carry so much in the way of historical and 'associative' resonance. One hears in its incantatory rhythms the Bible; the hallelujahs and interjections of black folk church-going (in Forrest's case it is also a mystic Catholic Christianity with origins in New Orleans French and Creole life and which displays a resemblance to the world of Flannery O'Connor in stories like 'Revelation' and *Wise Blood*); phrasings taken from Jazz and the great Blues and Spirituals; and traits learnt from Joyce and Faulkner (especially the Faulkner of *The Sound And The Fury*) and of the major black writers, from Jean Toomer and Ralph Ellison. But, for all of these influences, Forrest's novels create, quite insistently, their own grain. They explore, time and again, the meanings of dynasty, of family and racial paternity which have been lost and intermeshed by the turns of American history as manifested in slavery, the Great Migration, the guilty racial ascendancy of one race over another. For Forrest, in both novels, has been endeavouring to write his own unique version of Yoknapatawpha, a fiction of 'roots' not as costume melodrama, but as a mythic modern diaspora, history not so much as a line of specific 'events' but as experience carried on the pulse and in the psyche of all black Americans. The effects of this endeavour can be crowded, difficult on first acquaintance to read steadily, but Forrest has put his own advice into practice. His 'form' is secure; his materials do 'fit'.

There Is A Tree More Ancient Than Eden is told through the consciousness of Nathan Witherspoon, detectably Forrest's own *persona*, here a boy present at his mother's funeral, a yellow-skinned mulatto child whose vivid imagination give the novel its form. Told in five parts, each a contributing dream, the novel seeks in different images of flight and of memory to establish perspectives on Nathan's family and on the legacies of race and history which have come down to him—in his own mixed colour and in the family myths and folklore. The 'story' that connects Nathan with his Dilsey-like mentor, Aunt Hattie Breedlove, and with the driven and often demented Witherspoon family, and especially with Nathan's slave-descended kin, James Fishbond, and which in turns send him 'journeying' down emblematic routes like 'DuSable Street' and 'Black Bottom Street', thus links him not only to his own individual past, but to a shared black community past. The violence of that past, its rapes and lynchings, its flights and ecstasies, which Nathan 're-sees' in his different dreams, is enacted in Forrest's language. The reader meets precisely 'word transitions' and 'symbolic connections' in such visions as Nathan's dream of

246

the crucifixion in which he sees the torture of black American slaves, or in Fishbond's experience as a fugitive and soldier, or in the following, where Fishbond gives an account of 'the uniqueness of our history':

> how much is demanded . . . in terms of forbearance, when a people's total soul has been ripped off, whored upon, misused, wracked, raped, ruptured, and mangled, and they are left with their asses set afire in the grass and their names gutted with a protoplasm soaked in dung and urine, and their breath choked off on the gallows and their sex spread and split down upon rust-bloodied hooks, like sausages . . .

Another character speaks of 'the larger questions, the major implications, the jaundice-soaked, riddle-whorings of our history . . . our collective history memory'—thereby referring the specific family and dynastic concerns of the Witherspoon line to a wider 'collective' experience. Nathan's mind acts as the staging-ground for all this 'history'. As each vision declares and exhausts itself, the novel moves to a final Joycean section, 'Wakefulness', which serves as a coda, a last recapitulation of what has gone before. Written in prose as cross-reference and impressionistic as Molly Bloom's soliloquy, it brings the novel to an ordering final point of meaning and insight.

In opening *There Is A Tree More Ancient Than Eden*, Forrest uses two lines from a Billie Holiday refrain:

> Southern tree bearing strange fruit—
> Blood on the leaves and blood at the root.

'Blood at the root' is an apt phrase for the world imagined in *The Bloodworth Orphans*, a novel conceived to the scale of *Ulysses* or Faulkner's Snopes Trilogy. Forrest again ranges over a wide canvas, which requires equally patient unravelling, offering a night-town vision of America as a genealogy of racial 'orphans' —all, one way or another, derived from the original slave-owning Bloodworths. The novel is uninhibited in its uses of myth, especially the Bible's myth of Genesis and the lost sons and daughters of Israel here adapted to America and its 'lost' and divided Afro–American progeny. Forrest again uses Nathan Witherspoon as a guiding consciousness (Fishbond and others from *There Is A Tree More Ancient Than Eden* also make appearances). The fate of the Bloodworth stock, whom Forrest depicts in a variety of incarnations and across two centuries of history, becomes almost a case-study in disaffiliation and radical human and racial confusion. The novel works over, exhaustively, the metaphor of a people treated as illegitimate offspring, born out of racial wedlock as it were, and refused the basic family obligations by white America. The Bloodworth lines of kinship Forrest shows as irretrievably tangled by miscegenation and rape—a violent, incestuous mingle over time of blood and pigment. The means by which Forrest renders his 'outcast' world, his different leaps of memory and gatherings of voices, could be thought congested, but he writes with a discernible sureness of aim, a deserved confidence in his overall design. The concluding dialogue between Nathan and his friend and fellow orphan, Noah Grandberry, serves especially to draw together the novel's proliferating allusions to parentage, lost kin, the nation's historical severance from its 'family' roots. Like Quentin Compson and Shreve McCannon in *Absalom, Absalom* they help to clarify the novel's contrapuntal movements of loss and abandonment, search and discovery. If Forrest's eddies of language and mythic allusion on occasion give the impression of 'style' in the grand manner, his novel nevertheless matches in performance the boldness of its conception. Forrest's sights are set ambitiously upon the mythic racial truths of American history, the truths of its inner blood and skin. *The Bloodworth Orphans* eloquently fulfils that ambition.

10

To speak of a contemporary black American novel is to acknowledge that, since *Invisible Man* and *Go Tell It On The Mountain*, there has emerged a vital new generation of imaginative talent. In giving attention to the fiction of writers like Demby, Wideman, Wright, Polite and Forrest, it is also to acknowledge that one manifestation of that talent lies in the novel of serious experiment, the willingness to take risks of voice and design. Others, to be sure, share in the endeavour, Himes from an earlier time, alongside Ishmael Reed, LeRoi Jones, William Melvin Kelley, Clarence Major and Gayl Jones notably. Further, it can be argued that, in one sense, they continue a tradition of experiment that was always there, in Jean Toomer, or Langston Hughes, or in an interwar satirist like George Schuyler, but which too often was made to appear outside the main line of Afro–American fiction by pigeon-holing debates about realism and protest. Ishmael Reed is clearly right in believing the novel to be no 'one thing'. It is, and always has been, 'many things', in black literary tradition as elsewhere. The writers I have given prominence to are ample testimony to that, especially in their determination to write free of all prescriptive ideologies, past and current.[15] And in 'making new', and in seeking to be neither 'one thing', nor for that matter simply 'another thing', their novels offer not only the opportunity to encounter new directions, but a new wisdom.

NOTES

1 First published in *Esquire* (May 1961) and reprinted in *Nobody Knows My Name: More Notes Of A Native Son* (New York, 1961).

2 'Nobody Knows My Name' in *Soul On Ice* (New York, 1968).

3 See *Nobody Knows My Name* (ibid.) and *Shadow and Act* (New York, 1964).

4 Murray's two important studies are *The Hero And The Blues* (University of Missouri Press, 1973) and *Stomping The Blues* (New York, 1976).

5 I'm conscious of many names not present in these notes: The following are novelists whose fiction deserves mention in any account of post-war black American fiction: Cecil Brown, Frank London Brown, Lloyd Brown, David Bradley, Ed Bullins, George Cain, Clarence L. Cooper, Paul Crump, George Davies, Owen Dodson, Bill Gunn, Henry Dumas, Sam Greenlee, Nathan C. Heard, Herbert A. Simmons, Henry Van Dyke, Gordon Parks, John Stewart, John McCluskey, Jane Philips. Special mention needs to be made of two veteran expatriate Afro–American writers, William Gardner Smith and Frank Yerby.

6 See, for instance, Addison Gayle Jr. (Ed.): *The Black Aesthetic* (New York, 1972); Addison Gayle Jr. (Ed.): *Black Expression* (New York, 1969); Mercer Cook and Stephen E. Henderson: *The Militant Black Writer In Africa And The United States* (Wisconsin, 1969); George Kent: *Blackness And The Adventure Of Western Culture* (Chicago, 1972); and the special issue of *MidContinent American Studies Journal*, Fall, 1972, Vol. XI, No. 2.

7 John Henrik Clarke: *William Styron's Nat Turner: Ten Black Writers Respond* (Boston, 1968).

8 Foreword to Leon Forrest: *There Is A Tree More Ancient Than Eden* (New York, 1973).

9   Ishmael Reed (Ed.): *19 Necromancers From Now* (New York, 1970).

10 Himes's publishing history is tangled. The main novels and publishing dates are as follows: *If He Hollers Let Him Go* (1945); *Lonely Crusade* (1947); *Cast The First Stone* (1952); *The Third Generation* (1954); *The Primitive* (1955); *Pinktoes* (1961); *Une Affaire de Viol* (1963); *For Love of Imabelle* (1957); *The Real Cool Killers* (1959); *The Crazy Kill* (1959); *Run Man Run* (1966); *The Big Gold Dream* (1960); *All Shot Up* (1960); *The Heat's On* (1966); *Cotton Comes To Harlem* (1966); *Blind Man With a Pistol* (1969); The detective series first appeared in French which explains the American dates of publication being somewhat out of sequence. I have tried to set out the history of these novels elsewhere. See 'Hurts, Absurdities and Violence: The Contrary Dimensions of Chester Himes' in *Journal of American Studies*, Vol. 12, No. 1, pp. 99–114, April 1978.

11 John A. Williams: 'My Man Himes: An Interview With Chester Himes', in *Amistad* 1, (New York, 1970).

12 John O'Brien: *Interviews With Black Writers* (New York, 1973), p. 214. A useful analysis of Wideman's fiction is Kermit Frazier: 'The Novels Of John Wideman', *Black World*, Vol. 24, pp. 18–38, June 1973.

13 Although the interview was given in May 1969, it didn't appear in *Black World* until March 1972, Vol. 21, pp. 4–22, 87–98.

14 *The Massachusetts Review*, Winter 1977, Vol. XVIII, No. 4, pp. 631–42.

15 Reed writes in his poem, 'Catechism of a neoamerican hoodoo church':

> Our pens are free
> do not move by decree, accept no memos
> frm jackbootd demogs who wd exile our minds.
> Dare tell d artist his role.

Index